Moving Images

Edinburgh Critical Studies in Victorian Culture

Series Editor: Julian Wolfreys

Volumes available in the series:

Visit the Edinburgh Critical Studies in Victorian Culture web page at www. euppublishing.com/series/ecve

Also Available:
Victoriographies – A Journal of Nineteenth-Century Writing, 1790–1914, edited by Julian Wolfreys.
ISSN: 2044-2416
www.eupjournals.com/vic

Moving Images

Nineteenth-Century Reading and Screen Practices

Helen Groth

EDINBURGH
University Press

© Helen Groth, 2013

Edinburgh University Press Ltd
22 George Square, Edinburgh EH8 9LF

www.euppublishing.com

Typeset in 10.5/13 Sabon by
Servis Filmsetting Ltd, Stockport, Cheshire,
printed and bound in the United States of America

A CIP record for this book is available from the British Library

ISBN 978 0 7486 6948 6 (hardback)
ISBN 978 0 7486 6949 3 (webready PDF)
ISBN 978 0 7486 6950 9 (epub)

The right of Helen Groth
to be identified as author of this work
has been asserted in accordance with
the Copyright, Designs and Patents Act 1988.

Contents

List of Illustrations

Series Editor's Preface

'Victorian' is a term, at once indicative of a strongly determined concept and an often notoriously vague notion, emptied of all meaningful content by the many journalistic misconceptions that persist about the inhabitants and cultures of the British Isles and Victoria's Empire in the nineteenth century. As such, it has become a by-word for the assumption of various, often contradictory habits of thought, belief, behaviour and perceptions. Victorian studies and studies in nineteenth-century literature and culture have, from their institutional inception, questioned narrowness of presumption, pushed at the limits of the nominal definition, and have sought to question the very grounds on which the unreflective perception of the so-called Victorian has been built; and so they continue to do. Victorian and nineteenth-century studies of literature and culture maintain a breadth and diversity of interest, of focus and inquiry, in an interrogative and intellectually open-minded and challenging manner, which are equal to the exploration and inquisitiveness of its subjects. Many of the questions asked by scholars and researchers of the innumerable productions of nineteenth-century society actively put into suspension the clichés and stereotypes of 'Victorianism', whether the approach has been sustained by historical, scientific, philosophical, empirical, ideological or theoretical concerns; indeed, it would be incorrect to assume that each of these approaches to the idea of the Victorian has been, or has remained, in the main exclusive, sealed off from the interests and engagements of other approaches. A vital interdisciplinarity has been pursued and embraced, for the most part, even as there has been contest and debate amongst Victorianists, pursued with as much fervour as the affirmative exploration between different disciplines and differing epistemologies put to work in the service of reading the nineteenth century.

Edinburgh Critical Studies in Victorian Culture aims to take up both the debates and the inventive approaches and departures from convention that studies in the nineteenth century have witnessed for the last half century at least. Aiming to maintain a 'Victorian' (in the most positive sense of that motif) spirit of inquiry, the series' purpose is to continue and augment the cross-fertilisation of interdisciplinary approaches, and to offer, in addition, a number of timely and untimely revisions of Victorian literature, culture, history and identity. At the same time, the series will ask questions concerning what has been missed or improperly received, misread, or not read at all, in order to present a multi-faceted and heterogeneous kaleidoscope of representations. Drawing on the most provocative, thoughtful and original research, the series will seek to prod at the notion of the 'Victorian', and in so doing, principally through theoretically and epistemologically sophisticated close readings of the historicity of literature and culture in the nineteenth century, to offer the reader provocative insights into a world that is at once overly familiar, and irreducibly different, other and strange. Working from original sources, primary documents and recent inter-disciplinary theoretical models, Edinburgh Critical Studies in Victorian Culture seeks not simply to push at the boundaries of research in the nineteenth century, but also to inaugurate the persistent erasure and provisional, strategic redrawing of those borders.

Julian Wolfreys

Acknowledgements

While writing this book over many years I have been inspired and challenged by conversations with many colleagues and friends. I would like to thank first my colleagues and students at the University of New South Wales; their corridor conversations, formidable work ethic and collegiality have created such a convivial environment in which to write, read and think over the last few years. Among them I would like to particularly thank John Attridge, Chris Danta, Penny Hone and Sean Pryor; all have read versions of chapters and offered insightful feedback. The argument developed in the following pages has benefited both implicitly and explicitly from conversations with many friends and colleagues over the years. Jumana Bayeh, Katherine Biber, Susan Conley, David Ellison, Matthew Gibney, Sam Glover, Ian Henderson, Syd Hickman, Lucinda Holdforth, Natalya Lusty, Nicole Moore, Wendy Parkins, Gillian Russell, Paul Sheehan, Mary Spongberg, John Sutton, Patrick Tarrant, Clara Tuite and Anthony Uhlmann have all contributed in their various ways to making the writing of this book possible. I would especially like to thank Michele Pierson, who always challenges me to be better and work harder, and Angela Dunstan, for coming to the rescue at pivotal moments.

Simon During, Kate Flint, Hilary Fraser, Jon Mee and Julian Murphet have written timely references or provided support at vital points in my career, for which I am very grateful. I would also like to thank Regenia Gagnier and Josephine McDonagh for inviting me to present early versions of this research at the University of Exeter and the University of Oxford. Both of these experiences came at a critical point in the project, and challenged me to reframe my work in significant ways. In addition, I would like to thank the editors of the journals *Textual Practice*, *Victorian Studies*, *South Atlantic Quarterly*, *English Literary History*, as well as the generous editorial invitations of Nicola Parsons, Kate Mitchell, Collette Colligan and Margaret Linley, for providing me with the opportunity to publish early versions of some of the chapters that appear here. This research would also not have been possible without the generous funding of the Australian Research Council and Macquarie University Research Grants, for the latter I owe an enduring debt to the support of Jim Piper. I would also like to thank Julian Wolfreys for his positive response to my work and strong support of this book, and to the patience and assistance of the editorial team at Edinburgh University Press.

Finally, to my family, I owe an incalculable debt. This book was interrupted in the best of possible ways by the birth of Joshua and the care of Alec and Connor. They have all contributed by constantly drawing me back to the wonders of everyday life. Fay Sprague and Joan Groth have kept us going in too many ways to name. To my husband Tim, only you can know how much I owe you. This book would not have been possible without your love and support. This book is for you and our boys.

For Alec, Connor & Joshua

Moving Images: Nineteenth-Century Reading and Screen Practices

In late 1895 the American author and critic Brander Matthews (1852–1929) published a short story in *Scribner's Magazine* entitled 'The Kinetoscope of Time'.[1] It tells the tale of a man who enters a strangely illuminated building on a deserted street in an unnamed city. Compelled down a darkened hallway by a mysterious force, he draws aside a velvet curtain at its end and finds himself in a large circular space. Only four kinetoscopes, Edison's popular pre-cinematic viewing device, furnish the room. Cued by a legend that appears fleetingly above one of the kinetoscopes, he looks through the eye piece and views a series of dance sequences from familiar historical and literary sources: *Salome*, Esmeralda's dances from Victor Hugo's *The Hunchback of Notre Dame*, Pearl dancing before her cursed mother Hester in Nathaniel Hawthorne's *A Scarlet Letter* and Topsy dancing from Harriet Beecher Stowe's *Uncle Tom's Cabin*. At the end of this sequence the narrator looks up, then follows another mysterious legend to a second kinetoscope where he views a sequence of military scenes drawn from fiction and history: the fight between Hector and Achilles, the tale of Saladin and the Knight of the Leopard from Sir Walter Scott's *The Talisman*, Cervantes' *Don Quixote*, Goethe's *Faust* and Custer's Last Stand. In both instances he remarks upon the proleptic nature of his viewing experience. He seems to know what he is about to see and the manner in which it will be projected before he has even looked into the viewer. He recognises the hiatus between one scene and another and waits expectantly for the next image to materialise, just as he recognises when each sequence has come to an end.

At the conclusion of the second sequence, the narrator becomes aware of a distinguished middle-aged man standing behind him. Clearly the proprietor, the man quizzes him on what he has seen, claiming to have been present at the scenes the narrator has just witnessed. This prompts the narrator to ask whether he is 'Time himself' (741). The man dismisses this idea as absurd before proceeding to offer the narrator a Faustian-style deal. He can look through the other two kinetoscopes, the first containing scenes from his past and the second scenes from his future, however in exchange 'for every ten years of the future which I may unroll before you here, you must assign me a year of life – twelve months – to do with as I will' (742). The narrator deems the price too high and is summarily ejected by the proprietor into the 'world of actuality' (743). Suffused with electric light and jarred by the clatter of the elevated railroad above, the shop front reveals the final clue, an engraved portrait of the kinetoscope's mercurial proprietor – 'Monsieur le Comte de Cagliostro' (744).

This story captures a number of issues that this book will examine; principally the way nineteenth-century writers explored the psychological aesthetics of moving images produced by new visual media. When Matthews' narrator looks through the lens of the kinetoscope he enters into a dreamscape filled with projected images generated by familiar literary and cultural narratives, loosely connected by association rather than narrative sequence. Unlike the recent scholarly emphasis on the parallel histories of early cinematic automatism and literary modernism, Matthews isolates the kinetoscope's projective mechanism from the automatic registration of the real.[2] The focus of the story is on the psychology of the moving image as an affective catalyst of memory and suppressed wish-fulfilment, creating an alternative temporality that diverges from the chronology of real time.[3]

Simultaneously, the story fictionalises an actual inter-medial connection between popular nineteenth-century visual formats, such as the kinetoscope, and the familiar textual sources on which they typically drew for content and legitimacy. Like Matthews' modern Cagliostro, those in the business of both early and pre-cinematic entertainment often combined literary and visual media in an endeavour to align the moving images on the screen with the moving images scrolling through the minds of their audiences. Echoing an enduring philosophical tradition of enlisting familiar optical devices to materialise the mechanisms of perception, memory, dreams, and associative streams of consciousness, these convergences between literary and popular visual media invited an analogical interplay between reading and viewing.[4]

This book considers the ways in which this inter-medial reciprocity aligns with a parallel history of the emergence of a modern psychology which was keen to understand and describe the dynamic processes that generate moving images in the mind, including reading, viewing and dreaming. As Rick Rylance has observed, one of the definitive characteristics of the new discipline of psychology was the multiplicity of viewpoints it generated from virtually all the major intellectuals of the period. Echoing his subjects' fascination with optical analogies, Rylance likens this multi-vocality to the 'organised multiplicity' of 'beautiful Victorian inventions' such as David Brewster's kaleidoscope or stereoscope.[5] Reading between these parallel histories of mind and media reveals a complex conceptual, aesthetic and technological engagement with the moving image that is both typically of the nineteenth century in its preoccupation with questions of automatism and volition (unconscious and conscious thought), spirit and materiality, art and machine, but also definitively modern in its secular articulation of the instructive and entertaining possibilities of making images move both inside and outside the mind.

Moving Images in the Mind

Elaborating on the processes of unconscious cerebration in his influential *Principles of Psychology* (1874), the nineteenth-century psychologist William Carpenter described reading as a form of automatism, an unconscious process of picturing or summoning images. While the mind is absorbed in thought the words on the page take on 'the appearance and proper sound of each word', while 'all the time we are not thinking of these matters . . . but of the argument of the author; or picturing the scene he describes'.[6] Formulating these ideas in response to his friend Frances Power Cobbe's 'graphic sketches' of 'the nightly miracles of unconscious cerebration' that fill the dreaming mind, Carpenter shared Cobbe's interest in the analogies between the moving images generated by reading, viewing and dreaming.[7] Both interpreted dreams as symptoms of the 'myth-making' tendency of the human mind and likened the distortive effects of the dream to turning the pages of a much-loved illustrated book, 'like those of M. Doré to the page of life which we have turned the day before', to invoke Cobbe (28). Transformed by the distortive lens of the dream into art by an agency beyond the dreamer's control, images taken from everyday life are animated by a mysterious agent that Cobbe whimsically dubs 'our Familiar':

> But our Familiar is a great deal more than a walking dictionary, a housemaid, a *valet de place*, or a barrel-organ man. He is a novelist who can spin more romances than Dumas, a dramatist who composes more plays than ever did Lope de Vega, a painter who excels equally well in figures, landscapes, cattle, sea-pieces, smiling bits of *genre* and the most terrific conceptions of horror and torture. Of course, like other artists, he can only reproduce, develop, combine what he has actually experienced or read or heard of. But

the enormous versatility and inexhaustible profusion with which he furnishes us with fresh pictures for our galleries, and new stories every night from his lending library, would be deemed the greatest of miracles, were it not the commonest of facts. (27)

Liberated from the constraints of will and moral judgement, the dreaming mind is rendered passive before a nightly profusion of images channelled into an infinite archive of stories presided over by a wish-fulfilling librarian.

Turning to the opiate-infused visions of Coleridge and De Quincey to further exemplify the vivid flow of dream images that fill the sleeping mind, Cobbe wrote with relish of the 'whole panoramas of beauty and horror' that expanded before the entranced reader's eyes in *Kubla Khan* and *Confessions of an English Opium Eater*.[8] The utter surrender of both writers to the lure of wish fulfilment, however, only reinforced Cobbe's 'conviction that the dreaming brain-self is not the true self for whose moral worthiness we strive' (523). Like Matthews' narrator, Cobbe's moral self must choose light over dark, the real over the illusory hold of the moving images of the mind.

George Eliot, who owned a copy of Cobbe's pamphlet 'Dreams as Illustrations of Unconscious Cerebration', narrates a similar ethical dilemma in *Middlemarch* (1874), creating a metaphoric network that invites her readers to associate the illusion of movement created by sequences of magic lantern images with the vivid scenes that threaten to overwhelm her heroine Dorothea's agonised reverie. As Dorothea contemplates the ruins of Rome and the broken shards of her own misguided idealism, Eliot's omniscient narrator observes:

> Forms both pale and glowing took possession of her young sense, and fixed themselves in her memory even when she was not thinking of them, preparing strange associations which remained through her after-years. Our moods are apt to bring with them images which succeed each other like the magic-lantern pictures of a doze; and in certain states of dull forlornness Dorothea all her life continued to see the vastness of St Peter's, the huge bronze canopy, the excited intention in the attitudes and garments of the prophets and evangelists in the mosaics above, and the red drapery which was being hung for Christmas spreading itself everywhere like a disease of the retina.[9]

As the accumulative phrasing of the second sentence in the above passage suggests, the unconscious associative mechanisms of emotion trigger the movement between one remembered image and another, guided by the invisible hand of the lanternist. Eliot's syntax also mimics the serial effects of the magic lantern sequence, using the machinery of language to move the reader's eye from image to image, from the vast domes of St Peter's, to the mosaics of the prophets and evangelists, to the red drapery that saturated all in an ominous festive hue.

It is only in retrospect, after many repeat viewings, that the underlying meanings of these images begin to make sense to Dorothea. Writing decades later, the psychologist James Sully, who was also a friend and critic of Eliot's, concurred with Eliot's account of the revelatory dynamics of such dream-like states and their perpetual re-visioning of scenes drawn from ordinary experience. Sully argued that the dream prolonged habits of rational reflection and moral self-criticism. According to his evolutionary model of the mind as palimpsest, the superficial 'kaleidoscopic transformations of the dream', or 'jumble of the nocturnal phantasmagoria', may run seemingly illogical scenes together, but in so doing the dream 'strips the ego of its artificial wrappings', bringing 'up from the dim depths of our sub-conscious life the primal, instinctive impulses, and discloses to us a side of ourselves which connects us with the great sentient world'.[10]

Both Eliot and Sully import optical devices into their prose to demonstrate the unconscious processing of images that are subsequently rationalised by the conscious mind, naturalising the connection between optical devices and dream-states, reverie and the role unconscious visualisation plays in reading and thinking. In turn, this drive to rationalise and instruct their readers connects their nuanced theorisation of the psychological mechanisms that drive the mind's perceptual and rationalising processes to an extensive network of contemporary nineteenth-century scientific explanation that enlisted optical devices to materialise or externalise the perceptual limitations of the human mind. David Brewster typifies this tradition. A prolific reviewer and theorist of his own and others' inventions, such as the kaleidoscope, the thaumatrope, the stereoscope and the magic lantern, Brewster vividly evoked the mind's perpetual struggle to distinguish the real from the illusory images fabricated by both intense emotion or technological ingenuity. As he observes in his much reprinted *Letters on Natural Magic*:

> When the eye in solitude sees before it the forms of life, fresh in their colours and vivid in their outline; when distant or departed friends are suddenly presented to view; when visible bodies disappear and reappear without any intelligible cause; and when it beholds objects, whether real or imaginary, for whose presence no cause can be assigned, the conviction of supernatural agency becomes under ordinary circumstances unavoidable . . . it is not only an amusing but a useful occupation to acquire a knowledge of those causes which are capable of producing so strange a belief, whether it arises from the delusions which the mind practises upon itself, or from the dexterity and science of others.[11]

Brewster is referring here to the demystifying rhetorical and optical devices of natural magic. Elaborating on the psychology of belief, Brewster invites his readers to question the deciphering powers of eye and mind. Whether the reader has fallen prey to the arts of a dexterous illusionist or their own emotion-infused reverie, Brewster promotes the utility of rational explanation, a descriptive apparatus that incorporates an array of optical devices to demonstrate the fallacies of perception and superstition. Moving fluidly between the spectral reveries of the isolated mind and ghost shows, including Paul de Philipstal's legendary phantas-magoria, Brewster reinforces the analogy between the moving images of the mind and those projected by mercurial impresarios, as well as by enlightened scientists, such as himself.

Addressed to Walter Scott, Brewster's *Letters on Natural Magic*, also explicitly aligned Scott's imaginative interrogations of the illusions of the mind with a history of philosophical toys and optical devices. In a notable sequence in the *Letters*, Brewster speculates on how the simple flicker effects or fusions created by the turning movements of the thau-matrope in which successive images appear to move with the turn of a hand, could be adapted to teach children to read, reiterating the literary framing of the device by its inventor John Ayrton Paris in his novelistic account of his invention, *Philosophy in Sport Made Science in Earnest*.[12]

As Tom Gunning has recently observed, the discourse surrounding philosophical toys such as the thaumatrope in the nineteenth century inaugurates 'a fundamental change in the nature of the image'.[13] Gunning describes this new 'technological image' as a product of a process of integrating word and image, speculating that it might even be said to realise 'a new process of reading and writing, one of whose future forms would be cinematography, the writing of motion' (497). For Gunning, the term 'technological image' means both machine-produced images, such as lithographs or prints, as well as images generated by a device – 'optically produced by it rather than simply reproduced' (500). He speaks of a 'modern environment of images', where unprecedented numbers of people had access to new technologies that revealed a newly labile conception of the 'technological/perceptual image' taking shape and dissipating with the turn of the hand, transforming 'the traditional static ideal of pictorial representation' (504). Implicit in Gunning's account is the assumption of a complex form of training of the human sensorium that enables a new way of seeing images as transitional, inher-ently unstable forms, and the translation of this concept of the image into other media and perceptual processes, such as writing and reading.

As the following study demonstrates, this is far from a speculative connection between new modes of visualising, conceptualising, reading and writing moving images. A distinctively modern conception of the moving image begins to emerge with the vibrant multi-medial formations of the Regency period, including the thaumatrope, the kaleidoscope, panoramas and dioramas. This newly labile concept of the image was correspondingly amplified by a vigorous print culture that fostered the integration of word and image in multiple forms, from illustrated books that literally mimicked the transitions and dissolves of magic lanterns shows, to the proliferation of optical tropes and metaphors in the work of writers compelled by the aesthetic and psychological effects of a heightened sense of visual contingency that pervaded the cultural landscape of early to mid-nineteenth-century London. Literature took its place from the late eighteenth century onwards, as Paul Keen has argued, in this dynamic commercial marketplace 'alongside a host of phenomena, from performing animals to the rage for air ballooning to scientific demonstrations which featured healthy doses of conjuring', simultaneously endorsing and parodying the 'pursuit of knowledge'.[14]

Responding to this profusion of new media, Regency and Victorian writers and booksellers were quick to see the profits to be made from expanding the illustrative potential of the codex. Appealing to the social aspirations of middle-class parents and beguiling the eye of consumers with instructive literary entertainments also reflected a corresponding shift towards child-centred theories of literacy and education in the early to middle decades of the century.[15] Fostering the experimental sensibility of the child under the close supervision of a watchful parent advocated by popular writers such as Maria Edgeworth, also stressed both the haptic and optic dimensions of reading. Likewise works of popular science by Jane Marcet, Paris and Brewster modelled domestic scenes of enlightened instruction where children were guided through experiments with optical devices, transforming libraries, parlours and gardens into sites of possibility and wonder.

By the 1830s popular illustrated magazines and periodicals traded in what Jacques Rancière describes as 'collective imagery' that functioned in dispersed but complimentary ways to create stabilising reference points and defined cultural typologies.[16] Amidst their miscellaneous offerings, publications such as *The Penny Magazine* (1832–45) converted the vertical planes of the popular serial format of 'Galleries of Illustration' into the horizontal planes of the cheaply printed page.[17] Illustrated series such as 'The Year of the Poets' and 'The Canterbury Tales' created the illusion of access and ownership by simulating 'an instantaneous and temporary social mobility', as Andrew King has argued in relation to *The London Journal*, a successor of *The Penny Magazine*, 'without the threats that actually challenging or changing cultural hierarchies would involve'.[18] Luisa Calè's reading of eighteenth-century 'Galleries of Illustration' as a proto-cinematic medium suggests a further dimension to the issue of mobility King raises.[19] By simulating the juxtaposition of moments of time in space, Calè argues with specific reference to Fuseli's illustration of Milton's *Paradise Lost*, 'Galleries of Illustration' created a 'dynamism of form' that animated 'a character's movement beyond the limits of the frame and into the next painting' (9). These kinetic effects, she suggests, are indicative of an emergent visual culture that turned readers into spectators as they moved between the sequencing devices of text and image, gallery space and printed page. Remediated in the early to mid-nineteenth-century popular penny press, the animating effects of these galleries of illustration were literally transported to the printed page. Typifying Bolter and Grusin's theory of the double logic of remediation these hybrid media simultaneously multiplied new illustrative forms, while erasing their differences, by fostering an isomorphic relation between image and word, viewing and reading.[20]

However, the desire to make images move, dissolve and cohere into a new form of 'visual story-telling', to use Joss Marsh's term, found one of its most dramatic and widespread forms in the dissolving magic lantern shows of the mid to late nineteenth century.[21] These multi-medial entertainments combined dramatic readings of familiar stories such as Lewis Caroll's *Alice in Wonderland*, Charles Dickens's Christmas tales, *Bluebeard*, Daniel Defoe's *Robinson Crusoe*, and *Ali Baba and the Arabian Nights*. Beginning in 1820s the dissolving effects created by the painter and lanternist Henry Langdon Childe, first at the Adelphi Theatre in London and then at the Royal Polytechnic from 1838–76, were a popular sensation that remediated iconic literary images as a series of spectacular transformation scenes that elevated the moving image into an object of wonder and instructive entertainment. Dissolving views, as Marsh rightly contends, 'were an entertainment whose time had come' (334). Primed by the scenic transformations of earlier visual formats, such as Philip James De Loutherbourg's Eidophusikon and Louis Daguerre's Diorama, Royal Polytechnic audiences, which included seminal figures of British early cinema such as Cecil Hepworth, relished the multiple visual effects and narrative possibilities of these new lantern shows. Hepworth recounted his avid retention of all the details of these entertainments in his autobiography *Came the Dawn*. He remembered his father, who was a lecturer there, transforming Dickens's world into an animated spectacle. He also marvelled at the then unremarked affinity between the 'intermittent movement' of the spectacular lantern images produced by the Polytechnic's fifteen magic lanterns and the cinematograph, 'fifteen years before anyone had a film to show'.[22]

Reading Moving Images

Reading Proust's description of the movement of magic lantern images across the wall of his childhood room at Combray in the opening sections of *Swann's Way*, Elaine Scarry remarks on 'the perceptual mimesis of solidity of the room' created by the 'impalpable iridescence' of the images moving across its surfaces.[23] In the passage Scarry reads, Proust writes of the lantern images of the figure of Golo, from the medieval legend of Genevieve of Brabant, 'advancing across the window-curtains, swelling out with their curves and diving into their folds':

> The body of Golo himself, being of the same supernatural substance as his steeds, overcame every material obstacle – everything that seemed to bar his way – by taking it as an ossature and embodying it in himself: even the door-handle, for instance, over which, adapting itself at once, would float irresistibly his red cloak or his pale face, which never lost its nobility or its melancholy, never betrayed the least concern at this transverberation.[24]

Scarry draws our attention to the way the thin impalpable lantern images cause the reader to linger on the wall just long enough to materialise their solidity. Prompted by these visual cues, the walls of the room solidify in the reader's mind creating a space for the 'projective act' of reading to continue without 'vertigo or alarm'.[25] By carefully reproducing the phenomenology of perception, this passage implicitly instructs or guides the reader through what Scarry describes as a 'process of directed image-making' in which images move about, brush across other images, rotate figures from upright to supine positions, and create openings through which the reader is instructed to look (31).

Reading in this sense is interactive, projective and somatic, training the mind to mediate visual stimuli in material three-dimensional forms. More significantly in the context of this study, by teasing out the intricacies of the way verbal images acquire the vivacity of perceptual objects, Scarry's cognitive theory of reading sustains a long tradition of writing about the kinetic materialising power of words that intensified in the early decades of the nineteenth century in the wake of the new science of mind and the profusion of technological transformations of the relationship between word and image.

Coleridge's famous letter to William Godwin on 'the power of words, and the process by which human feelings form affinities with them' expresses a similar interest in the vivacity of the verbal arts.[26] Coleridge poses a series of questions to Godwin:

> 'Is Logic the *Essence* of Thinking?' in other words – is *Thinking* impossible without arbitrary signs? & – how far is the word 'arbitrary' a misnomer? Are not words &c part and Germinations of the Plant? And what is the Law of the Growth? – In something of this order I would endeavour to destroy the old antithesis of *Words* and *Things*, elevating, as it were, words into Things, & living things too. (1:625–6)

The 'thingness' of words exists in a vital and often antagonistic relation to thinking according to Coleridge – a generative antagonism that, in turn, results in the striking vivacity of mental images. This productive dissonance between the materiality of writing and the vivid images generated by the act of reading also recurs in poems, such as 'The Garden of Boccaccio', where as Peter Otto has recently argued, reading is transformed into 'an experience of immersion and interactivity'.[27]

> Thanks, gentle artist! now I can descry
> Thy fair creation with a mastering eye,
> And all awake! And now in fix'd gaze stand,
> Now wander through the Eden of thy hand;
> Praise the green arches, on the fountain clear
> See fragment shadows of the crossing deer;
> And with that serviceable nymph I stoop
> The crystal from its restless pool to scoop.
> I see no longer! I myself am there,
> Sit on the ground-sward, and the banquet share.[28]

Dwelling on the materialising power of Boccaccio's words, as Scarry does with Proust, Coleridge guides the reader's eye towards the fragmented reflection of a deer flickering in and out of focus, as the scene takes shape in his own mind. In the process he describes the lapse from conscious perceptual mastery into the illusory flow of reverie as intrinsic to his reading experience.

Reflecting on the immersive nature of this reading experience, Otto suggests an alternative history linking this scene to a romantic aesthetics of the virtual that extends into the sphere of popular immersive entertainments, such as the panorama, and through to contemporary theorisations of virtual reality. The unfettered escape from the real into the sensual pleasures of the virtual, however, is always complicated for Coleridge by a didactic compulsion to guide the eye of his ideal reader to abstract and animate what they see or read, moving from simply attending to what is already known to the voluntary analysis of the 'state of consciousness' evoked.[29] Simply attending to what one sees or reads pales in comparison to the retrospective and analytical vitality of thought. As Coleridge observed of the art of portraiture: 'it is not the likeness for actual comparison, but for recollection'.[30] According to this idealised internalised version, the portrait, as Christopher Rovee notes, 'is not a fixed outline but a flickering essence that tells more about the beholder of the portrait than about the portrait itself'.[31]

This dynamic re-visualising becomes more conflicted when the idealising power of thought breaks drown, as it does in a letter Coleridge wrote to his friend James Gilman in which the kaleidoscope becomes a figure for the disintegrating effects of failed inspiration. Bereft of ideas, the poet's ink turns to mud as his uninspired mind transforms once vital impressions into 'kaleidoscopic freaks':

> Alas! That Nature is a wary wily long-breathed old Witch, tough-lived as a Turtle and divisible as a Polyp, repullulative in a thousand Snips and Cuttings, *integra et in toto!* She is sure to get the better of LADY MIND in the long run, and to take her revenge too – transforms our To Day into a Canvass dead-coloured to receive the dull featureless Portrait of Yesterday; not alone turns the mimic Mind, the ci-devant Sculptress with all her kaleidoscopic freaks and symmetries! Into clay, but *leaves* it such a *clay*, to cast dumps or bullets in; and lastly (to end with that which suggested the beginning –) she mocks the mind with its own metaphors, metamorphosing the Memory into a lignum vitae Escrutoire to keep unpaid Bills & Dun's Letter in, with Outlines that had never been filled up, MSS that never went further than the Title-pages, and Proof-Sheets & Foul Copies of Watchmen, Friends, Aids to Reflection & other *Stationery* Wares that have kissed the Publisher's Shelf with gluey Lips with all the tender intimacy of inosculations! – Finis![37]

In this instance, nature's wonders elude Coleridge's power to idealise and abstract. Inadequate simulations – poor copies of the spells of a witch who no longer does his bidding – disfigure his vision. And yet, assimilated into a metaphorics of aesthetic crisis, the kaleidoscope becomes a generative site of resistance, not unlike the 'pressure of reality' that the portrait exerts on the observer's idealising powers.[33] The negation of the literal constraints of everyday objects in this sense becomes a catalyst for active analytical thought and creative reflection.

One finds a similar dynamic in play in Dugald Stewart's roughly contemporary philosophical speculations on the visualising powers of unconscious thinking in dream states and reverie. Unconstrained by the ordinary demands of waking life, the dreaming mind moves associatively between images, an experience Stewart likens to looking through a peep-show or show-box. Operating on a similar principle to Edison's kinetoscope, the show-box required the spectator to look through a lens into a box in which a series of illuminated images scrolled with the aid of an operator pulling a string or turning a lever:

> If the representation be executed with so much skill as to convey to me the idea of a distant prospect, every object before me swells in its dimensions, in proportion to the extent of space which I conceive it to occupy; and what seemed before to be shut up with the limits of small wooden frame is magnified, in my apprehension, to an immense landscape of woods, rivers, and mountains.[34]

Stewart, like Coleridge, narrates a transition between conscious perception and a contained surrender to the virtual world created by human invention. Like the visual effects of Boccaccio's poem, the peep-show analogy allows Stewart to materialise the way the mind generates images that simultaneously exceed and retain a vital and critical connection to the signified, an analytical process that correspondingly transforms the peep-show into a multiply signifying epistemological figure that functions both discursively and as a part of a network of cultural practices. Thus reframed the peep-show becomes what Gilles Deleuze would call an assemblage: a cultural formation that is 'simultaneously and inseparably a machinic assemblage and an assemblage of enunciation', a discursive construction and a literal manipulable technology.[35]

There are also revealing parallels between Stewart's rhetoric and twentieth-century film/mind analogies, Hugo Munsterberg being an obvious early example.[36] However, the more illuminating parallel is between Stewart and Alexander Kluge's account of the associative cognition that takes place in the mind of the film spectator as a template for a counter-public sphere:

> Cinema is a program that is a relationship of production – if for no other reason than that this relationship exists in the experiences of the spectators which constantly recreate the cinema's experiential horizon. The multitude of films in the mind of the spectators will continue to be infinitely richer than what can be seen in the cinema until all number of directors work at combining their professional skills and temperaments, their most personal feelings and impulses . . . all people relate to their experience like authors – rather than managers of a department store.[37]

According to Kluge, since the Ice Age or earlier, 'streams of images, of so-called associations have moved through the human mind', prompted by what he calls 'an anti-realistic attitude', protesting against an 'unbearable reality' (209). This spontaneous stream is sparked by the competing energies of laughter, memory and intuition that predate modern institutional formations, such as the school: 'This is the more-than ten-thousand-year-old-cinema to which the invention of the film strip, projector and screen only provided a technological response' (209). But while this reciprocity between the screen and associative spectator may seem to embrace a virtual world that exceeds temporal and moral constraints, Miriam Hansen reminds us that Kluge's careful revision of Walter Benjamin's account of the desacralisation of art in the age of mechanical reproduction tries to salvage 'the experiential possibilities of the disintegrated aura for a secularised, public context' by allowing for the possibility of the spectator returning the gaze of the film through the medium of inter-subjectivity and memory.[38] To quote Hansen:

> Thus the reciprocity between the film on the screen and the spectator's stream of association becomes the measure of a particular film's use value for an alternative public sphere: a film either exploits the viewer's needs, perceptions, and wishes or it encourages their autonomous movement, fine-tuning, and self-reliance. (13)

Stewart's peep-box analogy entertains a similar possibility of self-reflexivity, of looking back into the viewing machine through the medium of memory or the dream, of being drawn into a process that resists the wish-fulfilment of a purposeless escape into a virtual world, in favour of an instructive movement between medium and mind.

To return to 'The Kinetoscope of Time', Matthews' story offers a complicated, but not unprecedented, take on this model of instructive reciprocity. Published in the pages of the highly profitable literary pictorial *Scribner's Magazine*[39] only a year after the first kinetoscope parlour opened in New York in 1894, Matthews literally transforms a first encounter with Edison's marvellous new viewing device into a morally instructive reading scene.[40] Vicariously viewing the seemingly random assortment of images along with the narrator, the reader engages in a parallel form of associative bricolage, drawing on a collective archive of inter-textual knowledge to make sense of the series of scenes.

By inviting the reader to identify with the narrator's recognition of familiar literary scenes, the tale also implicitly normalises the necessary combination of diegetic and extra-diegetic material that was intrinsic to early cinematic experience, reinforcing the new medium's dependence on established traditions of story-telling – literary formations well-represented in the pages of *Scribner's Magazine*, which included contributions from Robert Louis Stevenson, Edith Wharton, Rudyard Kipling and Arthur Conan Doyle.[41] Taking pleasure in this fusion of memory, fantasy and novelty, the narrator and reader operate both inside and outside the kinetoscope's representational logic as Matthews evokes it. While the tale narrates a transient loss of agency as the narrator and reader are drawn by the combined dynamics of suspense and cinematic illusion into the dark magical sphere of Count Cagliostrio, Matthews ultimately valorises the power of the individual will to resist the allure of wish-fulfilment and forbidden knowledge.

Gerald Graff describes Matthews, who was also the first Professor of Drama at Columbia University and an early cinéphile, as 'a middlebrow populariser'.[42] As his quick uptake of the idea of the kinetoscope suggests, Matthews was keen to channel the instructive potential of the new medium, an enthusiasm that led to the incorporation of film into Columbia's adult education classes from as early as 1913 and the establishment of its first film course 'Photoplay Composition' taught by his student Victor Oscar Freedburg.[43] Modelling his teaching of screen writing on Matthews' 'great books' courses, Freedburg drew on a Ruskinian hermeneutics, training students to read and re-read films as they would literary classics.[44] In practice, Freedburg's pedagogy was ultimately more concerned with speeding the adaptation of his predominantly migrant students to the industrial rhythms of American life, facilitated by the didactic combination of the universal language of cinema and 'the best that has been thought and said', to quote the Arnoldian phrase that Columbia's promotional literature transformed into a slogan.[45] Miriam Hansen reminds us however, through her reading of Kluge, that this ideologically driven discursive construction of spectatorship, whether in the form of the textually inscribed subject or the commercially targeted consumer, must be understood in a plural sense, not in terms of a 'socially contingent individual', but 'as an audience endowed with historical concrete contours, conflicts and possibilities'.[46] As Hansen and Kluge suggest, there are always historically particular spaces for resistance, experiment, and the formation of counter-publics that read and see otherwise, seizing upon images, objects and experiences, and generating alternative streams of images in the mind.

Differentiating Movements

Writing of his travels in Italy, Dickens invoked a series of visual analogies that assumed a modern understanding of the technologically generated moving image. As Kate Flint observes, Dickens 'presents Italy like a chaotic magic-lantern show, fascinated by the spectacle it offers, and by himself as spectator'.[47] His senses deranged and over-stimulated, he moves from one vivid Italian scene to the next 'in a sort of a dream' or reverie.[48] Describing his chapters as pictures or 'Rapid Dioramas', Dickens guides his reader through a progression of dissolving images, as a magic lantern lecturer might have done. He also exploits the psychological resonances of these optical allusions, such as in the opening paragraph of his picture of 'An Italian Dream':

> The rapid and unbroken succession of novelties that had passed before me, came back like half-formed dreams; and a crowd of objects wandered in the greatest confusion through my mind, as I travelled on, by a solitary road. At intervals, some one among them would stop, as it were, in its restless flitting to and fro, and enable me to look at it, quite steadily, and behold it in full distinctness. After a few moments, it would dissolve, like a view in a magic lantern; and while I saw some part of it quite plainly, and some faintly, and some not at all, would show me another of the many places I had latterly seen, lingering behind it, and coming through it. This was no sooner visible than, in its turn, it melted into something else. (77)

The magic lantern dissolve, like the cinematic dissolve, was created by slowly diminishing the illumination of one slide while simultaneously illuminating another so that the second slide appeared to be magically emerging from the previous slide projected on the screen. A similar effect was used at the Diorama, which opened in London in 1823, by backlighting the screen to reveal a second scene, or transforming scenes from day to night through a process of progressive illumination.[49] The key element of these transformations being the intermittent movement between still and moving images that Dickens compares to the oscillations between the momentary stasis of an image illuminated by memory, and its gradual dissolution as another image surfaces from the 'streams of consciousness', to invoke the term coined by George Henry Lewes.[50]

While Lewes famously observed that Dickens's characters were like 'frogs whose brains have been taken out for physiological purposes', the concept of the mind as palimpsest that Dickens materialises through the metaphor of the magic lantern parallels Lewes's own preoccupation with the dynamic relation between perceptual cognition and the 'streams of consciousness'.[51] Indeed Lewes, in a more generous vein, conceded that Dickens was a 'seer of visions', who, like no 'other sane mind' he had observed, possessed a 'vividness of the imagination approaching so closely to hallucination'.[52] The mind, for Lewes, is a 'sensitive mechanism' that registers present sensations that are subsequently transformed by the accumulation of past experiences. Lewes writes in *Problems of Life and Mind*, that the mind:

> is not a passive recipient of external impressions, but an active co-operant. It has not only its own laws of action, but brings with it that very elementary condition of Consciousness which most theorists attempt to derive *ab extra*. I mean that the sensitive mechanism is not a simple mechanism, and as such constant, but a variable mechanism, which has a *history* . . . the sensitive subject is no *tabula rasa*: it is not a blank sheet of paper, but a palimpsest.[53]

Lewes, as Michael Davis has noted, argued against both a philosophical realism that assumed 'the direct projection of images of things onto the mind' and a Kantian idealism that insisted that the mind 'projects order onto the external world'.[54] Instead, Lewes speculated that our minds resemble a chaotic collage of 'impressions, imperfect memories, echoes of other men's voices, mingling with the reactions of our sensibility'.[55] Assimilated into these multiple associative streams of consciousness, 'Social Forms, scientific theories, works of Art, and above all, Language' are incessantly impressed and assimilated into an 'existing mass of residual impressions'.[56]

Read through the lens of Lewes's psychological aesthetics, Dickens's structural and metaphoric play with magic lantern motifs in *Pictures from Italy* intersects with a parallel theorisation of the mind as a 'sensitive machine'. As E. S. Dallas, Lewes's fellow reviewer and friend, observed, 'as a photograph, the mind refuses nought'.[57] Sustaining the metaphor in his reading of Wordsworth, Dallas continued, in a 'moment at a single jet the picture is in the mind's eye complete to a pin's head with all the perfectness of an imaginative work' (1:222). 'One blow, one flash is all we are conscious of' he writes, while we remain 'unconscious of the automatic energy within us until its work is achieved and the effect of it is not to be resisted' (1:222). Dickens dramatises a like perceptual process in *Pictures from Italy*; images flash upon the retina, are arrested and then dissolve. He knows not how or why this happens, but in dramatising the process as a sequence of instructive visual affects that gradually and inexplicably transform his own consciousness, he guides his readers through the projective act of reading. To return to Scarry, Dickens animates the two-dimensional monotony of reading 'small black marks on a white page' with the aid of the magic lantern and diorama's familiar visual effects (5). Turning the page becomes the equivalent of moving between one magic lantern slide, or illuminated screen, and another – an analogy that didactic Regency writers, such as Ann and Jane Taylor, as we shall see in the following chapter, enlisted to engage a new class of readers. The materiality of the book disappears as the stream of images evoked by the associative play of word and image 'acquire the vivacity of perceptual objects'.[58]

This study begins with a series of curious works produced during the Regency period that explicitly play with the analogy between reading books and operating optical devices, such as the camera obscura, the peep-show, and the magic lantern, beginning with Jane and Ann Taylor's *Signor Topsy-Turvy's Wonderful Magic Lantern* (1810) and culminating with Marguerite Gardiner, Countess of Blessington's first anonymous publication *The Magic Lantern; or, Sketches of Scenes in the Metropolis*

(1823). Sustaining this Regency focus, Chapter 2 traces the circulation of Byronic fragments through a series of media networks that extract and transform his work into associative iconic sequences, moving from panoramic re-mediations to the dioramic effects of Victorian spectacular theatre. The latter, George Henry Lewes would later object in a scathing review of a mid-century adaptation of *Sardanapalus*, reduced Byron to a series of magic lantern images. Yet despite such high-minded protests, Byron was very much a creature of the commercial culture of Regency London. His work fed off its worst and best excesses, fashions and visual predilections, including the dynamic illusionism of the kaleidoscope that animates his famous description of the celestial rainbow that appears after the iconic shipwreck scene in the second canto of *Don Juan*. Such allusions inadvertently drew him into a media network that included the kaleidoscope's inventor, David Brewster, who actively promoted the aesthetic, commercial and scientific applications of his work, as Chapter 3 will discuss with particular reference to psychologically speculative scenarios narrated in *Letters on Natural Magic, addressed to Sir Walter Scott*. The spectre of Brewster's inventions also haunts the analysis in Chapters 4 and 5 of magic lantern adaptations of Dickens's Christmas tales and Carroll's multiple iterations of Alice in the multi-medial space of the Royal Polytechnic. The afterlife of Brewster's kaleidoscope can even be traced through the late nineteenth-century journalism of George Sims, whose proto-cinematic journalism, as I discuss in Chapter 6, drew on both the seminal urban ethnography of Henry Mayhew and the early cinematic actualities of Robert Paul. Returning to Dickens and Carroll, the final chapter examines the complex interplay between reading and viewing that shapes early cinematic experience, through a close analysis of Cecil Hepworth's (1901) adaptation of *Alice's Adventures* and Paul's adaptation of Dickens's *A Christmas Carol* (1903).

In a recent historical reframing of his seminal work on the 'adjacent inscriptive media of film and literature'[59] Garrett Stewart claims the 'motor thrills' of Victorian 'everyday reading' as a precursor to theatrical cinema, 'with no news yet of moving pictures, they had made pictures move in their head'.[60] According to Stewart, the mental afterimages sparked by the 'psychodynamics' of cinematic viewing, to invoke the earlier formulations of *Between Film and Screen*, owe all to the 'ocular suppression' of the differential relationship between static and moving images that one finds in verbally portrayed visuality or ekphrasis (4). The following chapters engage with the suppressed material and conceptual history of reading and thinking through moving images that Stewart's image of the 'motor thrills' of 'everyday reading' as a form of making images move in the mind assumes and perpetuates.

Richard Rorty attributes a fundamental shift from classical and medieval descriptions of the observer to Locke and Descartes' spatial visualisation of the human mind 'as an inner space in which both pains and clear and distinct ideas passed in review before an Inner Eye'.[61] The 'unblinking Eye of the Mind', Rorty continues, oversees a writing scene in which the tabula rasa of the mind is imprinted, 'all the knowing gets done, so to speak, by the Eye which observes the imprinted tablet, rather than by the tablet itself' (143–4). The Cartesian/Lockean eye of the mind systematically rationalises what it sees into a coherent unity – a stable 'world picture' to invoke Heidegger.[62] But viewed through a post-Kantian frame, this world picture begins to destabilise and move. Countering the Cartesian model of perceptual objectivity, Kant argued in the preface to the second edition of the *Critique of Pure Reason* (1787): 'our representation of things as they are given, does not conform to these things as they are in themselves, but that these objects as appearances, conform to our mode of representation'.[63] This ideal subjective projection of order on the external world, however, becomes more contingent and labile with the emergence of more physiological conceptions of the machinery of observation in the nineteenth century. As Jonathan Crary has argued, an increasingly technical model of the observer was described in greater detail by 'the empirical sciences of the nineteenth century', and 'posited by various romanticisms' and 'early modernisms as the active, autonomous producer of his or her own visual experience'.[64] As we shall see in the next chapter, this multivalent stress on the active physiological production of visual experiences can be traced through a range of inter-medial experiments with training eyes to self-consciously visualise what and how they are reading as they read.

Notes

1. Matthews, 'The Kinetoscope of Time', pp. 733–44.
2. David Trotter argues for the importance of the parallel histories of literary modernism and the automatism of early cinema in *Cinema and Modernism*.
3. Mary Ann Doane explores the implications of the tale's Faustian pact in the context of the late nineteenth-century fascination with 'the representability of time' that early photographic and cinematic technologies inspired, drawing on familiar motifs of 'immortality, the denial of the radical finitude of the human body, access to other temporalities, and the issue of the archivability of time', in *The Emergence of Cinematic Time: Modernity, Contingency, the Archive*, p. 2.
4. Martin Jay provides a formidable narration of this history in *Downcast Eyes: The Denigration of Vision in Twentieth-Century French Thought*.

5. Rylance, *Victorian Psychology and British Culture 1850–1880*, p. 14.
6. Carpenter, *Principles of Psychology*, p. 526.
7. Cobbe, 'Unconscious Cerebration. A Psychological Study', p. 25.
8. Cobbe, 'Dreams, as Illustrations of Unconscious Cerebration', p. 519. This essay was also reprinted, along with 'Unconscious Cerebration. A Psychological Study', in Cobbe's *Darwinism in Morals and Other Essays* (London: William and Norgate, 1872).
9. Eliot, *Middlemarch*, p. 226.
10. Sully, 'The Dream as a Revelation', p. 358.
11. Brewster, *Letters on Natural Magic, addressed to Sir Walter Scott*, p. 99.
12. Brewster, *Letters on Natural Magic*, p. 28. Paris, *Philosophy in Sport Made Science in Earnest, Being an Attempt to Illustrate the First Principles of Natural Philosophy by the Aid of Popular Toys and Sports*, vol. 3, p. 6. I have previously considered Paris and Brewster's discussion of the thaumatrope as a potential technological supplement to teaching children to read in the context of Victorian domestic discourse in Groth, 'Domestic Phantasmagoria: The Victorian Domestic and Experimental Visuality', pp. 147–69.
13. Gunning, 'Hand and Eye: Excavating a New Technology of the Image in the Victorian Era', p. 496.
14. Keen, *Literature, Commerce, and the Spectacle of Modernity, 1750–1800*, pp. 13–14.
15. Alan Richardson discusses the broader cultural implications of the emergence of child-centred pedagogy in *Literature, Education, and Romanticism: Reading as Social Practice, 1780–1832*.
16. Rancière, *The Future of the Image*, p. 16.
17. Patricia Anderson provides a detailed account of the visual image in popular periodicals and magazines, including *The Penny Magazine* in *The Printed Image and the Transformation of Popular Culture 1790–1860*.
18. King, 'A Paradigm of Reading the Victorian Penny Weekly: Education of the Gaze and *The London Journal*', p. 83.
19. Luisa Calè mobilises Sergei Eisenstein's 'filmic eye' to restore the visual dimensions to Romantic reading practices in *Fuseli's Milton Gallery: 'Turning Readers into Spectators'*, p. 5.
20. Jay David Bolter and Richard Grusin distil the double logic of remediation thus: 'Our culture wants to multiply its media and to erase all traces of mediation: ideally, it wants to erase its media in the very act of multiplying them.' *Remediation: Understanding New Media*, p. 5.
21. Marsh, 'Dickensian "Dissolving Views": The Magic Lantern, Visual Story-Telling, and the Victorian Technological Imagination', pp. 333–46.
22. Hepworth, *Came the Dawn: Memories of a Film Pioneer*, p. 18.
23. Scarry, *Dreaming by the Book*, p. 11.
24. Proust, *Remembrance of Things Past*, vol. 1, pp. 10–11.
25. Scarry, *Dreaming by the Book*, p. 12.
26. Coleridge, *Collected letters of Samuel Taylor Coleridge*, vol. 1, pp. 625–6.
27. Otto, *Multiplying Worlds: Romanticism, Modernity, and the Emergence of Virtual Reality*, p. 9.
28. Coleridge, 'The Garden of Boccaccio', in *Poems*, pp. 473–6, lines 57–66.
29. Coleridge, *The Friend*, vol. 1, pp. 16–17.

30. Coleridge, 'On Poesy or Art', in *Biographia Literaria, with his Aesthetical Essays*, vol. 2, pp. 259–60.
31. Rovee, *Imagining the Gallery: The Social Body of British Romanticism*, p. 39.
32. To James Gilman (Surgeon, Highgate), 9 October 1825. Coleridge, *Collected letters*, vol. 5, p. 496.
33. Rovee, *Imagining the Gallery*, p. 39.
34. Stewart, *Elements of the Philosophy of the Human Mind*, vol. 3, p. 315.
35. Deleuze and Guattari, *A Thousand Plateaus: Capitalism and Schizophrenia*, p. 504.
36. Munsterberg, 'The Photoplay: A Psychological Study' in *Hugo Munsterberg on Film. The Photoplay: A Psychological Study and Other Writings*, pp. 1–161. See also Noel Carroll on the limitations of the film/mind analogy in 'Film/Mind Analogies: The Case of Hugo Munsterberg', pp. 489–99.
37. Kluge, Levin and Hansen, 'On Film and the Public Sphere', *New German Critique* 24/25, p. 207.
38. Hansen, *Babel and Babylon: Spectatorship in American Silent Film*, p. 13.
39. Scribner's Magazine ran from 1887 until 1889, publishing writing by Arthur Conan Doyle, Edith Wharton, Robert Louis Stevenson, Rudyard Kipling, alongside lavish illustrations and heavily supplemented by advertisements.
40. The kinetoscope was the combined invention of Thomas Edison and his employee, William Kennedy Laurie Dickson. Edison first invented a camera called the kinetograph that could display rolls of 35 mm wide celluloid film on a continuous loop at an even speed. Dickson then developed a viewer for the films that he called the kinetoscope, consisting of a viewing piece attached to the top of a box, which a single viewer could look through to watch the film that ran continuously. Edison's earliest films lasted around 20 seconds. The kinetoscope was first exhibited at the Chicago World's Fair in 1893 and in London in 1894.
41. P. Adams Sitney notes that 'the cinematic experience during the silent period was one of an alternation of reading and looking at images in an illusionistic depth', in 'Image and Title in Avante-Garde Cinema', p. 103.
42. Gerald Graff contextualises Brander Matthews' contribution to the history of literary studies in America in *Professing Literature: An Institutional History*, p. 128.
43 Hansen analyses the 'civilising' ideology that shaped the education of predominantly women and migrants in film literacy programmes of this kind in *Babel and Babylon*, pp. 76–86.
44. Peter Decherney identifies these Ruskin-derived techniques in 'Film Study and Its Object', p. 446.
45. Hansen, 'Universal Language and Democratic Culture: Myths of Origin in Early American Cinema', in *Myth and Enlightenment in American Literature*, p. 45.
46. Hansen, *Babel and Babylon*, p. 14.
47. Flint, Introduction to Charles Dickens, *Pictures from Italy*, p. vii.
48. Dickens, *Pictures from Italy*, p. 25.
49. Richard Altick provides a detailed account of the diorama's effects in *The Shows of London*.
50. Lewes, *The Physiology of Common Life*, vol. 2, p. 66.

51. Lewes, 'Dickens in Relation to Criticism', *Fortnightly Review* 11 (February 1872), p. 148.
52. Lewes cited in Collins, *Dickens: The Critical Heritage*, p. 571.
53. Lewes, *Problems of Life and Mind*, vol. 1, p. 162.
54. Davis, *George Eliot and Nineteenth-Century Psychology: Exploring the Unmapped Country*, p. 136.
55. Lewes, *Problems of Life and Mind*, vol. 4, p. 166.
56. Lewes, Problems of Life and Mind, vol. 4, p. 167.
57. Dallas, *The Gay Science*, vol. 1, p. 213.
58. Scarry, *Dreaming by the Book*, p. 5.
59. Stewart, *Between Film and Screen: Modernism's Photosynthesis*, p. 266.
60. Stewart, 'Curtain Up on Victorian Popular Cinema; Or, The Critical Theater of the Animatograph', http://www.branchcollective.org/, p. 3.
61. Rorty, *Philosophy and the Mirror of Nature*, p. 49.
62. Heidegger, 'The Age of the World Picture', in *The Question Concerning Technology and Other Essays*, p. 154.
63. Kant, *Critique of Pure Reason*, pp. 24–5.
64. Crary, *Techniques of the Observer: On Vision and Modernity in the Nineteenth Century*, p. 59.

Chapter 1

Moving Books in Regency London

Regency London, or the 'Romantic Metropolis', has come to be known in recent scholarship as a site of dramatic social and technological transformation.[1] With a population exceeding one million by 1800, a figure that doubled by 1850, no European city compared to its scale or cosmopolitan scope. Describing the radical impact of this social transformation, with its attendant 'gross and violent stimulants', Wordsworth wrote:

> For a multitude of causes unknown to former times are now acting with a combined force to blunt the discriminating powers of the mind, and unfitting it for all voluntary exertion ... the encreasing [sic] accumulation of men in cities, where the uniformity of their occupations produces a craving for extraordinary incident which the rapid communication of intelligence hourly gratifies. To this tendency of life and manners the literature and theatrical exhibitions of the country have conformed themselves.[2]

Networked as never before by new systems of information, dwelling in increasingly confined urban spaces, distracted by novel entertainments that fed off immediate sensation, Wordsworth's Londoners are passive instruments of an insatiable undiscriminating media machine.

Nor was this an atypical response to the sheer density and disorientating accelerations of this new urban life. One of the defining characteristics of London during the Napoleonic wars, as Daniel Headrick observes, was the technological transformation of information systems, such as the telegraphic communication of news, heightening the sense of porous boundaries between nations, as well as minds, as Wordsworth's anxious reflections on the state of modern poetry suggest.[3] Yet, as James Chandler and Kevin Gilmartin, and more recently Peter Otto, remind us in their readings of the panoramic scope of 'Composed Upon Westminster Bridge', Wordsworth's dynamic visualisations of Regency London are necessarily a part of the modern media ecology that he feared was transforming active reading and viewing into passive consumption.⁴ Indeed, Peter Otto claims that the following lines from Wordsworth's sonnet establish 'a homology' (217) between the reader, the poem, and the generic form of the sonnet, on the one hand, and the spectator, visual representation, and the panorama (or Eidophusikon's) optical environment on the other:

> Earth has not anything to show more fair:
> Dull would he be of soul who could pass by
> A sight so touching in its majesty:
> This city now doth, like a garment, wear
> This beauty of the morning: silent, bare,
> Ships, towers, domes, theatres, and temples lie
> Open unto the fields, and to the sky;
> All bright and glittering in the smokeless air.⁵

Ironically, given the critical assessment of contemporary 'literary and theatrical exhibitions' in the above passage from the *Lyrical Ballads*, the transformation of London into a sublime 'show' in these lines evokes the visual experience of contemporary popular exhibitions, such as Robert Barker's panorama of London, and Thomas Girtin's panoramic painting of London, which the latter advertised as the *Eidometropolis*.⁶ Inviting the spectator to scan the city in all its vivid density, Girtin and Barker's panoramic views of London conveyed a sense of suspended animation, a moment taken out of time, paused so that the overwhelming detail of the scene could be processed. While identifying the affinities between this visual experience and Wordsworth's panoramic view, Otto also distinguishes a subtle variation from the 'prepared script' of the conventional panoramic experience. Wordsworth's stress on the contingency of the panoramic view as a 'passing reality' produced by a specific 'perceptual environment', Otto suggests, created unprecedented ways of interacting with the spectacle of modern London (218).

These interactions seem less unprecedented, however, when filtered through the implicit passivity of Wordsworth's nostalgia for a premodern world. As Paul Keen observes of the 'sophisticated but implicitly passive accounts' of Wordsworth's immediate literary precursors, such reactionary responses to the spectacle of modernity constituted only one of many modes of literary engagement in this period of radical cultural and social transformation. Other writers, publishers and readers who adopted more resourceful, witty and self-conscious approaches to the role of literature in the new media landscape of Regency London, were less concerned with questions of aesthetic expression and power than with engaging with the challenges and possibilities it represented to rethink 'what kinds of knowledge' literary forms should aspire to 'and what kind of reading public this ought to entail'.⁷

The following chapter examines three such witty and resourceful responses to the dynamic media environment of Regency London that vary significantly from Wordsworth's magisterial aesthetic interaction with the panorama as a mechanism for the sublime transfiguration of the landscape of London into a natural wonder. The first, Jane and Ann Taylor's *Signor Topsy-Turvy's Wonderful Magic Lantern: or, The World Turned Upside Down* (1810) emanates from a network of writers and publishers that channelled Lockean models of the mind as an inscriptive surface into experimental interactions between visual and verbal media.[8] The second example, Marguerite Gardiner, Countess of Blessington's first anonymous publication *The Magic Lantern; or, Sketches of Scenes in the Metropolis* (1823) enlists the fluid dissolve of one lantern slide into the next to materialise the associative flow of reverie inspired by her digressive wanderings through Regency London's profuse and various attractions.[9] Operating as a structural and meta-phoric conceit designed to create the illusion of life unfolding in real time, Blessington's magic lantern strives to capture 'the living, active thickness' of the historical world, to adapt William James.[10] The third and final example is Pierce Egan's playful alignment of reading and looking through a camera obscura in his enduringly popular *The True History of Tom and Jerry; or The Day and Night Scenes, of Life in London* (1821).[11] Recalling reading Egan as a child, William Makepeace Thackeray described *Life in London* as an invitation to let his mind wander through the long-gone diversions of Regency London. Like Blessington's magic lantern sequences, Egan's camera obscura images license, according to Thackeray, drifting from one scene to another, a kinetic process that triggers nostalgic associations.[12] Thackeray's anec-dotal account of reading Egan also resonates, as we shall see, with an emerging psychological preoccupation with the involuntary aspects of reading and viewing (the unconscious turning of a page or involuntary decoding of sequences of black marks on a white surface) as analogous to the mind's dynamic generation of moving images in states of reverie or dreaming.

Regency Reading Scenes

Signor Topsy-Turvy's Wonderful Magic Lantern is an idiosyncratic convergence of print and visual media produced by two writers who were immersed not only in contemporary pedagogic theory, but also in the traditional technologies of book production. Born into a prominent dissenting family of writers and engravers with both provincial and

London-based literary networks, Ann and Jane Taylors' literary ambitions and engraving skills were nurtured by their parents, who combined writing didactic books of various kinds with managing the family engraving business.[13] Notably in the context of his daughters' later interest in visual technologies, Isaac Taylor devised educational flash cards of plants and animals and engraved outlines for students to colour in and label with names of anatomical and botanical parts.[14] Likewise, Isaac Taylor Jr, best known for his extraordinarily successful *Natural History of Enthusiasm* (1830), wrote a remarkable defence of home education that drew together contemporary psychological debates with a close analysis of the visual dimensions of reading.[15]

Ann and Jane Taylors' first literary collaboration, *Original Poems for Infant Minds* (1804) was quickly followed in the next seven years by nine other children's books, including *Signor Topsy-Turvy's Wonderful Magic Lantern*. The sisters' first venture into adult verse, *The Associate Minstrels* (1810) continued their prolific and positively received collaboration. The poems in this volume also reflect an emergent mutual preoccupation with gendered theories of mind, the history of scientific ideas and pedagogic practice. Organised around the motif of sexual difference, Ann Taylor's poem 'Remonstrance' exemplifies these shared concerns, rhythmically calibrating the contributions of male philosophers and female pedagogues:[16]

> Boyle, Locke, and Newton, deep in lore,
> *Man's* lofty records trace;
> Edgeworth, and Hamilton, and More,
> *Our* living annals grace.
>
> *His* soul is thoughtful and profound;
> *Hers*, brilliant and acute; –
> Plants cultured, each, in different ground
> And bearing different fruit.[17]

Despite modelling an implicitly conservative and intractable gender division of the spheres of knowledge, aligning the masculine with the reason and abstraction, and the feminine with the applied knowledge of lived experience, these lines also position Ann Taylor within what Niklas Luhmann would characterise as a 'self-referential system' of writers who perpetually re-described their connection to one another and to their precursors, while reflexively producing increasingly complex understandings of the discursive construction of their collective object of inquiry – the experiential configuration of the mind.[18] Taylor's allusions to Boyle, Locke and Newton summon associations with an empirical insistence on 'tracing' the development or history of phenomena through close observation and experimental induction, while the triumvirate of Maria Edgeworth, Elizabeth Hamilton and Hannah More were all synonymous with the education of women and writings on the domestic.[19]

Maria and Richard Edgeworth's popular *Practical Education* typifies the circulatory mechanisms of this new system of scientific education, with its explicit debt to Locke's conception of the malleability of the child – born a tabula rasa and subsequently shaped by experience.[20] This ethos is materialised by the organic metaphor of culturing plants in different grounds in Ann Taylor's second stanza. Integral to this 'culturing' of the child's mind is the fostering of an experimental sensibility as part of an engagement with everyday objects in their environment. Edgeworth writes: 'When children are busily trying experiments upon objects within their reach, we should not, by way of saving them the trouble, break the course of their ideas, and totally prevent them from acquiring knowledge by their own experience' (19). These words echo Locke's own advice that children be granted 'free liberty in their recreations'.[21] The Edgeworths also recommended that parents read Joseph Priestley's experiments with optics from his *History of Vision* to their child to foster 'habits of observation and attention' through various experiments with the magic lantern, the telescope, as well as reflected light on everyday things such as bubbles and windowpanes (35). But this self-referential educational system was not an open one. It was closed, the Edgeworths insisted, to the parallel world of 'parlour tricks' masquerading as enlightening experiments (32). William Hooper's *Rational Recreations* (1774), for example, typified this competitive alternative system of magic and illusion.[22] Notably, Hooper's work went through multiple editions and reprints throughout the nineteenth century. His name was also synonymous with elaborate home entertainment devices. These included a magic theatre consisting of a lantern and moving slides inside a box that projected narratives designed to 'render useful learning, not dull, tedious and disgustful', to quote Hooper, 'but facile, bland, delightfully alluring, captivating'.[23]

Such captivating digressions into virtual worlds also fell outside the Taylor sisters' pragmatic engagement with the lessons to be learned by engaging with the then novel technology of the illustrated book. Reinforcing their mutual commitment to guiding their readers' eyes through a world of rational pleasures, the sisters published *Signor Topsy-Turvy* in Benjamin Tabart's Juvenile Library series. Editors of this series included leading figures in debates about the education of women; Mary Wollstonecraft, Eliza Fenwick and Mary Jane Godwin. Fenwick also contributed *Visits to the Juvenile Library; Or, Knowledge*

Proved to be the Source of Happiness (1805), which was an elaborate fictional advertisement for Tabart's Bond Street bookstore, 'The Juvenile and School Library'.[24] Fenwick was a proto-feminist who earned a living by her pen, hence her agreement to sing Tabart's praises. Yet this commercial pragmatism was complicated by her sincere belief in the vital role of pleasure and imagination in the instruction of children. *Visits to the Juvenile Library* accordingly told the story of a family of orphaned children who arrived in England from the West Indies with an aversion to reading.[25] They soon learn the error of their ways, however, when their guardian Mrs Clifford exposes them to the wonders of Tabart's bookseller's shop, 'entirely filled with books that are written purposely for the instruction and entertainment of children' (21).

The subsequent descriptive passages are worth quoting at length as they provide us with a perspective, albeit a vested one, on the fusion of commerce and education that defined Tabart's Juvenile Library, which would soon include the Taylors' *Signor Topsy Turvy* on its overcrowded shelves:

> All the young gentlemen and young ladies that I am acquainted with, think they cannot go there too often; as for prettiness . . . the neat arrangement of an immense quantity of books, handsomely bound in red or green leather, and lettered on the back with gold letters together with globes, maps, and little ornamented book-cases, of various sizes, fine painted and varnished, have a pleasing effect on the eye. Besides, the library is generally full of well-dressed ladies, accompanied with blooming boys and girls, who are eagerly hunting for books of knowledge, or looking at the pictures of entertaining stories; (24)

This alluring description, however, pales in comparison to the real wonders of Tabart's bookshop:

> The carriage was in readiness, and the children leaped into it with bounding hearts, and were whirled away to Bond Street. Notwithstanding they had heard so much said in praise of the Juvenile Library, they found it far exceeded their utmost expectations. *What all these books written for children!* They were ready to exclaim . . . they were puzzled amidst the endless varieties that presented themselves. They took up first one book and then another, examined the globes, peeped into the boxes of dissected maps, and wished again and again, that they could carry the whole shop away with them. (32)[26]

Beautiful bindings compete for the attention of fashionable mothers and privileged children in this marvellous consumer phantasmagoria packed with alluring objects and wonderful toy-books.

Grimly viewing similar scenes, Robert Southey was scathing in his assessment of what would become known as 'the bibliomania' of the

Regency period. 'Books are now so dear', he lamented, 'that they are becoming rather fashionable articles of *furniture* more than anything else; they who buy them do not read them, and they who read them do not buy them.'[27] Countering Southey's distinction between serious readers and undiscriminating bourgeois collectors, Fenwick presents an argument for pleasurable tactile encounters with the materiality of books as a conduit to potentially reading their contents with an open, engaged mind.

Contemporary engravings of the Juvenile Library suggest multiple ways of engaging with the space, all sanctioned by Tabart of course, in which children read or are read to, thumb through bookshelves, engage in conversation with interested adults, and gaze longingly through the shop's windows from the street outside.[28] Fenwick also licenses the pleasures of collecting and displaying beautifully bound books on ornamental shelves, rather than puritanically reducing such acquisitiveness to undiscriminating fashion. Describing the emotional and sensual thrills of collecting, Walter Benjamin writes of the mysterious

> relationship to objects which does not emphasise their functional, utilitarian value – that is, their usefulness – but studies and loves them as a scene, the stage, of their fate . . . One has only to watch a collector handle the objects in his glass case. As he holds them in his hands, he seems to be seeing through them into their distant past as thought inspired.[29]

Looking and touching beautiful books triggers a state of reverie and childlike renewal, according to Benjamin, that recalls more juvenile forms of acquisitiveness, 'from touching things to giving them names' (63).

Signor Topsy-Turvy's Wonderful Magic Lantern was a less luxurious object than Fenwick describes, but it nevertheless conforms to Tabart's fusion of commerce, entertainment and instruction. As the sisters reassured their readers:

> Those grandmammas and aunts who are versed in the nursery learning of fifty years ago, may perhaps recollect a little volume entitled, 'The World Turned Upside Down': The Biographers of Signor Topsy-Turvy, and his Magic Lantern, beg leave to apologise for having stolen a few ideas from that learned original, which they had been recommended to revise for the amusement of modern nurseries.[30]

In what amounts to false advertising, the Taylors avow a debt to a tradition of 'world upside down books' before turning that tradition on its head. The specific volume to which they refer, *The World Turned Upside Down: or The Folly of Man Exemplified in Twelve Comical Relations Upon Uncommon Subjects* (1750) was an anthology of illustrated verse

FRONTISPIECE

Figure 1.1 Frontispiece, Jane and Ann Taylor's *Signor Topsy-Turvy's Magic Lantern*

in which pictorial inversions were corrected by accompanying didactic poems.[31] Yet the engraved frontispiece of the Taylors' volume playfully reframes the 'upside down' tradition (Figure 1.1).

Inviting the eye to move backwards as part of moving forward into the text, the engraving imitates a magic lantern slide that, in turn, represents a lantern slide show in progress. A lecturer, surrounded by a group of children in various states of distraction and attention, gestures towards an illustration of an upside down figure playfully balanced on an illuminated globe. The scene creates a three-dimensional effect, an illusion of a story-telling space opening out before the reader and set in motion by their hand turning the page.

The Taylors' introductory poem sustains the playful inversion of their eighteenth-century source. The opening poem from *The World Turned Upside Down* began with the following attack on the astronomical discoveries of Tycho Brahe:

Philosophers of old will tell us,
As Tycho, and such merry fellows,

That round this habitable ball
The beamy sun did yearly fall;
No wonder then the world is found
By change of place Turn'd Upside Down:
If revolutions strange appear
Within the compass of the sphere;
If men and things succession know,
And no dependence reigns below;
Since 'tis allow'd the world we dwell in,
Is always round the sun a sailing;
Experience to our knowledge brings;
That times may change as well as things,
And art than nature wiser grown,
Turns every object upside down,
Whim's epidemic takes her rise,
And constancy's become a vice.

Here the upside down motif negatively associates epistemological and moral uncertainty with a history of experimental science synonymous with technological invention and natural magic. Tycho Brahe's famed observational precision and refinement of the telescope to more accurately record orbital patterns and anomalies is erroneously associated with the Copernican revolution to serve the author's satirical attack on the devices of rational explanation.[32] Characterised as a 'merry fellow' Tycho Brahe becomes synonymous with a new world order in which moral certainties are turned upside down by the relative perspective and inconstant character of the individual observer. This wilful misrepresentation is also a throwback to the association of the telescope with natural magic, the seemingly miraculous revelation of the wonders of nature by 'men of learning'.[33] Indeed, the first known sketch of a telescope is attributed to Giambattista della Porta, the author of *Natural Magick* (1558).[34] Like the telescope, from its first appearance in 1659 the magic lantern was synonymous with disrupting the 'succession' by which men know; literally turning things upside down, it was an optical device that the Taylors playfully exploit to divert and engage their readers.

In contrast to their eighteenth-century inspiration, and as Lewis Carroll would do over half a century later in the Alice books, the Taylors embrace the epistemological uncertainties that arise from viewing familiar moral topoi from a technologically altered perspective. Their introductory poem, following on from their frontispiece, reproduces a magic lantern performance in which an audience actively embraces illusionistic inversion over verisimilitude. The poem begins anecdotally with the protestation, 'I can't tell the story for truth', before proceeding to tell the tale of the first inventor of the magic lantern who, perplexed by its inverse projections, loses patience with the travails of scientific explanation and promotes his invention to the 'nobility, gentry and public at large' as a 'shew': 'So wonderful, magical, comic and new, /As nothing in nature could equal' (5). To his surprise the public throng to his 'rare exhibition':

> And nought could exceed the huzzas and encores,
> As houses, and horses, and people, and doors,
> With their feet in the air, and their heads on the floor,
> Past by, – 'twas so droll a position! (6)

This unqualified embrace of inverted magic lantern images as 'original thought' by 'people of rank and intelligence', as well as the general public, is matched only by the intensity of resistance to the actions of a 'shrewd fellow', who resenting the 'philosopher's fame' destroys the entertainment:

> At length a shrewd fellow from college that came,
> Who envied, 'twas said, the philosopher's fame,
> (As cross and conceited as could be),
> Stole up to the sliders, and *turning them round*,
> To the company's grief and dismay it was found,
> That now, they were seen as they *should be!*
>
> The tumult was dreadful, – the gentlemen rose,
> And said they *would* see *upside down*, if they chose,
> They came with no other intention;
> And begg'd that, upon a philosopher's word,
> He would not let any one be so absurd
> Again, as to spoil his invention.
>
> Now lest there may still be some pedant in town,
> To laugh at this turning the world upside down,
> With argument witty and weighty,
> We've taken the trouble, at wonderful cost,
> To copy the sliders (long thought to be lost),
> And appeal to the whole literati. (7)

The Taylors' self-acknowledged anachronism lightly rewrites the magic lantern's provenance as both an entertainment and a device to aid in the demonstration of experimental physics.[35] In contrast to seventeenth-century audiences encountering the highly regarded physicist Christiaan Huygens' invention for the first time, the Taylors' intended audience would have been very familiar with primitive versions of the domestic magic lantern, as well as more spectacular recent phantasmagoric reincarnations in both Paris and London. The magic lantern motif would also have appealed to a well-established market for children's books that cleverly exploited the growing popular interest in optical devices, such as John Newbery's extraordinarily successful foray into pseudonymous publication under the name *Tom Telescope*.[36] Tom Telescope's diverting account of Newtonian philosophy for the child reader had gone through nine editions by the end of the eighteenth century and is an important precedent for the Taylors' volume and Benjamin Tabart's Juvenile and School Library.[37]

Another notable feature of the Taylors' introductory poem is its enactment of a scenario of consensual consumption that correlates with the new child-centred pedagogy's advocacy of engineered consent rather than overt repression.[38] Continuing the stress on rationality and independent judgement promoted by Wollstonecraft, Barbauld, Edgeworth and others, the members of the Taylors' fictional audience interact with and determine the course of their entertainment, preferring to engage with the magic lantern on their own terms. This scenario thus serves as the ideal introduction to the following series of 'sliders' of playful, predominantly animal–human inversions promoted to 'appeal to the whole literati'. For example, in the first slider, 'The Cook Cooked' – an engraving of a cook on a spit being slowly roasted and basted by a hare, a turtle, and a turkey – is accompanied by a poem that imagines sedition, treason and revolution in the pantry (Figure 1.2).

In a thinly veiled political allegory, the cook's various delicacies, renamed 'patriots', which also include a Carroll-like company of eels, oysters, as well as the ring-leading hare and turkey, pledge to 'murder every cook they saw' and proceed to do so in the final stanza of the poem (8–10). This anthropomorphic representation of animals confronting humans with the cruelty of their everyday treatment is sustained throughout the volume.

In a later slider, 'The Fish Turned Fishers' the hunted plot revolution against the hunters in an absurd scenario that again suggests the anthropomorphic inversions of Carroll's much later satire (Figure 1.3):

On the banks of a lake by a forest o'erhung,
One day a rebellion began,
The tenants of wood and of water among,
Against the dominion of man;

The partridge and rabbit, the pheasant and hare,
Were met for a chat on the shore,
And a fish or two ventur'd their gills in the air,
To listen, and put in their oar.

'My friends of the forest,' the partridge begun,
'Just lords of these beautiful shades,

Figure 1.2 'The Cook Cooked'

Figure 1.3 'The Fish Turned Fishers'

'You know that a great living thing with a gun,
'Our rightful domain invades.' (13)

This whimsical politicising of animal rights and implicit critique of the excesses of the landed gentry is consistent with the Taylors' non-conformist resistance to worldly excess. The sisters were active abolitionists and tireless philanthropists.[39] After her sister's marriage Jane Taylor became even more outspoken in her political views, writing openly as a dissenter in two popular volumes addressed to young people, *Display: a Tale for Young People* (1815) and *Essays in Rhyme* (1816). When criticised for her openly dissenting stance she rejected the idea that women should remain silent on controversial topics, acerbically remarking in her memoirs: 'Whoever blamed Mrs. [Hannah] More for poking the steeple into almost every page of her writings?'[40]

The Taylors' reworking of the conventions of licensed misrule in the form of a magic lantern slide sequence is indicative of their canny targeting of aspirant middle-class interest in the education of the child as a register of social status. Anthropomorphism and inversion were popular devices of illustrated children's books published during the Regency period.[41] The Taylors themselves were only too well aware of this market, given their ambitions to start a school for girls in London and their commercial relationship with their publisher Benjamin Tabart, who ran one of many juvenile libraries competing for market share at this time. Others included the successful juvenile library of John Harris who made his reputation with the much reprinted *The Comic Adventures of Old Mother Hubbard, and Her Dog*.[42] As J. H. Plumb argues in his account of the emergence of the child as a discrete literary consumer, by the end of the eighteenth century a new children's literature had emerged that was designed to attract adults by projecting 'an image of those virtues which parents wished to inculcate in their offspring, as well as to beguile the child'.[43] In this context, the Taylors' overt featuring of the technology of mediation conforms to another practice Plumb identifies, the decoying of the child into reading by appealing to the eye. By sustaining the association of the act of turning each page with the projection of a new slider, the familiar didactic narrative of the upside-down book and the engraved illustrative plates are imbued with an aura of novelty. This also meant that the magic lantern's contradictory associations with science and magic became an integral part of how the text was consumed. The volume's title and frontispiece explicitly associate a private act of reading with the sphere of early nineteenth-century public visual entertainments that were synonymous with the strategic intensification of audience affect.

The instrumental extension of the senses was a familiar one to early nineteenth-century consumers, readers and pedagogues, as was the correlative idea that what was seen and heard required interpretation by a watchful parent, tutor or lecturer. Instruments such as the telescope, the microscope and the magic lantern provided useful distortions that made the previously hidden visible, but they also generated increasingly heated debates about the relative epistemological implications of exact or distorted duplications of human perception. These debates were particularly heated later in the century in the case of the stereoscope, but they are also pertinent to early nineteenth-century conceptions of the magic lantern as an instructive device.[44] Notably, Locke reinforced the association of instruments, such as the magic lantern, with natural magic. He distrusted the distorted mediation of the natural world by philosophical instruments with the same intensity that he rejected the false insinuations and passions of figurative language. According to Locke, both language and instruments introduced distorting lenses that cheated the eye and mind creating false analogies between words and things.

This philosophical distrust of distorting illustrative media, however, did not penetrate into the profitable commerce in explicitly inter-medial forms, such as moveable illustrated books, which invited readers to read, view, touch and move pages in and out and back and forth to create literal three-dimensional scenes. While early forms of these books began to appear in the middle of the eighteenth century, such as John Sayer's extraordinarily popular turn-up books which simulated the sequence of the Harlequinade, progressively revealed by the child turning down the flaps on each page, moveable books reached the height of their popularity in the middle to late decades of the nineteenth century.[45] Often described as toy books, these volumes encouraged reading as a form of interactive episodic play, transforming the codex into an instructive miscellaneous entertainment where extracts and abridgements of familiar tales, legends and myths could be endlessly recycled. Dean and Sons' popular series of toy books, for example, included enticing titles such as *Dame Wonder's Transformations* (1840). Later more elaborate publications explicitly drew on peep-show and proto-cinematic formats, featuring popular works such as *Little Red Riding Hood, Robinson Crusoe, Cinderella* and *Aladdin* – typical titles included *The Scenic Fairy Tales of Cinderella and her Glass Slipper* (1876), *The Scenic Effect of Robinson Crusoe and his man Friday* (1877) and *The Motograph Moving Picture Book* (1898).[46]

Blessington's Magic Lantern

In contrast to her more didactic precursors, Marguerite Gardiner, Countess of Blessington's first anonymous publication *The Magic Lantern; or, Sketches of Scenes in the Metropolis* (1823) mobilises the conceit of the book as viewing device for the light entertainment, as opposed to the instructive edification, of the adult middle-class reader. Devoid of illustrations the printed text depicts a series of four crowd scenes viewed from different perspectives – an auction, the opera, spectators at Belzoni's tomb and walking in Hyde Park. Projecting herself and the reader into these disparate environments, Blessington attempts to capture the contingency of life unfolding in real time. As she moves through varying states of conscious attention and associative reverie, recording overheard conversations, impressions of objects, faces, the stress on the contingency and ephemerality of modern metropolitan life intensifies.

Contemporary reviewers played on this notion of ephemerality as well. Christopher North's (John Wilson) decidedly ambivalent review of *The Magic Lantern* in *Blackwood's* describes himself looking at and then opening the covers of Blessington's 'long, lean, blue-looking volume', which an anonymous reader passed on after it 'had amused him on his voyage down from London in the James Watt steam-boat'.[47] This intentionally diminishing aside aligns reading Blessington's five-shilling volume with an icon of industrialised transport – the then novel steamboat that had only commenced transporting people between London and Leith in 1819.[48] Like the railway that would follow in its wake, the advent of the steam engine signalled the acceleration of daily life, a self-conscious modernity typified by new temporalities of travel through time and space. Consumed in transit, Blessington's 'slim' and 'lively' volume provided an easy distraction. North reinforces this equation of reading Blessington with the ephemerality of modern industrial experience by stressing the 'coarseness of this paper over which we are now drawing our forefinger', and summoning associations with other cheap stereotypically feminine genres, such as the domestic guide or cookbook:

> Had this been a matronly treatise on household frugality, an attempt to undersell Mrs Rundle's System of Cookery, such paper and such boards would have been in good-keeping – its outward appearance seems to remind one more of the kitchen than the drawing table. (715)

Imbued with the 'aesthetics of the machine', to use James Secord's suggestive phrase, Blessington's *Magic Lantern* exhibits scenes of London

life that prove a little too realistic for North.[49] Oscillating between praising Blessington's 'colloquial piquancy' and playfully co-opting the motif
of the magic lantern to evoke the experience of reading Blessington's
scenes, the ultimate impression this review gives is of ambivalence:
'Indeed, the work throughout, exhibits our fellow-beings, perhaps, too
much as they actually are, and of course in a less favourable point of
view than that in which any of us would wish to be seen' (716).

Although she would achieve some fame for her *Journal of Conversations
with Lord Byron* (1833) and her contributions to annuals, Blessington's
scandalous private life and reputation as a self-styled salonnière over-
shadowed her various literary enterprises.[50] *The Magic Lantern* was
never intended to secure Blessington enduring fame. As North's dismissive assessment reinforces, ephemerality was as integral to the material
design of Blessington's volume, as the motif of the magic lantern was
to its metaphoric structure. Blessington herself pre-empted such an
evaluation in the volume's epigraph:

> For thee, my little book, I feel no dread,
> The chances are – thou never wilt be read.[51]

Rhetorical gestures to contingency and chance shape each scene.
Blessington's fragmentary anecdotal prose embraces an aesthetic of
the accidental, moving through spaces and seizing on random objects,
exchanges and events. At best this collage of details strives to simulate
the indeterminate perpetual becoming of everyday rituals unfolding in
real time – attending an auction, going to the park, visiting an exhibition,
frequenting the opera.

Each scene begins as if the magic lantern is a camera obscura transiently capturing street scenes in motion, rather than a projection device
that progressively illuminates a series of arrested images. In the case of
the auction, Blessington's eye is drawn into the scene by the 'sight of
a bustling crowd' in front of a doorway as she walks by (2). Curious,
she wanders into the house and through each room scanning its contents and recording overheard conversations. The instability of tenses,
moving between past and present, materialises the associative flow of
her impressions. In a sequence that begins with her eye being caught
by 'a very beautiful filigree box' surrounded by a group of fashionable
young men 'of the effeminate race which has, for the last few years, been
known by the appellation of Dandy or Exquisite', Blessington casually
evokes the performative banalities of polite conversation (6–7):

> The box, as I anticipated, soon attracted their attention, and, 'O dear, how
> pretty!' 'How very elegant!' 'How monstrous charming!' with innumerable

other ejaculations of admiration, were all uttered with great animation, and at nearly the same moment, by the ladies; while their attending beaux, between a languid smile and a suppressed yawn, merely said 'Do you think so?' 'is it so very pretty?' or, 'Do you wish to bid for it?' (7)

The alienation of the reader from the inherent instability of values – both moral and material – in this phatic conversational exchange is assumed. Exclamatory effusion and unanswered questions register the disruptive affects and failed communication of a conversational mode driven by object exchange. Unlike Blessington's 'magic lantern' the anonymous speakers only selectively identify and instantly commodify the residuum of the past inhabitants of the house. By contrast, the magic lantern in this context, like the archival temporality of photography and the early actualities of Edison, Lumière and others, registers the ontological contingency of private familial histories. The 'spectacular household failure' of the bankruptcy auction, as Jeff Nunokawa argues, serves notice of the 'ubiquitous insecurity' that underwrites nineteenth-century fictions of the sanctity of the domestic realm.[52] Even the contents of the family library come under the hammer. One potential bidder observes that the bankrupted owner's 'books were well chosen and well bought' (16). Again, Blessington's moral lens captures the skewed values of a social milieu in which books are exchanged, rather than read.

The subsequent scenes in Hyde Park, Belzoni's tomb and the opera present equally ambivalent impressions of the diurnal rhythms and rituals of metropolitan life. Sketching, the other mode of transcription evoked in Blessington's title, licenses the haste and incomplete impressions that capture the frenetic crowds promenading around Hyde Park on a Sunday afternoon. As she puts it – 'the reader's mind will supply all that I have omitted' (54). Echoing her casual wandering through the auction, Blessington's lantern passes through, as if by chance, recording otherwise ephemeral scenes in an accumulative listing prose:

> Carriages of every description were to be seen, from the splendid *vis-à-vis* and elegant chariot, down to the vulgar city coach and more vulgar gig: next to the well-appointed curricle followed a shabby-hired whiskey; while the *cabriolet*, with its Dandy driver, was contrasted by its next neighbour, a vehicle partaking the joint qualities of a taxed-cart and Irish jaunting-car, conducted by a butcher-like looking man, accompanied by a large female, whose cheeks might in colour out-view his primest ox beef . . . while the promenade, at each side, is a moving mass, in which hats and bonnets, with occasional peeps of pretty faces, are alone visible. (26–7)[53]

The chaotic press of bodies moving through space, transgressing class and decorum verges on an urban grotesquery that 'would require the pencil of Hogarth', Blessington observes (31). As with Hogarth, inscription is a form of intervention, whether pencil on paper, or the projection of a magic-lantern slide sequence of metropolitan scenes. Indeed Blessington's stress on how the machinery of inscription interposes between the reader and representation nicely exemplifies the ways in which 'different media and varied forms, genres, and styles of representation', as Lisa Gitelman argues, 'act as brokers among acculturated practices of seeing, hearing, speaking, and writing'.[54] While this may seem a grand way to describe Blessington's slim volume of lantern scenes, her appropriation of the technology of the magic lantern as a representational style playfully negotiates between the auditory, optical and tactile dynamics of reading – from turning the page to eliciting similar projections within 'the reader's mind' (54).

The final two scenes of the volume – the tomb and the Italian opera – accentuate this reflexive interplay between 'acculturated practices of seeing, hearing, speaking and writing'.[55] Both scenes provide ample opportunity for what Blessington describes as 'daily observation' of English character and manners. In contrast to the desensitisation that Richard Sennett ascribes to the modern mobile individual whose 'desire to move freely has triumphed over the sensory claims of the space through which the body moves', Blessington's evocations of crowded London spaces are intended to sensitise and inspire the reader to register and engage with impressions of urban life in motion.[56] However, there are parallels between Sennett's account of Goethe's solidifying individualism felt more deeply in the midst of the crowd and Blessington's descriptions of crowded rooms through which she drifts stimulated yet aloof from the moving bodies that her lantern records. After describing the sensation of threading 'one's way through an immense and ever-moving crowd' as a peculiar and salutary experience in the *Italian Journey*, Goethe writes that 'anyone who looks about him seriously here and has eyes to see, must become *solid*; he must get a conception of solidity such as never so vivid to him before'.[57] He also speaks in a proto-cinematic way of seizing 'things one by one as they come', then retrospectively editing them – 'they will sort themselves out later' – as he wanders through the streets of Rome.[58] Blessington expresses a similar desire for solidity and retrospective stability, but it remains an elusive ideal.

Blessington accordingly begins her description of the crowded space of William Bullock's Egyptian Hall, where Belzoni's tomb was exhibited, by dramatising a 'reflecting mind' struggling to sort through 'the ever-varying scenes of this mutable world' (56). One such scene is of an earnest governess 'sententiously reading extracts from Belzoni's description' to her young charges in answer to her own question: 'If there ever existed men with lions', apes', and foxes' heads?' (58). Like Robert Burford prompting his customers to read Byronic extracts while viewing sublime vistas of Mount Blanc at the Leicester Square Panorama, to which I will return in the following chapter, the Governess compliantly reproduces acculturated practices of viewing and reading which Blessington records. A page later Blessington endorses this textual filtering of Belzoni's spectacular archaeological artefact in her description of a tutor and his two young charges, 'attentively examining the model, and comparing it with Belzoni's Narrative' (59). Such seriousness, she observes 'showed a spirit of enquiry and intelligence pleasing to witness' (59). However, a less ideal reading scene succeeds this in which an old lady with the aid of 'a pair of spectacles' struggles and fails to decipher a definition of a pyramid from Belzoni's description:

> Unfortunately she has got at a wrong page, and having puzzled herself for some time, at last, gives up the task in despair; and in answer to one of the children's questions of 'Grand-mama, what is a Pyramid?' the good old lady replies, 'Why a pyramid, my dear, is a pretty ornament for the centre of a table, such as papa sometimes has instead of an epergne. (61)

Exemplifying the lowbrow middle-class audience that frequented the Egyptian Hall, Blessington's hapless grandmother is unable to decipher the meaning of cultural artefacts that fall outside the familiar sphere of banal domestic experience. In contrast, the reader is left to assume, to the cosmopolitan sophistication of their authorial guide.

Blessington herself provides little detail of Belzoni's archaeological spectacle. Her concern is with enumerating familiar English types as they move through the exhibition space, momentarily pausing before each display. At first this response seems to align with Jane Austen's earlier account of visiting the Egyptian Hall in 1811. In a letter to her sister Cassandra, Austen wrote that while she derived 'some amusement' from Bullock's exhibits, her 'preference for Men & Women, always inclines me to attend more to the company than the sight'.[59] Blessington shared Austen's social preoccupations, enumerating further misuses of Belzoni's description, including a mother who bribes her children to cease asking questions with the promise of a copy of the description on their return home, and a woman who loudly pronounces that Egypt must be near Venice. Recoiling from the 'historical, geographical and chronological' ignorance of the 'greater part of the visitors', Blessington concludes judgementally that they were clearly only there to pass the time and meet acquaintances, rather than to draw any 'moral inference' from what they were viewing:

Wrapt up in their own self-satisfied ignorance, the works or monuments of antiquity boast no attraction for them; and, strange, to say, the metropolis of a country that professes to surpass all others in civilisation and morals, presents, in some of its inhabitants, examples of ignorance and want of reflection scarcely equalled in any other part of the civilised world. (74)

Giovanni Belzoni, a Bartholomew Fair strongman-turned-archaeologist, who had filled the upper floor of the Egyptian Hall with reconstructed ancient Egyptian sites, had failed to civilise the world with his grandiose imperial vision, according to Blessington at least.[60] Popularity equalled mass distraction in her assessment, in contrast to one reviewer in *The Times* who effused: 'Every eye must be gratified by this singular combination and skilful arrangement of objects so new and in themselves so striking.'[61]

Blessington's scathing account of Belzoni's tomb paralleled her Romantic contemporaries' ambivalent engagements with the wonders of the modern metropolis. Like Coleridge and Wordsworth, she registers the shock effects of its 'crowding images' and 'onrushing expressions'.[62] She is equally guilty of conveniently obscuring complex social relations in her fixation on the 'panoramic view', or the pleasurable illumination of isolated moments and scenes, as Deborah Epstein Nord has observed of other Regency writers such as Pierce Egan, Charles Lamb and Thomas De Quincey.[63] She also shares their preoccupation with the way the mind unconsciously registers and processes impressions of the external world. But, rather than selecting the sublime panoramic overview, her magic lantern slides favour close-up portraits of faces, bodies and objects. They parallel her own intermittent focus, which moves from simulating the affects of reverie to consciously attending to present sensations, shifting modalities that provide her with an expedient means of guiding her reader's attention from one scene to the next.

Thomas Brown observed in his contemporaneous lectures on the philosophy of mind, 'when *in reverie*, our conceptions become peculiarly vivid, and the objects of our thought seem almost to exist in our presence', but, he continues, 'if only we stretch out our hand, or fix our eyes on the forms that are permanently before us, the illusion vanishes'.[64] This contingent experience of perceptual vivacity is precisely the effect Blessington wishes to create through the visual reveries induced by her magic lantern – the involuntary generation of 'peculiarly vivid' images of London in her readers' minds. To return to Elaine Scarry, Blessington's magic lantern illuminates the complex reciprocity between the ordinary process of perceptual mimesis and the power of writing of a reflexively literary kind 'to incite us to bring forth mental images' that resemble our own 'perceptual acts'.[65] To be sure these vivid images generated by the reveries of the reading mind may evaporate with the touch of a hand. The complex interplay between reading black marks on a page 'devoid of *actual* sensory content' (5) and the vivid mental images reading generates remained a vexing one for Brown and his immediate Scottish Enlightenment precursors, such as Thomas Reid and Dugald Stewart. The parallels between Scarry and Reid are particularly striking on this question. Observing the fundamental difference between external moving objects and the mind's registration of those movements, Reid invokes the analogy of the way the material medium of writing, or sequences of sounds that constitute various speech acts, excite images in the mind:

> Such is the nature of mind, that, by its very constitution, when certain bodily motions take place, certain thoughts immediately arise, that have no resemblance whatever, as images, to the motions in consequence of which they arise. The thoughts which words, written or spoken excite, have surely no resemblance to the words themselves. A slight change of motion of a pen may produce, in the reader, affections of mind the most opposite.[66]

Writing has no visual or acoustic contents. Its tactile aspects are, as Scarry notes, limited to the 'weight of its pages, their smooth surfaces, and their exquisitely thin edges' (5). In fact, as Reid suggests above, the materiality or thingness of words may be antagonistic to the mental images they evoke. All this is not to overstate the philosophical claims of Blessington's self-consciously ephemeral writing, but to identify the parallel history of philosophical inquiry into the process of visualisation that her text literalises in its drive to propel the reader into a space beyond the material constraints of writing.

Egan's Camera Obscura

Thackeray wrote nostalgically of reading Pierce Egan's *Life in London* as a boy in his 'Roundabout Papers' (1860):

> What is that I see? A boy, – a boy in a jacket. He is at a desk; he has great books before him, Latin and Greek books and dictionaries. Yes, but behind the great books, which he pretends to read, is a little one, with pictures, which he is really reading. It is – yes, I can read now – it is the *Heart of Midlothian*, by the author of *Waverley* – or, no, it is *Life in London, or the Adventures of Corinthian Tom, Jeremiah Hawthorn, and their friend Bob Logic,*' by Pierce Egan; and it has pictures – oh! such funny pictures! As he reads, there comes behind the boy a man, a dervish, in a black gown, like a woman, and a black square cap, and he has a book in each hand; and he seizes the boy who is reading the picture-book, and lays his head upon one of his books,

and smacks it with the other. The boy makes faces, and so that picture disappears.[67]

In addition to being a punitive example 'that books can be subjected to uses other than reading', as Leah Price reminds us, Thackeray's memory of reading Egan is triggered by an inscription on another devalued form of currency – a Regency coin:

> Any contemporary of that coin who takes it up and reads the inscription round the laurelled head, "Georgius IV. Britanniarum Rex. Fid. Def. 1823," if he will but look steadily enough at the round, and utter the proper incantation, I daresay may conjure his life there. (502)[68]

The first image conjured by this nostalgic phantasmagoria is of an orientalised Regent which then dissolves to reveal the above image of Thackeray in a previous incarnation – absorbed in a book and oblivious to his schoolmaster's looming figure.

Before this scene dissolves, when the young Thackeray's head is slammed between the offending books, the pleasure of reading Egan's funny pictures draws him into a reverie filled with vivid images of Tom and Jerry's rakish perambulations through a variety of well-known Regency attractions. As Nicholas Dames has observed, such scenes of solitary reading, often abruptly punctuated by the demands of the present, are a recurring motif in Thackeray's work (73). Indeed the initial illustration for the 'Roundabout Papers' series published in the first issue of the *Cornhill Magazine* in 1860 depicted a 'Lazy Idle Boy' reading, according to Thackeray's description,

> a little book . . . held up to his face, and which I daresay so charmed and ravished him, that he was blind to the beautiful sights around him; unmindful, I would venture to lay any wager, of the lessons he had to learn for tomorrow; forgetful of mother waiting supper, and father preparing a scolding; – absorbed utterly and entirely in his book.[69]

Holding the book close in a state of entranced reverie, the idle boy, like the young Thackeray, is serenely indifferent to the claims of family and school. Yet despite the inevitable and brutal interruption that will follow, as Dames observes, Thackeray implicitly licenses the boy's 'wilful inattention' as a welcome, indeed necessary, liberty that momentarily frees him from the conscripted attentiveness that society requires.[70]

The parallels between these reading scenes and contemporary accounts of the necessarily unconscious dimensions of reading, as Dames also notes, are striking. Reflecting on the way the mind gradually learns to read, George Henry Lewes argued in *The Physical Basis of Mind* that we

learn to read with conscious effort; each letter has to be apprehended separately, its form distinguished from all other forms, its value as a sign definitely
fixed, yet how rarely are we 'conscious' of the letters when we read a book?
Each letter is perceived; and yet this process passes so rapidly and smoothly,
that unless there be some defect in the letter, or word be misspelled, we are
not 'conscious' of the perceptions. Are we therefore reading automata?[71]

Reading necessarily requires a habituated degree of distraction that can
easily lapse into the more expansive interludes of reverie and dreaming, according to Lewes. As E. S. Dallas argues in *The Gay Science*, the
machinery of the mind continues to operate 'independent of our care' as
we read, to the extent that the reader can fall asleep and continue to read
aloud as if awake (1:224).

This automatism correlates with Dallas' analogy of reading with
photography. Dallas argues that while the child may not understand
what they learn to read as a child 'the memory of things not understood
may be vital within us' (1:213). Accordingly, these memories may be
activated by what Dallas saw as the unprecedented dynamism of new
technological forms of literature and art that synchronise with these
involuntary impulses:

> The stereotype, the photograph, wood-engraving, the art of printing in
> colour, and many other useful inventions have been perfected – making the
> printed page within the last thirty years what it never was before. At the same
> time the railway and the steamship, the telegraph and the penny postage, by
> daily and hourly bringing near to us a vast world beyond our limited circles,
> and giving us a present interest in the transactions of the most distant regions,
> have enormously increased the number of readers, have of themselves created
> a literature, and through that literature have had a mighty influence upon the
> movement of the time. (2:312)

As Dallas' modern readers scan these new multi-medial forms they
gradually become habituated to new systems of information and new
understandings of literature as a multi-medial experience. As Matthew
Rubery observes, the boundaries between journalism and literature
that we assume made little sense in the nineteenth century, indeed the
modern novel was generated by a 'competitive literary economy' that
'pitted the two forms against each other for attention and profit'.[72]
Correspondingly, this struggle to capture the attention of this new
community of readers was necessarily complex and chaotic, despite
Dallas' vision of an increasingly standardised reading experience that
mirrored the technological accelerations of a modern media landscape.
As Thackeray suggests, certain books absorb the reader, momentarily
freeing the mind from the relentless attentiveness required by modern
life.

Reading Egan, as Thackeray describes it, no longer requires the material presence of the book itself. The 'literary contents of the book', he informs the reader, 'have passed sheer away'.[73] Egan's 'striking descriptions' retain their value as a record not only of life in Regency London, but because 'all London read it and went to see it in its dramatic shape' (4). In this context the satiric images of Isaac Robert and George Cruikshank that illustrated Egan's text assume an archival status, a series of remembered images reactivated by the associative mechanisms of nostalgia. Reinforcing Egan's obsolescence, Thackeray claims that he was unable to purchase a copy by the 1860s.[74] Nostalgia also informs Thackeray's enumeration of the Cruikshanks' depictions of wandering through a London that no longer exists:

> Away for the career of pleasure and fashion. The park! delicious excitement – the theatre! the saloon!! the green-room!!! Rapturous bliss – the opera itself! And then perhaps to Temple Bar . . . now they are at Newgate, seeing the irons knocked off the malefactor's legs previous to execution. What hardened ferocity in the countenance of the desperado in yellow breeches! What compunction in the face of the gentleman in black (who, I suppose, has been forging) . . . Now we haste away to merrier scenes: to Tattersalls . . .[75]

Thackeray represents his memory of the text as a series of moving images that capture the live action of life in London viewed from a comfortable distance. In this sense he is Egan's ideal reader. Egan recommended precisely this mode of responsiveness in his second chapter, evocatively titled 'A Camera Obscura View of the Metropolis, with the Light and Shade attached to "seeing Life"' (46).

Egan informs his readers that he has chosen to provide them with a '*Camera Obscura* View of London, not only from its safety, but because it is so *snug*, and also possessing the invaluable advantages of SEEING and not being *seen*' (46).[76] On the following page he is even more explicit, comparing the technology of the Camera Obscura, to the machinery of the codex:

> The *Camera Obscura* is now at work; the table is covered with objects for the amusement of my readers; and whenever it is necessary to change the scene it is only requisite to pull the string, *i.e.*, to turn over leaf after leaf, and LIFE IN LONDON will be seen without any fear or apprehension of danger either from *fire* or *water*; avoiding also breaking a limb, receiving a *black* eye, losing a pocket-book, and getting into a watch-house; (47)

Like Thackeray's cluttered schoolroom desk, Egan materialises the process of reading *Life in London* in the form of a table crowded with potentially distracting objects and surfaces to be read. Objects, like the camera obscura itself, are intentionally placed on the table to be animated by the reader's hand. Snugly ensconced in this familiar domestic scene, the dangerous, unpredictable and unknowable elements of urban everyday life can be progressively illuminated at a speed determined by the reader's own proclivities. The only movement required is pulling the string, or turning the page, to bring Egan's images to life.

The remainder of the chapter plays on this voyeuristic dynamic. Egan describes London as 'the looking-glass for TALENT' in which 'the faithful emporium of the enterprising, the bold, the timid, and the bashful' can view themselves 'at full length' (48). He speaks of the 'extremes, in every point of view' that daily confront the denizens of London's streets. Of 'seeing life' as one peeps, strolls, struts, lounges, trots and pauses in an overtly masculine performance of getting 'out into the world' (65). The next chapter similarly plays with the mechanism of 'taking a likeness' in the process of sketching out the character of Corinthian Tom (68). This chapter concludes by assuring the reader that this likeness 'was not taken with a machine', although produced with speedy voracious consumption in mind (79). Consistent with his earlier invocation of the camera obscura, Egan's work turns here on multiple senses of image making, seeming to embrace the industrial temporalities of mechanical reproduction, while cleaving to artisanal narrative and visual techniques.

By the 1820s the camera obscura was a ubiquitous metaphor that harked back to eighteenth-century evocations of the relation of a perceiving subject to an external world. The optical geometry it materialised, as Geoff Batchen has observed, 'at once ideal and natural, was taken as an empirical confirmation of the truth of its Enlightenment worldview'.[77] What distinguishes this eighteenth-century ideal of the camera obscura and Egan's version of the metaphor is a proto-photographic interest in the temporality of image production that Batchen identifies as emerging in the second decade of the nineteenth century (84). In 1817 Coleridge, who was familiar with his friend Humphrey Davy's experiments with fixing the images produced in the camera obscura, associated his poetic ideal of creation with arresting images of a flash of sunlight: 'creation rather than painting, or if painting, yet such, and with such co-presence of the whole picture flash'd upon the eye, as the sun paints in a camera obscura'.[78] That said, as Alexandra Neel argues, Coleridge was equally critical of the absence of an 'active thinking subject' inside the camera obscura's darkened chamber.[79] In a footnote in the *Biographia Literaria* Coleridge extends the camera obscura metaphor to evoke, in Neel's words, 'a vision of the reader and author as one and the same – somnambulant figures with camera-like empty heads, nothing more than machines of production and reception' (211):

For as to the devotees of the circulating libraries, I dare not compliment their *pass-time*, or rather *kill-time*, with the name of *reading*. Call it rather a sort of beggarly day-dreaming, during which the mind of the dreamer furnishes for itself nothing but laziness and a little mawkish sensibility; while the whole *materiel* and imagery of the doze is supplied *ab extra* [from without] by a sort of mental *camera obscura* manufactured at the printing office, which *pro tempore* [for a time] fixes, reflects and transmits the moving phantasms of one man's delirium, so as to people the barrenness of an hundred other brains afflicted with the same trance or suspension of all common sense and all definite purpose. (399)[80]

Coleridge and Thackeray diverge in their estimation of killing time with little picture books. According to Coleridge, the 'mental camera obscura' of popular writing reduces reading to the passive registration of visual images. More noxiously still, from Coleridge's viewpoint, popular writing transmitted an identical image to multiple minds, an inert illiterate collective assimilation that accounted for 'nine-tenths of the reading public' (211).

Four decades later, Thackeray nostalgically implicates himself in the collective reverie generated by Pierce Egan's camera obscura images of London life. He nevertheless concludes his autobiographical reflections with a characteristically Victorian retreat into the domestic. Leaving the streets of the city behind, he returns to his sleeping family, reinforcing the association of looking through Egan's camera obscura with self-indulgent reverie in defiance of more quotidian demands.

Marx and Engels' invocation of the metaphor of the camera obscura in *The German Ideology* provides an illuminating negative counterpoint to this alignment of the flickering inverted images of the camera obscura with the self-protective illusions of bourgeois distraction:

If in all ideology men and their circumstances appear upside-down as if in a *camera obscura*, this phenomenon arises just as much from their historical life-process as the inversion of objects on the retina does from their physical life-process.

In direct contrast to German philosophy which descends from heaven to earth, here we ascend from earth to heaven. That is to say, we do not set out from what men say, imagine, conceive, nor from men as narrated, thought of, imagined, conceived, in order to arrive at men in the flesh. We set out from real, active men, and on the basis of real-life process we demonstrate the development of the ideological reflexes and echoes of this life process.[81]

According to Marx and Engels, ideology generates the illusion of the independence of consciousness and history from the material conditions of 'real, active men'. The antidote to this inversion of the order of things is a counter-inversion that reveals the 'true' origin of the real-life processes that ideology obscures. But while this may seem to affect an irrefutable divide between the images produced by the camera obscura and the unmediated authenticity of the real world, this distinction is far murkier than it appears.

'All these specular metaphors', as Sarah Kofman suggests, problematically imply the existence of original meaning, sounds and light that pre-exist consciousness:

> The history of sciences shows us that the camera obscura imposes itself as a model for vision in order to do away with that Euclidean conception according to which it is from the eye that emanates the luminous ray. The model of the camera obscura thus implies the existence of a 'given' which would offer itself as already inverted. Thus, even when Marx seems to *want* to use his own, specific language, metaphors join together as system and weigh down upon him ... Where ... from within ideology, comes the illusion of independence? The camera obscura and other specular metaphors all imply a relationship to the real. [82]

Marx and Engels perform their own metaphoric sleight of hand by transforming the transparent copy that the camera obscura produces into a baroque simulation that, to quote Kofman, 'disguises, burlesques, [and] blurs real relationships' to which they then 'oppose the values of clarity, light, transparency, truth, rationality' (14–15). In this sense, Marx and Engels' profound distrust of the technological image is symptomatic of a far more profound disavowal of the mediated nature of their own social vision and its dependency on visual rhetoric to re-present and persuade their readers of the true material condition of 'real, active men'. Notably, given the fourth chapter of this study's focus on the narrative and technological inventions of David Brewster, the kaleidoscope is treated with similar distrust as analogous to the passive reflective politics of Saint-Simon, which Marx and Engels dismiss as a 'kaleidoscopic display ... composed entirely of reflections of itself' (1:109–11). Saint-Simon, they argue, created the illusion of progressing from one idea to another, whilst sustaining the same position – the result being the complacent inertia of a politics of self-reflection. As we shall see, David Brewster also adapted the metaphoric potential of his miraculous new invention to suit his own polemic, typifying its intrinsically labile power to evoke both mass distraction and avid attention.

The following chapter will examine the convergence of panoramic technologies and the multi-medial system of what came to be known as Byronism. Byron, in contrast to his Romantic contemporaries, embraced the chaotic social world of London's streets, salons and entertainments. Rather than presenting a distant panoramic view from Waterloo Bridge, Byron's poetry conveyed a more intimate, implicated, often scandalous perspective on contemporary Regency life. But the consequent celebrity was both a trial and an intoxicant. Continuous with this interplay between spectacle and intimacy, Byronic fragments circulated in multiple forms, including popular writing on the mind. Predictably, this literature was dominated by anecdotes of Byronic superstitions and excesses culled from his life and work, cementing the Victorian association of the poet with surrendering to the sensual and exotic in defiance of the more prosaic demands of the real.

Notes

1. Chandler and Gilmartin (eds), *Romantic Metropolis: The Urban Scene of British Culture, 1780–1840*.
2. Wordsworth, Preface, 1800 version, *Wordsworth and Coleridge: Lyrical Ballads*, p. 294.
3. Headrick, *When Information Came of Age: Technologies of Knowledge in the Age of Reason and Revolution, 1700–1850*, pp. 181–216.
4. Otto, *Multiplying Worlds: Romanticism, Modernity, and the Emergence of Virtual Reality*.
5. Wordsworth, *William Wordsworth: The Poems*, vol. 1, pp. 574–5.
6. The history of the panorama has been told many times: see Hyde, *Panoramania!: The Art and Entertainment of the 'All-Embracing' View*; Oettermann, *The Panorama: History of a Mass Medium* and Alison Griffiths, *Shivers Down Your Spine: Cinema, Museums and the Immersive View*. Thomas Girtin's Eidometropolis is described in Smith, *Thomas Girtin: The Art of Watercolour* and by Chandler and Gilmartin, 'Introduction: Engaging the Eidometropolis', in Chandler and Gilmartin (eds), *Romantic Metropolis*, pp. 1–44.
7. Keen, *Literature, Commerce, and the Spectacle of Modernity, 1750–1800*, p. 2.
8. Jane and Ann Taylor, *Signor Topsy-Turvy's Wonderful Magic Lantern: or, The World Turned Upside Down*.
9. Marguerite Gardiner, Countess of Blessington, *The Magic Lantern; or, Sketches of Scenes in the Metropolis*.
10. See William James's description of the real in 'Bergson and His Critique of Intellectualism', in *A Pluralistic Universe*, p. 261.
11. Egan, *The True History of Tom and Jerry; or The Day and Night Scenes, of Life in London*.
12. Dames writes extensively on 'cognitive drift' in Thackeray in *The Physiology of the Novel: Reading, Neural Science, and the Form of Victorian Fiction*, pp. 73–122.
13. Isaac Taylor (1759–1824) also supported his considerable family through his work as an Independent minister to a small congregation in Colchester.
14. Davidoff and Hall provide a detailed account of the family life and literary practices of the Taylor family in *Family Fortunes: Men and Women of the English middle class 1780–1850*, pp. 59–69.

15. Taylor, *Home Education*.
16. Like the Brontë sisters' planned school, this venture failed due to lack of capital.
17. Gilbert, 'Remonstrance', in Josiah Conder (ed.), *The Associate Minstrels*, p. 23.
18. Luhmann, *Social Systems*, p. 9.
19. Locke, *Some Thoughts Concerning Education* (1693) refers to the child's mind as 'white paper' (325). See Locke, *The Educational Writings of John Locke: A Critical Edition with Introduction and Notes*, p. 212.
20. Maria and Richard Lovell Edgeworth, *Practical Education*. Further references are provided in-text.
21. Locke, *The Educational Writings of John Locke*, p. 212.
22. Hooper, *Rational Recreations, in which the principles of numbers and natural philosophy are clearly and copiously elucidated, by a series of easy, entertaining, interesting experiments. Among which are all those commonly performed with the cards.*
23. Hooper, *Rational Recreations*, vol. 1, p. 50.
24. Fenwick, *Visits to the Juvenile Library Or, Knowledge Proved to be the Source of Happiness*.
25. Alan Richardson analyses the colonial politics of some of the central reading scenes in Fenwick's text in *Literature, Education, and Romanticism: Reading as Social Practice, 1780–1832*, p. 135.
26. The italics are Fenwick's.
27. Letter to C. W. W. Wynn, 25 June 1805, in Southey, 'State and Prospects of the Country', *The Emergence of Victorian Consciousness, the Spirit of the Age*, p. 239.
28. These illustrations are reproduced in Evans, *Tabart of Fonthill: From England to Van Diemen's Land*, p. 27.
29. Benjamin, 'Unpacking my Library', in *Illuminations*, p. 62.
30. Jane and Ann Taylor, *Signor Topsy-Turvy's Wonderful Magic Lantern*, n. p.
31. Ronald Reichertz discusses the tradition of 'upside down books' in *The Making of the Alice Books: Lewis Carroll's Uses of Earlier Children's Literature*, Chapter 4.
32. Tycho Brahe did not accept the heliocentric theory of Nicholas Copernicus due to his unwavering belief in Aristotelian physics which depends upon the universal centrality of the earth; Thoren, *The Lord of Uraniborg: A Biography of Tycho Brahe*.
33. Della Porta, *Natural Magick* (Naples, 1558), p. 2.
34. Hankins and Silverman, *Instruments and the Imagination*, p. 4.
35. The earliest reference to the magic lantern is in the correspondence of the seventeenth-century physicist Christiaan Huygens. Huygens first projected images through a magic lantern in 1659 as part of his experiments with optics. He was dismissive of the actual device, which quickly became synonymous with popular entertainment and the sphere of travelling showmen in both Europe and England. It was not until the eighteenth century that the magic lantern began to be taken seriously as a device to aid in the demonstration of experimental physics. See Hankins and Silverman, *Instruments and the Imagination*, Chapter 3.

36. John Newbery's successful publishing enterprise began in 1742 with the *Pretty Little Pocket Book* and expanded to include an extensive list of titles that went through numerous reprints and ranged from simple guides to reading, writing and arithmetic to Newton's philosophy digested for young minds by Tom Telescope.

37. Tom Telescope, *The Newtonian system of philosophy adapted to the capacities of young ladies and gentlemen and familiarized and made entertaining by objects with which they are intimately acquainted: being the substance of six lectures read to a select company of friends.*

38. Valerie Walkerdine identifies this conflict in the early nineteenth century: the 'new technologies of power based on engineering consent rather than overt repression were often advocated by the more progressive elements of society in the name of professionalisation, utility and secularisation'. See Walkerdine, 'Developmental Psychology and the Child-Centered Pedagogy: The Insertion of Piaget into Early Education', in *Changing the Subject: Psychology, Social Regulation and Subjectivity*, p. 165.

39. Both sisters embraced the seclusion of provincial life after the failure of the venture to start a school in London in 1810. They also maintained an ambivalent attitude to paid literary work, despite their extraordinary success. *Original Poems* and *Original Hymns* would go through over 100 editions in England and America throughout the nineteenth century and would remain in print until the 1930s.

40. Jane Taylor, *Memoirs, correspondence, and poetical remains of Jane Taylor*, p. 154.

41. Examples of anthropomorphic themes in Regency illustrated children's books, which were often called toys, are reprinted in Iona and Peter Opie, *A Nursery Companion*. An indicative title of this period was published by J. Harris and Son in 1819, *Cock Robin, A Pretty Painted Toy for either Girl or Boy; suited to Children of All Ages.*

42. Sarah Catherine Martin provided the original text for this popular illustrated volume initially titled: *The Comic Adventures of Old Mother Hubbard, and Her Dog: Illustrated with Fifteen Elegant Engravings on Copper-plate.* It was subsequently reissued by Harris with a new title and with any reference to Martin removed as part of his 'Cabinet of Amusement and Instruction'. The attraction of the volume was patently visual with new coloured engravings – *The Comic Adventures of Old Mother Hubbard, and Her Dog: in which is shewn the Wonderful Powers that Good Old Lady possessed in the Education of her Favourite Animal.*

43. Plumb, 'The New World of Children in Eighteenth-Century England', *Past and Present* 67 (May 1975), p. 80.

44. Jonathan Crary analyses the debates surrounding the stereoscope in *Techniques of the Observer: On Vision and Modernity in the Nineteenth Century*, Chapters 3 and 4.

45. John Sayer's *The Witches or Harlequin's Trip to Naples* (August 1772) is reprinted in Haining, *Movable Books: An Illustrated History*, p. 10. John Plunkett provides an extensive history of nineteenth-century moveable books in Plunkett, 'Moving Books/Moving Images: Optical Recreations and Children's publishing 1800–1900', 1–27.

46. Peter Haining provides a history of Dean and Sons' publications and

those that followed in their wake during the heyday of the movable book in the second half of the nineteenth century in *Movable Books: An Illustrated History*. These included the late nineteenth-century German publisher Ernest Nister's illustration of an adapted verse version of *Alice in Wonderland* (1890) that featured six dissolving views. According to Haining, each dissolving view 'was made up of six interlocking sections which, when a tab in the frame was pulled, slid away to reveal a kaleidoscopic effect', p. 111.

47. Christopher North (John Wilson), 'The Magic Lantern, or Sketches of Scenes in the Metropolis', *Blackwood's Edinburgh Magazine* 11:65 (June 1822), p. 715.
48. Laxton, 'Steam Navigation', *Journal, Scientific and Railway Gazette*, 10 (April 1847), p. 117.
49. Secord, *Victorian Sensation: The Extraordinary Publication, Reception, and Secret Authorship of 'Vestiges of the Natural History of Creation'*, p. 54.
50. Susanne Schmid discusses the implications of this scandalous celebrity in 'The Countess of Blessington: Reading as Intimacy, Reading as Sociability', pp. 88–93; Ann R. Hawkins analyses Blessington's contributions to literary annuals in 'Marketing Gender and Nationalism: Blessington's *Gems of Beauty/l'Ecrin* and the mid-century book trade', pp. 225–40.
51. Gardiner, Countess of Blessington, *The Magic Lantern*, n. p.
52. Nunokawa, *The Afterlife of Property: Domestic Security and the Victorian Novel*, p. 5.
53. The italics are Blessington's.
54. Gitelman, *Scripts, Grooves and Writing Machines: Representing Technology in the Edison Era*, p. 3.
55. Gitelman, *Scripts, Grooves and Writing Machines*, p. 3.
56. Sennett, *Flesh and Stone: The Body and the City in Western Civilization*, p. 256.
57. Goethe, *Italian Journey* [1786], p. 202.
58. Goethe, *Italian Journey* [1786], p. 124.
59. Cited in Altick, *The Shows of London*, p. 235.
60. Gillen D'Arcy Wood evocatively describes Belzoni's spectacular construct as 'a veritable dreamscape of mocked-up tombs, statues, and sarcophagi, with the tomb of Seti as the exhibit's crowning glory', in *The Shock of the Real: Romanticism and Visual Culture, 1760–1860*, p. 2. John Whale analyses the inherent cultural imperialism of the exhibition in 'Sacred Objects and the Sublime Ruins of Art', in *Beyond Romanticism*, pp. 227–35.
61. *The Times*, 30 April 1821. Cited in D'Arcy Wood, *The Shock of the Real*, p. 2.
62. Simmel, 'The Metropolis and Mental Life', in *The Sociology of Georg Simmel*, p. 410.
63. Epstein Nord, *Walking the Victorian Streets: Women, Representation, and the City*, p. 48.
64. Brown, *Lectures on the Philosophy of the Human Mind*, vol. 1, p. 273.
65. Scarry, *Dreaming by the Book*, p. 7
66. Cited in Brown, *Lectures on the Philosophy of the Human Mind*, vol. 1, p. 406.

67. Thackeray, 'De Juventute – Roundabout Papers No. VIII', *Cornhill Magazine* 2:10 (October 1860), pp. 502–3.
68. Price, 'From the History of a Book to a "History of the Book"', *Representations* (Fall 2009), p. 123.
69. Thackeray, *Roundabout Papers, Little Travels, and Roadside Sketches*, p. 4.
70. Dames, *The Physiology of the Novel*, p. 73.
71. Lewes, *The Physical Basis of Mind*, p. 397.
72. Rubery, *The Novelty of Newspapers: Victorian Fiction after the Invention of News*, p. 11.
73. Thackeray 'On the Genius of George Cruikshank', cited in the bookseller John Camden Hotten's introduction to his 1869 edition of Pierce Egan, *Tom and Jerry. Life in London or the Day and Night Scenes of Jerry Hawthorn, Esq. and his elegant friend Corinthian Tom in their Rambles and Sprees through the Metropolis* (London: John Camden Hotten, 1869), p. 4. All references to Egan's *Life in London* will be to this edition.
74. Gregory Dart contradicts this assumption in a recent article which addresses the lasting popularity of Egan in '"Flash Style": Pierce Egan and Literary London 1820–28', *History Workshop Journal* 51 (2001), pp. 181–205.
75. Thackeray, 'De Juventute', p. 510.
76. The emphases and capitalisations are Egan's.
77. Batchen, *Burning With Desire: The Conception of Photography*, p. 82.
78. Coleridge, *Biographia Literaria; or, Biographical Sketches of My Life and Opinions* [1817], pp. 528–9.
79. Neel, '"A *Something-Nothing* Out of Its Very Contrary": The Photography of Coleridge', *Victorian Studies* (Winter 2007), p. 208.
80. The italics are Coleridge's.
81. Marx and Engels, *The German Ideology*, vol. 1, p. 47.
82. Kofman, *Camera Obscura of Ideology*, pp. 3–4.

Chapter 2

Byronic Networks: Circulating Images in Minds and Media

In 1837 Robert Burford presented a new panorama of Mont Blanc at the Leicester Square Panorama. Exploiting the Byronic associations with Mont Blanc, the accompanying guide included appropriately suggestive fragments from *Childe Harold's Pilgrimage* (1812–18) and *Manfred* (1817).[1] Burford simply assumed an homology between Byron's iconic scenes and his own panoramic images, although only a few years earlier he had framed the relationship between the panorama and the verbal arts in more competitive terms:

> Travellers speak of [the Niagara Falls] in terms of admiration and delight, and acknowledge that they surpass in sublimity [sic] every description which the power of language can afford; a Panorama alone offers a scale of sufficient magnitude to exhibit at one view (which is indispensable) the various parts of this wonderful scene, and to convey an adequate idea of the matchless extent, prodigious power, and awful appearance, of this stupendous phenomenon.[2]

Competitive gestures aside, Burford was too much of an entrepreneur not to realise that Byron's language had the potential to extend the scope of his panoramic vision into the public's collective fascination with the scandals and romance of the poet's life. As a reviewer remarked of the third canto of *Childe Harold* when it was published in 1816:

> Indeed it is the real romance of [Byron's] life, immeasurably more than the fabled one of his pen, which the public expects to find in his pages, and which not so much engages its sympathy, as piques its curiosity, and feeds thought and conversation. The Noble Poet, in the mean time, is content with – it should be said is ambitious of – this species of distinction; the bookseller, printers, and stationers, all profit by the traffic to which the exhibition gives rise; and thus every party is a gainer in this remarkable phenomenon of the time.[3]

Like the avid readers of *Childe Harold*, Burford participated in what Jerome Christensen has described as the 'literary system of Byronism'.[4]

As this reviewer suggests, Byron was complicit in the 'exhibition' of his life that accompanied each new foray into publication. He implicitly directed his readers, indeed habituated them, to move associatively between the page and the knowledge of 'the real romance' of Regency social mores that his verse triggered in their minds.

This chapter reads the popular nineteenth-century mediation of Byron's work in a range of panoramic formats as a multi-medial extension of already established practices of visual and linguistic mediation. Byron is transformed by this circulatory network into a fungible medium, a flickering figure that moves in and out of focus, guiding the reader to attend to a series of familiar privileged scenes, events and spaces, while holding out the prospect of intimate access, of speaking the same language as the poet. Addressing this specific dynamic, Friedrich Kittler entertains the reflexively anachronistic possibility of capturing the poet writing on film in what he calls the discourse network of 1800. By 'turning the motion-picture camera' onto the poets, Kittler suggests, taking inspiration from a nearly literary screenplay, a figure can be seen nervously moving around a room.[5] 'He writes a line on a piece of paper that has been folded in odd ways. He stands in front of the mirror and reads the line and admires himself. He lies down with evident satisfaction on a couch' (112). Film may have been lacking in the writing system of 1800, Kittler contends, but film's formidable automatism was foreshadowed by the dramatic technological and social transformations wrought by 'the condition of general alphabetisation' (112). Writing in 1800 no longer required 'the ascesis of a learned class', Kittler writes:

> It could become a skill of the fingers, which could write on through dreams, drunkenness, or darkness. Without disturbance or channel interference, without delay or transmission losses, the medium of writing transported pure signified or – fixed ideas. Alphabetisation in the flesh made possible an automatic writing that was not automatic. (112)

The affinity between Kittler's account of the automatism of writing and nineteenth-century analyses of the automatism of writing, reading, viewing and dreaming is striking. Correspondingly, as this chapter will argue, the enlisting of visual and linguistic Byronisms in a range of popular entertainments depended upon acknowledged or assumed patterns of automatic recognition that subsumed both poet and audience into the same media network.

Walter Cooper Dendy, a well-reputed surgeon, for example, enlisted Byron in his popular study of the psychology of mystery to teach his readers how to read their own dreams and perceptual illusions, moving back and forth between the poet's life and work to decode the mind's

erroneous automatic response to visual stimuli. In one anecdote Dendy
cites a man who dreamed he was Byron, which he compares to reading
Byron's equally superstitious account in a note to the *Giaour* of his
dervish Tahiri who prophesied an attack of the Mainotes that failed to
transpire.[6] In another anecdote, Dendy enlists Byron again to exemplify
how even great minds can fall prey to superstition:

> Even in minds of superior natural energy, from the instilment of superstitious
> ideas *in infancy*, a blind faith will often become paramount. Such a mind,
> and so influenced, was Byron's; and on such faith he once stole an agate bead
> from a lady, who had told him it was an antidote to love. It failed: had it not,
> Byron might have been a happier man; but the world would have been 'reft of
> poesy, the brightest, yet the darkest, that ever flashed on the heart and mind
> of man. (439)

Lifted from Thomas Moore's *Life of Lord Byron* (1835), this anecdote
simultaneously reproduces the romantic myth of involuntary genius
'flashing' forth, while drawing Byron into a functionalist psychology
that was ultimately more concerned with identifying commonalities
between reflexive and adaptive responses to visual stimuli, than hierarchies of intellect.

  Filtered through Moore's biographic interpretation, Dendy's anecdote
also typifies what Tom Mole has described as a new 'hermeneutic of
intimacy'.[7] This new hermeneutic, according to Mole, 'figured celebrity
texts as conduits' or mediums that cultivated intimate identifications
with remarkable or famous people (156). Dendy's series of Byronic
scenes conforms to this dynamic, redescribing already famous moments
from the poet's life to exemplify common psychological phenomena.
Walter Scott's much-cited encounter with Byron's ghost in the hall of
Abbotsford, for example, is enlisted to illustrate the perceptual distortions that can arise when the mind, in an already heightened emotional
state, responds involuntarily to momentarily inexplicable phenomena.
Interrupted from his reading by a sudden sound, Scott claimed that
he had encountered the '*eidolon*' of his dead friend. Apparently the
'intensity of the illusion' was so strong that he remained fixated on the
movements of the 'skins, and scarfs, and plaids, hanging on a screen
in the gothic hall of Abbotsford' (61). Dendy also cites John William
Polidori's account of the 'reading phantasmagoria' generated by Byron
and the Shelleys' notorious ghost story-telling sessions by the side of
Lake Geneva (73). Shelley's delirious response to this experience, Dendy
concludes, typified the dissociative effects that interludes of 'intense
reading' could have on an imaginative mind, potentially severing the ties
between illusion and reality (73).

Dendy's diagnostic reframing of Byron may be of a very different order to Burford's commercially driven borrowings, nevertheless, both participate in a form of deregulated reading and interpretation that is 'peculiar to modernity', to invoke Wai-Chee Dimmock's economic rhetoric.[8] Emerging in the early decades of the nineteenth century, this newly deregulated economy of reading practices revolved around an increasingly complex relationship between two mutually constitutive competitive systems, according to Dimmock. On the one hand, the indiscriminate 'World of Readers', as Coleridge described them, buffeted by world events and overwhelmed by an increasingly indecipherable media system, and on the other, an emergent class of professional interpreters and critics who were united in their characterisation of the voracious appetite of this new mass reading public, but divided on its social implications.[9] While Coleridge and Wordsworth recoiled at the prospect of a mass reading public, for example, their contemporary Hazlitt saw liberty, enfranchisement and progress: 'The reading public', Hazlitt contested, 'laugh at it as we will, abuse it as we will – is after all (depend upon it), a very rational animal, compared with the feudal lord and his horde of vassals.'[10] The only danger that lay in 'every one, high and low, rich and poor' being able to read and write, Hazlitt speculated, was if they all should turn author 'and the whole world be converted into waste paper' (17:327).

Hazlitt was equally dismissive of his contemporaries' erroneous assessment of Byron's popular legacy:

> When a certain poet was asked if he thought Lord Byron's name would live three years after he was dead, he answered, 'Not three days, Sir!' This was premature: it has lasted above a year. His works have been translated into French, and there is a *Caffe Byron* on the Boulevards. Think of a *Caffe Wordsworth* on the Boulevards! (17:209)

The blatant commercialism that the image of a Café Byron evoked, however, only reinforced Byron's worldly image, as Hazlitt well knew. Indicatively, Keats, compared Byron's 'worldly, theatrical, and pantomimical' exhibitionism to Napoleon Bonaparte.[11] While Leigh Hunt observed, 'there was no doubt whatever in my mind that Byron was all the time strutting about as on a stage'.[12] Indeed, this prevalent emphasis on Byronic self-dramatisation from critics and enthusiasts alike, as James Buzard has observed, 'made it difficult to think of the wandering poet without reference to theatres, stages, 'pageants', and so forth'.[13] Theatricality, as Buzard concludes, became the predominant feature of Byron's fame. Burford's unceremonious lifting of lines from Byron thus appears in this context as merely an extension of a complex multi-medial commerce that became inseparable from the act of reading Byron.

Given this immediate reception history, George Henry Lewes' 1853 negative review of Charles Kean's disrespectfully spectacular adaptation of Byron's *Sardanapalus* (1821) seems naïve and anachronistic. Lewes wrote in disgust: 'Is the Drama nothing more than a Magic Lantern on a large scale? Was Byron only a pretext for a panorama? It is a strange state of Art when the mere *accessories* become the aim and purpose of representation.'[14] Drama on a panoramic scale however, was precisely how many of Byron's nineteenth-century readers viewed his work and life. Even Ruskin, recounting his adolescent travels through Italy in the 1830s with a volume of Byron in hand, compared reading the poet to a form of visual reanimation: 'Byron told me of, and reanimated for me, the real people whose feet had worn the marble I trod on.'[15] Byron's scenic descriptions create a moving panorama of significant sites for Ruskin, infused with the drama of *Childe Harold's Pilgrimage*, *The Prisoner of Chillon*, *Mazeppa* and *Beppo*.

Nor was Ruskin exceptional in this regard, a commercial fact that John Murray, Byron's publisher cleverly exploited, publishing a pocket-sized *Lord Byron's Poetry*, 'so as to enable Travellers to carry it with their other HANDBOOKS'.[16] Murray also published an illustrated companion volume to his 'First Complete and Uniform Edition of Lord Byron's Life and Works' which was issued in instalments of five engravings per month, 'depicting places mentioned in "Childe Harold" and other of Byron's poems, together with portraits of himself and his associates', as well as quotations from his letters and diaries.[17] Another of Murray's savvy commercial ventures was the incorporation of carefully selected verse fragments from Byron's least controversial works into his best-selling guides to Italy and the Continent, 'knowing how much the perusal of [such passages] on the spot, where the works themselves are not to be procured, will enhance the interest of seeing the objects described'.[18] As James Buzard argues, Murray realised the profit to be made from his famous client's status as 'a moving tourist attraction' tracked across the Continent by voyeurs with telescopes and gossips rushing every salacious anecdote and opportune sighting into print (117).

This chapter begins with the circulation of extracts from Byron's poems in early panoramic guides and reviews of various Leicester Square Panoramas and concludes with the spectacular use of panoramic technologies in mid-nineteenth-century adaptations of one of Byron's many controversial historical fictions, *Sardanapalus*. Despite Lewes's insistence that Byron should be removed from the taint of such vulgar entertainments, they nevertheless perpetuated existing practices of reading Byron in fragments that were well suited to the multiplying perspectives of the magic lantern, the panoramic format, as well as galleries of illustration and the popular discourse on optical illusions. As Francis Jeffrey remarked in his positive review of *The Giaour*, Byron had produced 'fragments thus served up by a *restauranteur*' that meant that 'the greater part of polite readers would now no more think of sitting down to a whole Epic, than to a whole ox'.[19] Byron both indulged and suffered from 'the transient fashions of the age' to quote Thomas De Quincey.[20] 'A window composed of Claude Lorraine glasses spreads over the landscape outside a disturbing effect, which not the most practiced eye can evade', De Quincey continues in the same essay, the '*eidola theatre* affects us all. No man escapes the contagion from his contemporary bystanders' (11:52). The contagion of multiplying views threatened the integrity of poetic truth, according to De Quincey. Consequently, over-stimulated by an excess of information, the undiscerning reader was unable to differentiate between 'the Literature of Knowledge' and the 'Literature of Power', the function of the former being to teach and the latter, to move (11:54). Byron's celebrity, according to De Quincey's schema, diminished the power and truth of his verse. Fragmented, recycled and extracted it circulated instead as a cultural commodity in a newly unregulated knowledge economy.

Remediated as part of a panoramic spectacle, Byron's romantic figures, scenarios and landscapes were endlessly reproduced as a conduit to a world of cosmopolitan possibilities that were both intimate and exotic; a process that aligns with Jay David Bolter and Richard Grusin's conception of the contradictory imperatives of remediation. Speaking of a contemporary media context, but equally pertinent here, Bolter and Grusin argue that our 'culture wants both to multiply its media and to erase all traces of mediation: ideally, it wants to erase its media in the very act of multiplying them'.[21] In these popular formations, poetry's intrinsic value, as De Quincey understood it, is subjected to the logic of capital as Marx described it: 'The constant continuity of the process the unobstructed and fluid transition of value from one form into the other, or from one phase of the process into the next.'[22]

Tony Bennett's theory of popular reading provides one model for thinking about what the endless citation and revision of Byron in panoramic guides, reviews and performances might mean. Bennett describes popular reading as a knowing 'productive activation' as opposed to an interpretive aesthetics that privileges a tutored response over the vernacular and uninitiated.[23] By shifting the focus from interpretation to activation, Bennett argues, we can begin to think about popular reading practices as generative, rather than lacking the necessary cultural value to count as anything more than aberrant curiosities. While it is impossible to know how Burford's audiences at the Leicester Square Panorama read his guides, if they read them at all, contemporary reviewers did make extensive use of them, often interleaved with miscellaneous citations mainly drawn from Scott, Wordsworth or Shelley. This implied continuity between literary and popular visual media suggests a more calibrated understanding of the panoramic experience – one that diverges from what one such reviewer described as the 'regulation anecdotes' of shock and wonder that have played such a formative part in the panorama's long reception history.[24]

Panoramic Reading

Writing in the *London Saturday Journal* of his first bewildered encounter with the panorama as a young boy in the immediate wake of Waterloo, a journalist described Burford's 1842 revival of the 'Panorama of the Battle of Waterloo' in the following nostalgic terms:

> As a boy of fifteen, we felt these influences, and the panorama of 1816 was to us almost a scene of unmixed gratification. But six-and-twenty years make strange alterations in habits of thought, and accordingly we regarded the new picture, a few days since, with very different feelings. As a scene of deep interest, its hold was stronger than ever, for we read in its sickening desolation a far more valuable lesson than history had ever taught us before.[25]

Reinforcing the 'strange alterations in habits of thought' that have occurred in the intervening decades, the reviewer impresses the passage of time on his readers by citing the concluding lines of Scott's *The Field of Waterloo* (1815):

> Yes! Agincourt may be forgot,
> And Cressy be an unknown spot,
> And Blenheim's name be new;
> But still in story and in song,
> For many an age remember'd long,
> Shall live the Towers of Hougoumont,
> And Fields of Waterloo.[26]

The 'unmixed gratification' of the senses that he had experienced as a boy surrendering to the simultaneity of panoramic space is itself the subject of nostalgia. What he experiences now, filtered through Scott's memorialising chronology and Burford's descriptive guide, is a lesson in time and about the nature of an historical event:

To Mr Burford's *Description* of the picture is prefixed a succinct account of the battle, interspersed with characteristic anecdotes and traits of the contending forces. Of course, this narrative, as well as the picture itself, must be much more perfect in its details than the first painted panorama, or its *Guide*. Scarcely a year has elapsed since 1815, without some additional light being thrown upon the mighty conflict, by officers engaged in it. The details of great events, we know, are sifted by time, in the same proportion as those of minor occurrences are left to dwindle into oblivion. (188)

This alignment of viewing and reading accords with Lisa Gitelman's description of the plural, decentred and indeterminate nature of pre-digital technologies as reciprocal products of textual practices, rather than simple causal agents of change.[27] Despite the hyperbole surrounding the panorama's visual effects it was quickly assimilated by existing media and assumed an aura of inevitability. As Stephen Oettermann argues in his history of the medium:

The panorama became obsolete with its first appearance. It concealed its anachronism by reproducing itself in countless and seemingly new variations with the most up-to-date subjects. In this way it continued for a century to meet the needs of a mass audience that had played no small role in its creation.[28]

Although Oetterman smooths over the decidedly uneven success of the panorama in the middle decades of the century, his point about its capacity to assimilate and be assimilated by other media is correct.

Robert Barker quickly recognised the need to promote the educational benefits of the panorama to ensure and maintain demand. Advertising this emphasis on instructive amusement Barker claimed in the *Morning Chronicle* in 1801 that he was

determined to spare no expense or trouble to bring forward scenes of useful information, as well as gratifying amusement; and the public may expect to have the most interesting Views and the most noticed cities in Europe, in due time, laid before them.[29]

The introduction of pamphlets and guides was part of this didactic manoeuvre, beginning in 1801 with the panoramas of Constantinople. In their first rudimentary incarnation these pamphlets were free and featured a basic anamorphotic outline of the panorama accompanied by a numbered key that identified objects of interest to guide the spectator's eye through the dense visual field. In a further effort to distinguish the Leicester Square Panorama from its commercial competitors, booklet-length guides were introduced at a cost of sixpence under the subsequent managements of Barker's son Henry Aston Barker, John Burford and his son Robert Burford. These were more ambitious productions that

synthesised historical and cultural details, anecdotes and suitably evocative literary citations. Guides, descriptive booklets and sometimes books
describing the events displayed would continue to be a feature of the
panoramic experience well into the century. By mid-century, moving
panoramas such as *Mr Charles Marshall's Great Moving Diorama
Illustrating the Grand Route of a Tour Through Europe* which appeared
at Her Majesty's Concert Room in 1851 condensed the various aspects
of the panorama into a far more fluid linear structure supplemented
by descriptive guides, a lecture and musical accompaniment.[30] Albert
Smith's *Ascent of Mont Blanc* at the Egyptian Hall, which dominated
the mid-nineteenth-century London entertainment scene, provided yet
another permutation of the panoramic format. This was a spectacular
multimedia performance, incorporating personal anecdote with an
entertainingly instructive lecture, illustrated guide, interactive toys and
parlour games. Smith also included caricatures of the snobbery and
consumerism of Byronised tourists as part of his repertoire.[31]

Robert Burford's *Description of A View of Mont Blanc, The Valley
of Chamounix and the surrounding mountains. From drawings taken
by himself in 1835* exemplifies the didactic guide format. Burford begins
with the following extract from the third canto of *Childe Harold*:

> . . . The Alps
> The Palaces of nature, whose vast walls
> Have pinnacles in clouds their snowy scalps,
> And throned eternity in icy halls
> Of cold sublimity, where forms and fall
> The Avalanche. The thunderbolt of snow!
> All that expands the spirit, yet appals,
> Gather around these summits, as to show,
> How Earth may pierce to Heaven, yet leave vain man below!

Lavishly gesturing towards the sublime, this extract serves as an exemplary instance of refined landscape appreciation which Burford's more
socially aspirant customers are encouraged to emulate. Burford's reproduction of Byron's view of Mont Blanc also pragmatically perpetuates
the exchange of cultural property that the publication of *Childe Harold*
so profitably facilitated. As Andrew Elfenbein notes, like earlier topo-
graphical poems '*Childe Harold* offered its version of upper-class tastes
commodified for the consumption of a wider reading public'.[32] Burford
simply perpetuated the commercial circulation of the Byronic oeuvre as
'an anthology of quotable vernacular phrases' fuelled by the animus of
Victorian Byronmania.[33] In theory, the compliantly static observer positioned on the central viewing platform would scan and synthesise both
poem and panorama into a coherently instructive identification with a

communal ideal of nature filtered through the respectable language of early nineteenth-century sentimental cliché.

By the 1830s the Byronic oeuvre had become a stock of commonplaces. Early nineteenth-century women's commonplace books, as William St Clair has shown, reveal patterns of copying out stanzas of Byron's works. Extracts from the second canto of *Childe Harold* recur most frequently in these commonplace books indicating its specific appeal as a conduit of refined sentiment.[34] Byron himself described *Childe Harold* as a 'poem of variety', a loosely constructed sequence of reflections and scenes well suited to selective fan-like identification and textual poaching.[35] The personalised anthological form of the commonplace book was forged out of the emulative drive to memorise, internalise and possess the cultural markers of civility and mobility. This synchronises with the reading process that Barker's and Burford's panoramic booklet-length guides were designed to facilitate in the context of the panorama's virtual tour of otherwise inaccessible locales. *Childe Harold* also provided a particularly attractive and 'ennobling repertoire of poetical attitudes', to use James Buzard's phrase, for the discerning Victorian traveller to assume when travelling abroad (115). According to Buzard, 'the general Byronic aura' significantly altered tourist conventions: 'For the tourist who could evoke it, the "Byronic" held out the promise of making Continental experience "live", of saturating it anew with poetical evocations, pathos, and even the *frisson* of sexual daring not for domestic consumption' (117).

Read in the broader context of popular miscellaneous genres of the period, the literary bricolage or textual poaching of Barker and Burford reproduces the familiar dynamics of early nineteenth-century fan culture and popular tourism, relying on the familiar sentiments of *Childe Harold* as a mechanism of distinction.[36] Like the cosmopolitan posturing that Murray's tourist guides encouraged, Burford's audiences could consume Byron at home and abroad as a memory prompt that retrospectively incorporated the panoramic experience into a private nostalgic reading process. *Childe Harold* was particularly well suited to instructive re-narration of this kind, Harold being the archetypal intelligent traveller shaped by a various mix of cultural encounters, historical events and sublime insights, such as the one cited by Burford from Canto III when 'All that expands the spirit, yet appals'. *Childe Harold* was also synonymous with the cultural phenomena of Byronic celebrity, as the poet himself observed to John Murray after the publication of the first two cantos in 1812: 'I awoke one morning to find myself famous.'[37] An early notice in the *British Review* is less mystifying, while reacting to the misleading chivalric resonances of the poem's title, the critic attributes the poem's appeal to its accessible contemporaneous 'narrative of a modern tourist'.[38] By excising Byron's satirical account of the Napoleonic wars from its immediate political context Burford therefore contributes to what Peter Manning describes as 'the ceaseless mechanical reduplication of the Byronic hero in the sphere of commodities, the seemingly unique, sublime experience transmogrified into the desires and gratifications of a carefully manipulated mass market'.[39]

The carefully manipulated mass market to which Manning refers, however, was far from passive and undifferentiated in its interest in Byron, actively consuming and memorising his verse as children and adolescents, to quote the illustrator Percival Skelton's elegiac pilgrimage to the home and grave of Byron published in the illustrated weekly *Once a Week* in 1860.[40] Beginning with a panoramic overview and illustration of 'the extensive prospect of Nottinghamshire', Skelton moves into the more intimate domestic environs of Newstead before concluding with his own memories of reading Byron:

> Our memory unconsciously went back to the time when the sensitive feelings of our childhood were moved to tears by the 'Prisoner of Chillon' – how we read it in later years with scarcely less emotion by the white castle 'on the blue Leman.' We remembered in school-boy days how the wet half-holiday was beguiled with the odd volume of his poems, – how we envied and admired the retentive memory of our favourite chum, who could charm the wakeful hours of the Long Chamber with the recital of 'Mazeppa,' and long quotations from the 'Corsair,' – how in after life we appreciated more and more the meaning and music of his sweet verse, till in our mature, and perhaps partial judgements, we considered 'Childe Harold' as the master-piece of modern poetry. (542)

Skelton associates reading Byron with emotional individuation, involuntary memories summon images of sensitive childish feeling, adolescent posturing and maturing appreciation. These interludes of playful memorising, holiday re-enactments and partial personal judgements also constitute acts of private ownership, refashioned as anecdotal gestures that appeal to an assumed community of readers with like tastes and experiences. Skelton's pilgrimage to Newstead thus perpetuates the conflation of reading and viewing the poet's biography and image that permeated Romantic visual culture.

Byronic Theatricality

Spectacular theatrical adaptations of Byron's *Sardanapalus* extended and capitalised on this convergence of mediated spectacle and intimate identification. Byron's representation of ancient Assyrian culture through the lens of the fictional ruler, Sardanapalus, and his benevolent refusal of the barbaric violence of martial spectacle, was both deliberately anachronistic and intimately connected to his own political vision. As his reference to the uncivil nature of English society in the preface to the play makes clear, Byron's primary concern was not historical authenticity and archaeological accuracy, but the parlous nature of British politics in the face of the Napoleonic threat. As Daniela Garofalo observes, Byron rejects 'the patriotic view of British political benevolence', implicitly arguing through his dramatisation of Sardanapalus's inability to balance the responsibilities of power with his distaste for war that the British were 'seduced by Napoleonic barbarism' despite their hypocritical claims to moral superiority.[41] Such cavalier rewriting of history in the interest of contemporary political critique suggests that Byron may have shared George Henry Lewes's aforementioned distaste for Charles Kean's commercially-driven historical literalism.

Recoiling from Kean's pandering to the current taste for spectacular martial displays favoured by the Leicester Square Panorama and other popular 'Galleries of Illustration', Lewes dismisses any claims to archaeological accuracy as a risible distraction from the serious business of producing an authentic adaptation of Byron's original text:

> If you read Charles Kean's playbills, you are for ever after lost in wide astonishment at his talk. In his bill displays you see a man who reads Xiphilin at breakfast, takes up the *Eyrbyggia Saga* with a biscuit and a glass of sherry at luncheon, and sups with Diodorus Siculus! Lo! I show you a miracle!
>
> Appalled at Charles Kean's erudition (which of course I believe in), I am not surprised to find he has 'learnt that scenic illustration, *if it have the weight of authority*, may adorn and add dignity to the noble works of genius.' Observe, *only* if it have the weight of authority! Scenic illustration is a mere pandering to the public eye unless it can cite its pedigree![42]

Lewes rails against Charles Kean's snobbish scholarly claims to archaeological accuracy, his efforts to distinguish himself from the showmanship of his theatrical peers and his bad acting, demanding at one point: 'Why not give drama up altogether, and make the Princess's Theatre a Gallery of Illustration?' (3:251). In contrast, Lewes attributes dramatic authenticity to William Charles Macready's more reverential performance of *Sardanapalus* at Drury Lane in 1834; however, this attribution was misplaced. While the latter may have lacked Kean's archaeological pretensions, it was still a blatantly commercial spectacle. Alfred Bunn, the manager of Drury Lane at that time, was an opportunistic showman who Thackeray would later satirise in *Pendennis* in the guise of Mr Dolphin. Bunn appalled Macready by initially suggesting that the actress

Charlotte Mardyn, who it was rumoured had had an affair with the poet, be offered the role of Myrrha, the mistress of Sardanapalus. This only intensified Macready's dislike of the play. He cut and simplified the plot, reducing the tension between Sardanapalus's compulsions to heroic action and his effeminising indolent propensities.

The play was ultimately performed in fairly shambolic fashion after only two rehearsals. This, in part, reflected Macready's ambivalence towards the irresolvable ambiguities of Sardanapalus's character. He noted in his diary on 16 April 1834: 'I cannot work myself into the reality in this part – I have not freedom enough to satisfy myself.'[43] One register of his unease was his attempts to replace the gender confusions at the core of Byron's drama and its classical source with the masculine stereotypes of conventional military spectacle. Byron's stress on his hero's latent masculinity gave Macready some licence in this regard. Byron was also guilty of selectively editing Diodorus Siculus, who portrayed Sardanapalus 'as a monstrous hybrid', to quote Susan J. Wolfson, 'a man not only effeminate, but also given to fetishistic transvestism and bisexuality'.[44] But again, historical accuracy was never Byron's priority, his dramatic interest in Diodorus's account of the last king of the Assyrians lay in the complex interaction between self and social convention that his 'effeminate character' represented.[45] Sardanapalus's preference for the luxuries of private pleasure over the virtuous asceticism of public duty was also a familiar Byronic theme that critics were quick to read through the lens of biographical allegory. The *British Review* dismissed as whimsical Byron giving 'lectures on social morality from the mouth of the effeminate King of Assyria' which attributed a 'probable union of such manners as history attributes to him by the poet'.[46] Francis Jeffrey was more scathing in his assessment: 'There is the same varnish of voluptuousness on the surface – the same canker of misanthrophy [sic] at the core . . . he does little but repeat himself.'[47] In Byron's version, Sardanapalus risks revolution by preferring to 'rule a harem' rather than 'sway his nations' and 'head an army'. He recklessly succumbs to the 'lulling instruments. The softening voices / Of women', and one in particular, the slave girl Myrrha, a sentimental stereotype of heroic feminine subservience who ultimately casts herself onto Sardanapalus's funeral pyre at the conclusion of the play.[48]

Unimpeded by the archaeological knowledge that Lewes reviles in Kean's production, Macready instructed Clarkson Stanfield, who was known for his popular 'Grand Moving Pictures', to paint panoramic scenery to create the illusion of Oriental grandeur, including a final scene inspired by John Martin's spectacular canvas *The Fall of Nineveh* (1829).[49] Martin was synonymous with the cult of immensity that dominated both Georgian high art and popular visual culture. Spectacular panoramic canvases such as Martin's *Belshazzar's Feast* (1821) competed with other attractions, such as Belzoni's Tomb, and had to be roped off to protect it from the press of the crowd.[50] *The Fall of Nineveh* and *The Last Judgement* (1853), both measuring almost 100 square feet, were equally popular examples of what Charles Lamb dismissed as 'the material sublime'.[51] Stanfield's homage to Martin, especially given Stanfield's own association with the popular 'Grand Moving Picture' format, would therefore have been readily legible to audiences who, as Richard Altick observes, inhabited a cultural landscape in which the demarcation between immense canvases and panoramas was imperceptible: 'Was a painting occupying say, three or four hundred square feet of canvas an object of fine art or a small-scale panorama? The charge made to see it was the same at least.'[52] Dwarfed by the panoramic vistas of Nineveh, Macready enacted his abridged version of the travails of Byron's androgynous monarch, beefing up the martial aspects of the plot which called for awkward onstage fighting and downplaying the hero's risible narcissism, omitting the scene where Sardanapalus admires his reflection before rushing off to war. The staging of Sardanapalus's ritualised suicide by fire to elude capture by his enemies was even more spectacular.

The funeral pyre that was constructed on stage, much to the audience's amusement, burst into a conflagration when lit by the dolorous Myrrha, consuming the walls of the palace to reveal the burning city beyond. Engineered by the machinist W. Bradwell, the fire was produced by a slow-burning combination of strontia, shellac, chlorate of potash and charcoal called Redfire that produced a fierce red light.[53] The sets were then collapsed by a mechanism operated from beneath the stage, creating the illusion of total destruction. Then, the final visual scenario painted by Clarkson Stanfield brought the audience back to the present with the depiction of an intimate reading scene. In place of the conventional green curtain, the descending screen depicted Newstead Abbey with Lord Byron reading in a boat on a lake. Reinforcing the impact of this visual denouement, the bills informed audiences to expect 'a view of Newstead Abbey, The Residence of the late Immortal Poet' to drop down at the end.[54] Reviewers also emphasised the image of the reading poet as a featured aspect of the entertainment. The *Observer* noted that, 'Lord Byron is represented sitting in a boat on the lake reading'.[55]

Edward Ziter argues that Macready's production provided two opposing images of Byron, 'the sexually transgressive adventurer and the inward aristocratic scholar', a visual dyad that 'would long structure ways of knowing the exotic as imagined in popular entertainment'.[56]

These images invited the audience to vicariously engage with a 'real' East just beyond the wings as seen by the archetypal poet/traveller. In this sense they elicit a literal desire to re-read and re-enact Byron, an identification reinforced by differential repetition and self-conscious recollection. This suggests an alternative to the 'emerging ambivalence to the visual' that Ziter argues shaped the increased craving of nineteenth-century audiences for 'a surfeit of detail in production' with little connection to plot and scripts full of references to foreign customs and manners (607). Rather than a desire for abstraction, the panoramic exoticism of both Macready and Charles Kean's even more sensational rendering of the exotic sites of Nineveh invited audiences to buy into the Byronic experience as self-culture, to view, read and then literally internalise his vision as part of accessing a new social and physical mobility. In this sense Stanfield's image of Byron reading is a spectacularly intimate rendering of the conflation of reading and viewing the poet.

Kean first attempted to stage *Sardanapalus* in 1834, but it was the 1853 production at the Princess's Theatre Royal in Oxford Street, where he had gained a reputation for staging spectacular Shakespeare revivals, that transformed the play into a panoramic spectacle. Capitalising on the interest generated by Sir Austen Henry Layard's illustrated account of *Nineveh and its Remains* (1849) Kean instructed Thomas Grieve, who had a reputation for historically accurate scene painting, to direct the creation of authentic Assyrian views on a grand scale. To ensure that this attention to detail was not lost on his audience Kean emphasised this point in the self-aggrandising handbill that inspired Lewes's contempt:

> To render visible to the eye, in connexion with Lord Byron's drama, the costume, architecture, and customs of the ancient Assyrian people, verified by the bas-reliefs, which, after having been buried for nearly three thousand years, have in our own day been brought to light, was an object that might well inspire the enthusiasm of one who has learnt that scenic illustration, if it have the weight of authority, may adorn and add dignity to the noble works of genius ... The Sculptures now in the British Museum have been rigidly followed; and where recent discovery has failed to give authority of minor detail, I have, wherever it has been possible, borrowed designs from surrounding nations, flourishing at the same epoch. In decoration of every kind, whether scenic or otherwise, I have diligently sought for *truth* ... It is a note-worthy fact that, until the present moment, it has been impossible to render Lord Byron's tragedy of 'Sardanapalus' upon the Stage with proper dramatic effect, because, until now, we have known nothing of Assyrian architecture and costume.[57]

Layard's discoveries infused Kean's version of *Sardanapalus* with a topicality that had been absent from Macready's adaptation. Layard advised on the production and Kean prided himself on its 'rigid' historical authenticity. The reviewer in the *Athenaeum* noted that Kean went as far as to align his own and the other actors' gestures and expressions with the contours of Layard's disinterred frescoes.[58] While acknowledging that some might find the desirability of this literal copying questionable, the 'adherence to pictorial authorities', according to this reviewer, 'adds strangely to the remote oriental character of the scene' (745). To achieve this level of verisimilitude Kean discarded the residual dramatic unity of Macready's version of Byron's text in favour of a spectacular series of panoramic scenes. These were loosely connected by a bowdlerised performance text that, as Lewes observed, resembled the instructive entertainment format of a magic lantern slide or moving panorama lecture.

The play was structured around three panoramic stage sets. The first set for the opening two acts was a panoramic vista painted by William Gordon depicting a terrace in Nineveh overlooking the river Tigris with the city ascending the facing bank. Thomas Grieve intensified the dioramic effect of a rudimentary wing-and-drop set by creating the illusion of perspective through the location of two-dimensional scenery in planes parallel to the proscenium and graduated gas lighting. Kean made extensive use of Grieve's lighting effects, at one point replacing a lyrical description of a sunset and the Chaldean stars in Act II with a lighting effect popularised by Daguerre's diorama.[59] As the sun set the stage gradually darkened and then light projected from behind a screen created the illusion of emerging stars. Daguerre had created a theatre-style auditorium in which two transparent and moveable painted screens lit from above and behind created the illusion of movement and a diverse array of scenic effects, most notably the transition from day to night. As a contemporary reviewer of Daguerre's diorama of 'Mount St Gotthard' observed, 'the effect of bringing the reality before the eye so vividly' excites 'those emotions and raise up those associations which a contemplation of the actual scene would produce in the mind'.[60]

The stage set for Acts III and IV was a lateral view of the Great Hall of Nimrod producing the illusion of infinite regression. Elaborately decorated with figured frescoes, the effect was of an infinite series of winged lions drawing the audience's eye along a trajectory into the space and beyond. A simulation of time travel much appreciated by the *Athenaeum*:

> 'And I too have been in' Assyria – the 'Arcadia' of Sardanapalus – was the feeling with which we left this theatre on Monday last. Our readers have already been made acquainted with Mr Kean's intention to produce an illustrated performance of Lord Byron's 'Sardanapalus,' in accordance with Messrs. Layard and Botta's discoveries at the ruins of the ancient city of

Nineveh . . . The whole is a moving and variable picture, comprehending innumerable phases of existence.[61]

Vicarious experience is the main attraction of Kean's 'illustrated' performance of a hybrid of Layard, Botta and Byron. Cued by the associated promotional rhetoric, the *Athenaeum*'s readers knew what to expect. Kean solicited attention through a multi-sensorial appeal to an audience trained to translate visual stimuli into consumable information. There is also something akin to Barthes's broader historical sense of the 'reality effect' implicit in the description of the performance as a 'moving and variable picture, comprehending innumerable phases of existence'. Barthes links the emergence of a distinctly modern understanding of history to 'the development of the realistic novel, the private diary, documentary literature, the news item, the historical museum, the exhibition of ancient objects and the massive development of photography whose sole pertinent feature is precisely to signify that the event has already taken place'.[62] While the panorama, both in its 360-degree and large canvas versions, was a non-photographic form it reinforced a newly affective comprehension of history of the kind Barthes describes. The result was as a heady mixture of spatial immediacy and temporal disjunction if contemporary reviewers are to be believed.

The final set of Kean's production depicted a roofless room looking out over the panoramic expanse of Nineveh. Framed on either side by enormous winged lions with human heads supporting the columns of the roof, this elaborate scene was designed to collapse as the conflagration of the funereal pyre consumed the stage. Even Byron's friends acknowledged the popular appeal of such a spectacle. John Cam Hobhouse observed that while it was 'a poor play badly acted . . . the scenery & decorations & conflagration at the end attract multitudes'.[63] Sylvester Clarence, a reviewer for the *Theatrical Journal* was less sanguine, referring readers to Byron's text and praising aspects of the performance that were true to his verse. Clarence shared Lewes's judgement of Kean's acting and pretensions to erudition, but echoed the *Athenaeum*'s praise of the re-animation of ancient Nineveh and Assyria:

Assyria and Nineveh made easy to the comprehension of the English student! The buried mysteries of a thousand years dug up and brought to light by Dr Layard! The palace of the Assyrian Kings erected – by means of pencil, canvas, and machinery – . . . The denizen of our 'tight little island' in the nineteenth century rubs his eyes to find whether he is thoroughly awake, on hearing that there existed – a thousand years ago, a kingdom, whose limits extended from the confines of Troy to Samarcand [sic] – from the mountains of Palestine to those of the Caucasus – whose wealth, pomp, and magnificence surpassed that of the present day, while its civilisation approached, if it did not equal it.[64]

Kean's panoramic scenery, according to this reviewer, presented the bleary-eyed denizens of London with a historical vista that extended far beyond the limited horizons and fragmented partiality of their quotidian perceptual experience, a simulated perceptual mastery over ancient Assyrian culture that successfully blurred the lines between entertainment and instruction, much as the imperial expansiveness of the Crystal Palace Exhibition had done only two years before. There is, nevertheless, considerable doubt about the critical capacities of the inhabitants of 'our tight little island' in this description. As their eyes strain to assemble the parts of Kean's spectacle into a cognisable unity, attention lags as mind and eye move between foci and registers. Notably, what they see, owing to Kean's stress on verisimilitude is a simulation of the actual, precisely the panoramic illusion of the real which Lewes condemned. Londoners accordingly scan Kean's 'illustration' like they would a panorama. It transports the audience through time and history by moving them through a carefully manufactured spatiality, a new experience that as Lewes observed broke with traditional theatrical unities to create an overtly technical seriality, what Henry James would later describe in his recollections of Kean's spectacular productions as 'costly scenic science'.[65]

Byronic Reveries

Lewes's objections to Kean's production reveal his debt to a Romantic tradition of theatre criticism that opposed illusionism to the ideals of naturalism and authenticity. As Charles Lamb observed,

> when the novelty is past we find to our cost that instead of realising an idea, we have only materialised and brought down a fine vision to the standard of flesh and blood. We have let go a dream, in quest of an unattainable substance.[66]

Shakespeare epitomised this ideal of dramatic authenticity for Lamb and for other Romantic critics, such as Hazlitt. Hazlitt argued that,

> In reading this author [Shakespeare], you do not merely learn what his characters say, – you see their persons. By something expressed or understood, you are not at a loss to decipher their peculiar physiognomy, the meaning of a look, the grouping, the by-play, as we might see it on stage. A word, an epithet paints a whole scene, or throws back whole years in the history of the person represented.[67]

Hazlitt imagined a form of involuntary thought transference between Shakespeare and his audience in which the poet not only passes from one character to another 'like the same soul, successively animating different bodies', but also knows how to transfer what is going on in his character's minds to the minds of his readers: 'whatever would have passed through their minds on the occasion, and have been observed by others, passed through his, and is made known to the reader' (95). This is precisely the ideal of mediation without 'disturbance or channel interference' that Kittler aligns with the Romantic discourse network of 1800 (112). Hazlitt praises Shakespeare's capacity to trigger the 'unconscious power of mind which is as true to nature as itself' (97). 'As in our dreams we hold conversations with ourselves, make remarks, or communicate intelligence, and have no idea of the answer which we shall receive', Hazlitt argues, 'so the dialogues in Shakespeare are carried on without any consciousness of what is to follow, without any appearance of preparation or premeditation' (98).

Lewes shared this idealism, while extending Hazlitt's model of Shakespeare's 'enlarged subjectivity', as Lynn Voskuil has argued, into a more collective understanding of the theatre as a mirror of the general state of the culture, and, correspondingly, theatre criticism as a form of social criticism.[68] It is this social commitment coupled with his unique and seminal psychological approach to acting theory that drove Lewes's fierce attack on the technological artifice of Kean's production.[69] Lewes was not only a theatre critic, writing a regular column for the radical newspaper, *The Leader*, which was where the Kean review was published; he also wrote for the stage and acted. As a result of that experience, he believed in 'acted drama' as a dynamic labile art form. The theatre was no place for dioramic effects or panoramic illusionism, as he wrote in his column in *The Leader* in 1851, 'The Drama, as an Art is the material representation of an ideal conception. It places before our eyes the progress and culmination of some passion, the story of some ideal life.'[70]

Lewes's theory of drama became more psychologically complex in tandem with his growing interest in the science of mind. Indeed, later in his career, while in the process of writing the third volume of *Problems of Life and Mind*, he revised his earlier theatrical reviews, including his scathing critique of Kean, in a popular collection of essays *On Actors and the Art of Acting* (1875) which aimed to demonstrate the 'psychological conditions on which [theatrical] effects depend'.[71] Lewes, as Joseph Roach has shown, also published articles on the theatre for *Blackwood's* and the *Pall Mall Gazette* throughout the 1850s and 1860s that drew on the same network of ideas as his contemporaneous scientific papers, such as 'Voluntary and Involuntary Actions', also published in *Blackwood's*, and 'Heart and Brain' in the *Fortnightly Review*.[72] Voskuil reinforces this point in her reading of Lewes's *Pall Mall* essays, suggesting rightly, that 'a clarified and refined self-knowledge' was one of the 'unvoiced goals of Lewes's drama criticism' (49).

Given these passionately held ideals, Lewes's description of Victorian audiences as 'a mass of amusement-seekers' with a small 'nucleus of intelligent spectators' in *On Actors* suggested a broader social malaise (vi). Charles Kean's panoramic devices and magic lantern effects typified the channel interference generated by this drive to amuse, disrupting the naturalistic mediation of Byron's text with 'pantomimic' formulas and mechanically reproduced 'signs'.[73] Summing up Kean's contribution to theatre along these lines, Lewes concluded:

> He has added nothing to the elucidation of the characters, he has given no fresh light to players or public; but he has greatly improved the scenic representation, and has lavished time and money on the archaeological illustration of the plays. He has striven for public applause. Those who, like myself, care a great deal about acting and very little about splendid dresses, must nevertheless confess that what Charles Kean professed to do in the way of scenic illustration, he did splendidly well. (22)

Lewes perceived Kean's entrepreneurial embrace of the technologies that appealed to the 'mass of amusement seekers' as continuous with the pervasive reliance on mechanical and stereotypical characterisation in contemporary fiction; a disquieting trend that he believed a successful literature should counteract by forging more vital connections between the imagination and the emotions. According to Lewes, while the imagination could only 'recall what Sense has previously impressed', its power lay in its capacity to trigger and recombine these remembered images into vital moving images, 'all these kaleidoscopic fragments are recomposed into images that seem to have a corresponding reality of their own'.[74] A great artist does not too literally materialise the characters and world she or he imagines: 'These are all visible, and their fluctuations are visible. He sees the quivering lip, the agitated soul; he hears the aching cry, and the dreary wash of waves upon the beach' (49). Likewise, great theatre requires 'fluctuating spontaneity' that draws the audience into 'a sequence of feeling', an action driven by emotion not technology.[75] These arguments are predicated on an assumed indivisibility of body and mind that informs Lewes's conception of the dynamics of performance as a powerful embodiment of emotion that involuntarily revives corresponding memories and emotion in the audience. 'We are all spectators of ourselves', he observes in *On Actors*, 'but it is the peculiarity of the artistic nature to indulge in such introspection even in moments of all but the most disturbing passion, and to draw thence the materials of art' (113).

Confronted by the technologically generated images of a newly dominant sphere of mass amusements, Lewes turned his focus to differentiating the function of art as a counteractive to the transient pursuit of individual pleasure. It was imperative, he believed, to differentiate the function of 'art as a social system', to use Niklas Luhmann's terminology, from the mass-entertainment system.[76] The problem being, as Lewes's own predilection for popular optical metaphors suggests, these systems overlapped in their operational drive to communicate with and engage a newly conceived audience who increasingly moved between media in more knowing and sophisticated ways.

Notes

1. *Description of A View of Mont Blanc, The Valley of Chamounix and the surrounding mountains* (London, 1837). John and Robert Burford, The Panorama of Leicester Square Tracts 1826–1849, British Library Collection.
2. 'Guide to the Panorama of Niagara Falls', in *A Collection of Descriptions of Views Exhibited at the Panorama, Leicester Square, and Painted by H. A. Barker, Robert Burford, John Burford and H. C. Selous, London, 1798–1856* (London: British Library), n. p.
3. Byron, '*Childe Harold's Pilgrimage, Canto III*', *Portfolio* 1:4 (23 November 1816), p. 73.
4. Christensen, *Lord Byron's Strength: Romantic Writing and Commercial Society*, p. xvi.
5. Kittler, *Discourse Networks 1800/1900*, p. 112.
6. Dendy, *The Philosophy of Mystery*, p. 45.
7. Mole, *Byron's Romantic Celebrity: Industrial Culture and the Hermeneutic of Intimacy*, p. 156; see also Christensen's seminal study of the forging of the Byronic brand in *Lord Byron's Strength: Romantic Writing and Commercial Society*.
8. Dimmock, 'Feminism, New-Historicism and the Reader', in *Readers and Reading*, p. 144.
9. Coleridge, *Lectures on Literature 1808–1819*, vol. 1, p. 186.
10. Hazlitt, *Complete Works*, vol. 17, p. 326.
11. Keats, *The Letters of John Keats*, p. 233.
12. Cited in Chew, *Byron in England: His Fame and After-Fame*, pp. 131–2.
13. Buzard, *The Beaten Track: European Tourism, Literature, and the Ways to 'Culture' 1800–1918*, p. 116.
14. Lewes, 'Charles Kean and Sardanapalus', reprinted in *Dramatic Essays*, vol. 3, p. 250.
15. Ruskin, *Praeterita: The Autobiography of John Ruskin*, p. 140.

16. Cited in Buzard, *The Beaten Track*, p. 119.
17. Brokedon, et al., *Finden's Illustrations of the Life and Works of Lord Byron*.
18. Murray, Preface, *A Handbook for Travellers on the Continent*, 3rd edn, n. p.
19. Jeffrey, 'Review of Lord Byron's *Giaour*', *Edinburgh Review* 21 (July 1813), p. 299.
20. De Quincey, 'On the Poetry of Pope', in *De Quincey's Collected Writings*, vol. 11, p. 52.
21. Bolter and Grusin, *Remediation: Understanding New Media*, p. 5.
22. Marx, *Grundrisse*, p. 501.
23. Bennett, 'Texts, Readers, Reading Formations', *The Bulletin of the Midwest Modern Language Association*, p. 3.
24. 'Panoramas and Dioramas', *Leisure Hour* (January 1886), p. 47.
25. 'Panorama of the Battle of Waterloo', *London Saturday Journal* 3:68 (16 April 1842), p. 188.
26. Scott, *The Vision of Don Roderick, the Field of Waterloo, and Other Poems*, pp. 224–5.
27. Gitelman, *Scripts, Grooves, and Writing Machines: Representing Technology in the Edison Era*, p. 2.
28. Oettermann, *The Panorama: History of a Mass Medium*, p. 47.
29. Robert Barker, *Morning Chronicle* (21 April 1801), cited in Wilcox, 'Unlimiting the Bounds of Painting', in Hyde, *Panoramania!: The Art and Entertainment of the 'All-Embracing' View*, p. 36.
30. Griffiths, *Shivers Down Your Spine: Cinema, Museums, and the Immersive View*, p. 55.
31. Smith performed *The Ascent of Mont Blanc* 2,000 times between March 1852 and July 1858. Thorington, *Mont Blanc Sideshow: The Life and Times of Albert Smith*, p. 192.
32. Elfenbein, *Byron and the Victorians*, p. 29.
33. John Guillory describes this process in his analysis of the peculiar canonical significance and notorious popularity of Thomas Gray's *Elegy Written in a Country Churchyard* in *Cultural Capital: The Problem of Literary Canon Formation* (Chicago: The University of Chicago Press, 1993), p. x. While Byron's status in the vernacular canon differs dramatically from Gray, the distributive mechanism Guillory encapsulates in this phrase can also be adapted to describe the vernacularisation, commodification and selective reproduction of Byron's works throughout the nineteenth century.
34. St Clair, 'The Impact of Byron's Writings: an Evaluative Approach', in *Byron: Augustan and Romantic*, pp. 52–62.
35. Throsby analyses this aspect of the poem in the context of early fan culture in 'Byron, commonplacing and early fan culture', in *Romanticism and Celebrity Culture, 1750–1850*, pp. 226–7.
36. This sense of textual poaching is derived from De Certeau, *The Practice of Everyday Life*, p. 174.
37. Letter to John Murray, 2 July 1812, cited in Smiles, *A Publisher and His Friends: Memoir and Correspondence of the Late John Murray*, vol. 1, p. 214.
38. *British Review* 3 (1812), 275–302; repr. in *The Romantics Reviewed*, ed. Reiman, Part B: *Byron and Regency Society Reviewers*, vol. 1, p. 396.

39. Manning, 'Childe Harold in the Marketplace: From Romaunt to Handbook', *Modern Language Quarterly* 52 (1991), p. 182.
40. Skelton, 'The Home and Grave of Byron', *Once a Week* 2:49 (2 June 1860), pp. 539–42. *Once a Week* was launched in 1859 to compete with Dickens's new magazine *All the Year Round*. While it never succeeded in this aim it was known for its quality illustrations by notable figures such as Hablot K. Browne, John Leech, Holman Hunt, John Tenniel and John Everett Millais.
41. Garofalo, 'Political Seductions: The Show of War in Byron's Sardanapalus', *Criticism* 44:1 (Winter 2002), p. 43.
42. Lewes, 'Charles Kean and Sardanapalus', vol. 3, p. 248.
43. Macready, *The Diaries of William Charles Macready 1833–1851*, vol. 1, p. 49.
44. Wolfson, '"A Problem Few Dare Imitate": Sardanapalus and "Effeminate Character"', *ELH* 58:4 (Winter 1991), p. 871.
45. Wolfson cites Hazlitt's essay on 'Effeminate Character' as a formative intertext for Byron's poem, p. 871.
46. Roberts, 'Rev. of *Sardanapalus*', *British Review* 19 (March 1822), pp. 72–3.
47. Francis Jeffrey, 'Lord Byron's Tragedies', *Edinburgh Review* 36 (1822), pp. 420, 424.
48. Byron, *Sardanapalus*, in *The Poetical Works of Lord Byron: Poetry*, vol. 1, 18–23.
49. Clarkson Stanfield was primarily known as a marine painter. His 'Grand Moving Picture of a voyage to the Isle of Wight including a visit to Cowes Regatta' was exhibited at Drury Lane in 1828. These moving pictures were painted on a continuous roll of material unwound from one giant spool onto another.
50. D'Arcy Wood provides a detailed account of the popular appeal of Belzoni's tomb in the broader context of Georgian visual culture in *The Shock of the Real: Romanticism and Visual Culture, 1760–1860*, pp. 1–15.
51. Lamb, 'The Barrenness of the Imaginative Faculty in the Productions of Modern Art', in *Complete Works and Letters*, vol. 3, p. 203.
52. Altick, *The Shows of London*, p. 187.
53. This description is drawn from Howell's description in *Byron Tonight: A Poet's Plays on the Nineteenth-Century Stage*, pp. 66–7.
54. Drury Lane bills, Theatre Museum London.
55. Theatre Notices, *Observer* (13 April 1834).
56. Ziter, 'Kean, Byron, and Fantasies of Miscegenation', *Theatre Journal* 54:4 (2002), p. 620.
57. Kean, *Sardanapalus. Adapted for representation by Charles Kean*, n. p. The capitalisation of Stage is Kean's.
58. Rev. of *Sardanapalus*, *Athenaeum* (18 June 1853), p. 745.
59. Altick describes this lighting effect in his chapter on the Diorama in *The Shows of London*, pp. 163–72.
60. Cited in Gernsheim, L. J. M. *Daguerre: The History of the Diorama and the Daguerreotype*, p. 24.
61. Rev. of *Sardanapalus*, *Athenaeum* (18 June 1853), p. 745.
62. Barthes, *The Rustle of Language*, p. 147.
63. Cited in Cole, *The Life and Theatrical Times of Charles Kean*, p. 66.

64. Clarence, 'Mr Charles Kean's Sardanapalus', *Theatrical Journal* (20 July 1853), p. 223.
65. James, *A Small Boy and Others*, p. 318.
66. Lamb, *The Works of Charles Lamb*, vol. 2, p. 351.
67. Hazlitt, 'On Shakespeare and Milton', in *Lectures on the English Poets*, p. 94.
68. Voskuil, *Acting Naturally: Victorian Theatricality and Authenticity*, p. 48.
69. Roach discusses the seminal influence of Lewes's acting theory on twentieth-century theories in 'G. H. Lewes and Performance Theory: Towards a "Science of Acting"', *Theatre Journal* 32:3 (October 1980), pp. 312–28.
70. Cited in Voskuil, *Acting Naturally*, p. 43.
71. Lewes, *On Actors and the Art of Acting*, p. 103.
72. Lewes, 'Voluntary and Involuntary Actions', *Blackwood's* 86 (1859), pp. 99–113 and 'Heart and Brain', *Fortnightly Review* 1 (1865), pp. 66–74.
73. Lewes, *On Actors*, pp. 176, 185.
74. Lewes, *The Principles of Success in Literature*, p. 64.
75. Lewes, *On Actors*, p. 114.
76. Luhmann describes the ways in which different social systems, organised in functional rather than stratified relationships, still share the same operational mode in *Art as a Social System*, p. 2.

Chapter 3

Natural Magic and the Technologies of Reading: David Brewster and Sir Walter Scott

Looking back at the popular craze that followed in the wake of his invention of the kaleidoscope in 1816, David Brewster portrayed a city consumed by a new type of moving image:

> You can have no conception of the effect which the instrument excited in London; all that you have heard falls infinitely short of the reality. No book and no instrument in the memory of man ever produced such a singular effect. They are exhibited publicly on the streets for a penny, and I had the pleasure of paying this sum yesterday; these are about two feet long and a foot wide. Infants are seen carrying them in their hands, the coachmen on their boxes are busy using them, and thousands of poor people make their bread by making and selling them.[1]

Melancholic indignation pervades Brewster's accounts of the scenes of frenzied consumption that begin each new edition of his kaleidoscope treatise, culminating in the final edition revised for publication in 1858. In the first edition of the treatise, Brewster casts himself as a traumatised witness paralysed by the marketplace's sublime indifference to the provenance of 'this inexplicably wonderful toy'.[2] Falling prey to the avarice of London and Paris instrument makers, Brewster mournfully speculates that 'no fewer than two hundred thousand' of these cheap, flawed instruments were sold in London and Paris in the first three months of 1817 (7).

Enlisting the empirical authority of the *Encyclopaedia Britannica*, Brewster expanded the imperial scope of his invention in the 1858 edition. Beginning with 'the sensation it excited in London throughout all ranks of people', poor and rich, old and young, he describes large cargoes of kaleidoscopes being sent across Europe and to the East Indies. Soon travellers wandering through the 'most obscure and retired village in Switzerland', he speculated, might discover a kaleidoscope in the hands of a child with no way of knowing where this marvellous toy had come from.[3] Faced with the daunting scale of this phenomenon, which Percy

Bysshe Shelley playfully dubbed 'Kalleidoscopism', Brewster claimed he felt responsible for supplying an account of its origins, its construction and its potential uses as an instrument of recreation.[4] The result was the multiple editions of Brewster's treatise on the kaleidoscope, which, along with his *Letters on Natural Magic. Addressed to Sir Walter Scott* (1832) and prolific publications on optics, the stereoscope and the magic lantern, generated an extensive and influential network of theories and applications of the moving image in the middle decades of the century.[5] Brewster was the consummate populariser of science, a role that also extended, in his capacity as a reviewer for major periodicals, into the new science of mind. Beginning with the multiple technological and metaphoric circulations of the kaleidoscope and culminating with the interplay between Walter Scott's *Letters on Demonology and Witchcraft* (1830) and Brewster's *Letters on Natural Magic,* this chapter explores the ways in which Brewster's inventions materialised a newly modern sense of visual and temporal contingency that entered into the collective descriptive rhetoric of writers, ranging from Byron to Dickens. Drawing on Walter Scott's supernatural anecdotes in *Letters on Demonology and Witchcraft*, Brewster's *Letters on Natural Magic* provides an alternative series of readings of Scott's popular psychology of belief, dreams and illusion. While explicitly indebted to Scott, Brewster's interest was driven by the optical dimensions of the psychological phenomena Scott described, leading to often vivid and speculative theorisations of analogous images generated by philosophical toys and optical devices, such as the kaleidoscope, the thaumatrope and the magic lantern.

Kaleidoscopes and Other Things

In 1831 the *Metropolitan Magazine* announced that the nineteenth century was an age when writers ignored the 'world of things' at their peril: 'The great business of the modern author is to seize his opportunity. He knows that the world will neither await his leisure, nor suffer him to "bestow all his tediousness" upon his readers. The age of things has arrived.'[6] Animating this world of things, according to this reviewer, was an indiscriminate crowd who consumed every new craze with a voracious appetite and paid little attention to the integrity of forms and sources. This is the polarising notion of the crowd that haunts Brewster's account of the mass popularity of the kaleidoscope, and motivates the critical recoil of his Romantic literary contemporaries to the indiscriminate tastes of the mass reader. These divergent responses are also symptomatic of a more fundamental shift in patterns of cultural consumption at this time, as Jon Klancher has argued, towards 'a larger collective landscape of interpretive acts within which to situate the solitary reader'.[7] Klancher's idea of reading as an evolving set of related, yet distinct, cultural practices is pivotal to this chapter's emphasis on the symbiotic relationship between nineteenth-century literary descriptive techniques and visual technologies; a symbiosis succinctly distilled by Klancher in his reading of Shelley's *Defence of Poetry* (1840) as an exemplification of the ways in which writers in the early decades of the nineteenth century felt challenged to forge a new imaginative language capable of 'apprehending the relations between things without becoming merely a collection of "things" itself'.[8] Generated by a productive tension between literary and material culture, this hybrid descriptive mode, as Jerome Christensen argues in the context of two other Romantic figures, Byron and Wordsworth, takes the form of a poetics of 'scattered intensities' characterised by competing assimilative and resistant responses to 'the world of things':

> For Byron, as for Wordsworth, the world in which the poet travels is a site of scattered intensities . . . The poem organises this body putting a face on it and making it into a book, thus capitalising on the attraction of those touching intensities . . .[9]

According to Brewster's accounts, the kaleidoscope was intended to achieve just such an effect – to illuminate the relationship between 'scattered intensities' for a new class of writers and artists. Initially intended as an instrumental demonstration of Brewster's celebrated experimentation with the polarisation of light, the kaleidoscope was legitimated by its inventor through a fusion of scientific, literary and magical terms.[10] Brewster described the visual effect of the kaleidoscope as a 'magical union of parts', a significant choice of words that confirms the kaleidoscope's place in a long tradition of natural magic. But, as Brewster himself discovered as he watched his beautiful instrument slip from his grasp, the harmonising of the dissonant fragments of the material world into a magical unity was not so easily achieved when the vagaries of the mass market were involved. Cheap and easily copied, kaleidoscopes soon proliferated across early nineteenth-century London moving freely from street to drawing room, to quote one of many contemporary poetic renditions:

> 'Tis a tube made of brass, pewter, copper, or tin,
> With a hole at one end of it where you look in,
> And see – gracious heavens! – you see such a sight,
> Should I try to describe it 'twould take me all night;
> The exquisite figures and colours you can see,

No painter can copy, no poet can fancy:
You see – what must all you've before seen surpass
You see – some *small old broken pieces of glass!*
Need I tell you, indeed, that with such preparation,
So lovely a bauble has caused a *Sensation?*[11]

As these lines suggest, the kaleidoscope was synonymous with experiment and perceptual instability rather than mastery. It was also primarily a domestic entertainment, designed to be taken home and enjoyed in the privacy of one's drawing room; a pleasure amplified by the agency given to spectators to construct their own kaleidoscopic slides out of the found objects in their immediate environment. Brewster's instructions encouraged consumers to put beads, hairs, wires, insects and other fragments into the glass slides that came with the kaleidoscope to increase the number and variety of visual effects. They could also transform the external world into a kaleidoscopic effect if the object plate was removed and the tube turned, to quote Brewster:

> The furniture of a room, books and papers lying on a table, pictures on the wall, a blazing fire, the moving branches and foliage of trees and shrubs, bunches of flowers, horses and cattle in a park, carriages in motion, the currents of a river, waterfalls, moving insects, the sun shining through clouds or trees, and, in short, every object in nature may be introduced by the aid of the lens into the figures created by the instrument.[12]

Addressing an increasingly scientific and technologically literate readership, the various editions of the kaleidoscope treatise register not only Brewster's conflicted relation to the extraordinary popularity of his invention, but an awareness of the growing demand for a more interactive and creative relationship with new forms of technological and visual mediation on the part of his readers; a demand which Brewster was well placed to register given his close involvement with the Great Exhibitions of 1851 and 1862. Indeed, he conducted many famous visitors around the former, including Charlotte Brontë, who subsequently incorporated references to the kaleidoscope into *Jane Eyre*.[13] Brewster also never missed an opportunity to expand upon the possible imaginative and technical adaptations of his marvellous invention. Fascinated by aesthetic affect, he claimed that the 'combinations of forms and colours may be made to succeed each other in such a manner as to excite sentiments and ideas with as much vivacity as those which are excited by musical composition'.[14] Variations in mood and feeling, in turn, could be induced by alternating between harmonic and dissonant colour and formal sequences; 'dull and gloomy masses, moving slowly before the eye' exciting 'feelings of sadness and distress', while 'the aerial tracery of light and evanescent forms, enriched with lively colours' inspired 'cheerfulness and gaiety' (160).

Brewster also suggested ways in which this experience could be transformed into a public spectacle by being projected onto a screen with the aid of an 'electric lime-ball', appropriate musical accompaniment and the transformation of the internal workings of the kaleidoscope itself into an elaborate magic-lantern-style apparatus:

> The coloured objects might be fixed between the long stripes of glass, moved horizontally or obliquely across the ends of the reflectors; and the effects thus obtained might be varied by the occasional introduction of revolving object boxes, containing objects of various colours and forms, partly fixed and partly movable. Similar forms in different colours, and in tints of varying intensity, losing and resuming their peculiar character with different velocities, and in different times, might exhibit a distinct relation between the optical and acoustic phenomena simultaneously presented to the sense. Flashes of light, coloured and colourless, and clouds of different depths of shadow, advancing into, or emerging from the centre of symmetry, or passing across the radial lines of the figure at different obliquities, would assist in marking more emphatically the gay or the gloomy sounds with which they are accompanied. (160)

This wonder-inducing spectacle recalls the hallucinogenic effects of Philipstal and Robertson's Phantasmagoria, which had been such sensations in Paris and London just over a decade earlier.[15] Unfortunately, there are no accounts of Brewster's kaleidoscopic phantasmagoria being realised, although handbills and programmes from the Royal Polytechnic Institute in London reveal that some version of Brewster's idea was produced there using dissolving views integrated into a lecture on kaleidoscopic vision given by Dr John Henry Pepper during the Easter Holidays of 1866 and later still by a popular lecturer called Mr Benjamin Malden, who ended his 'scientific' lectures with a display of the kaleidoscopic effects of the chromotrope.[16] Whether Pepper or Malden's illusions were true to Brewster's vision, the visual experience potentially offered by the kaleidoscopic phantasmagoria remains a tantalising one, steeped in the spectacular traditions of natural magic and the sensual pleasures of optical revelation.

Natural Magical Reading

The frontispiece of Sir David Brewster's *A Treatise on Optics* (1831) depicts a highly stylised domestic scene (Figure 3.1). Five cherubic boys in various stages of undress appear absorbed by a selection of optical

Figure 3.1 Frontispiece to David Brewster's *A Treatise on Optics*

devices: a magic lantern, a kaleidoscope, a telescope and a mirror. Two boys project an image of Harlequin and Columbine on the back wall of the room, while two others hold a kaleidoscope and telescope up to a window. The only boy facing the reader looks admiringly at himself in a mirror. In a text otherwise illustrated by scientific drawings of ocular phenomena and optical devices, this frontispiece provides a more whimsical portrayal of reading as play. Whether Brewster had a hand in selecting this illustration or not, it identifies his volume as part of a more general trend towards instructive entertainment in the first half of the nineteenth century.

Entrepreneurial publishing ventures abounded during the 1830s, addressing a range of readerships – the popular, the familial, the radical, the aspirant middle-class – through a range of print media, including John Limbird's successful weekly pictorial miscellany the *Mirror of Literature, Amusement and Instruction* (1823), Charles Knight and Henry Brougham's various diffusions of useful knowledge and John Murray's ambitious but ill-fated Family Library series.[17] In the same year that Brewster published *A Treatise on Optics*, he also published the first of two volumes for Murray's Family Library series, *The Life of Sir Isaac Newton* (1831). This was followed a year later by the far more successful *Letters on Natural Magic. Addressed to Sir Walter Scott* (1832), which followed on from Scott's marginally better selling *Letters on Demonology and Witchcraft. Addressed to J. G. Lockhart* (1830). Illustrated by George Cruikshank, Scott's volume was sold as a Christmas book during a period of intense interest in gothic and super-natural tales. In the guise of a reverential supplement Brewster's volume extended Scott's antiquarian reflections on the psychology of belief and the explained supernatural into the domain of physiological experimen-tation and the instrumental extension of the senses.

By the late 1820s John Murray was one of the most distinguished publishers in London. Inspired by predecessors such as the Society for the Diffusion of Useful Knowledge (1826) and Constable's *Miscellany* (1827), Murray commissioned new non-fiction works to be published in a cheap format for the common reader. Commencing publication in 1829, the Family Library consisted of fifty-three volumes, of which Scott and Brewster's volumes were among the more successful.[18] Scott Bennett goes so far as to argue in his financial history of the Family Library that these books could even be read as 'counter-revolutionary documents' (142). According to Bennett, Murray explicitly set about creating an audience that crossed class lines, unifying any potentially dissenting voices in support of the common cause of enlightenment and the progress of knowledge.

Dwindling sales records reveal, however, that with the exception of the relative success of Brewster's volume in the latter years, the Family Library failed to inspire a revolution in reading practices. Recognising defeat, Murray remaindered the library to the notoriously opportunis-tic bookseller Thomas Tegg, who subsequently bequeathed the Scott and Brewster volumes, amongst others, to his son William Tegg, who continued to publish cheap reprints of both volumes.[19] Significantly, Cruikshank's illustrations are absent from the later editions of Scott published by both Teggs. According to Albert Cohn, the option to purchase the volume with or without illustrations had been available from the first edition.[20] This meant that Cruikshank was free to publish a much-reprinted abridged version of Scott's text designed to feature his illustrations in the same year.[21]

Written in the final years of Scott's life *Letters on Demonology and Witchcraft* was intended as a 'chatty book on the supernatural' cater-ing to the market for family reading.[22] Lockhart himself suggested the volume to Murray as a welcome change in register for his illness-ravaged friend. Yet despite Lockhart's good intentions, the book became an arduous chore for Scott, who grimly noted in his journal that he felt compelled to finish it because he needed the money.[23] Scott aptly records in his journal on 17 July 1830: 'I have finished the *Demonology* and have a mind to say Damn it, but the subject is damned to my hand.'[24] Given the physical and economic exigencies under which Scott laboured at this time, the results were predictably inconsistent. Lockhart noted that the *Demonology* 'contains many passages worthy of his best day – little snatches of picturesque narrative and the like – in fact, transcripts of his own fireside stories'.[25]

The majority of reviewers shared Lockhart's positive assessment of these aspects of the *Demonology*. In what amounts to a puff piece, the *Athenaeum* reproduced selected highlights three months prior to the volume's publication interspersed with breathless praise for Scott's descriptive ability to bring past superstitions to life:

> We have neither ate, drank, slept nor spoke since this book was put into our hands. The subject is most alluring, and the manner in which it is handled is magical: a spell is thrown upon the reader little less powerful than a page of the Book of Grammery, which was buried in the grave of Michael Scott, the wizard.[26]

Associated here with the familiar gothic drama of *The Lay of the Last Minstrel* (1805), Scott's miscellaneous supernatural anecdotes are transformed into dynamic performances that simulate the feeling of actually being there. The reviewer speaks of being 'possessed', of sensory affect 'all that we see and hear is of it and through it', and active identification, 'We see visions', 'we have walked . . . with Major Weir's magic staff in our hand', 'we rode on a broomstick of the Witch of Endor', and 'finally, we have kept watch by the sinner's side who had a skeleton for an attendant, with a sceptical physician who trembled if he did not believe' (577). This reviewer's only reservation was that 'many a worthy family' should ignore Scott's sceptical treatment of ghosts as forms of spectral illusion and immerse themselves in the 'poetic' charms of the spirit world that still eludes rational explanation: 'Spirits have more discretion than to come to be questioned and dissected by philosophers and materialists' (577).

One exception to the chorus of praise that met Scott's volume was an anonymous essay published in *Fraser's Magazine*. Noting the typically heightened expectations surrounding a Scott publication, the reviewer dismisses the volume as a cynical commodification of Scott's considerable literary powers. The 'depth of research and calmness of investigation' required to produce a credibly synoptic account of 'the origin, progress, and connexions of the belief in demons and witches' are 'inconsistent with the thinness and superficial rapidity which are necessary in a popular work, designed for no other end than to supply the market with ware that may be already existing'.[27] Not only is Scott guilty of producing a derivative 'popular miscellany' designed for rapid consumption, he also falls foul of this reviewer's scathing assessment of 'popular libraries' such as Murray's:

> This 'general diffusion of knowledge,' however imperfect, may well be the subject of sincere and legitimate congratulation, and we heartily wish that real knowledge were a thousand fold more diffused amongst us; but is there not, we may be allowed to ask, great reason to apprehend that these 'popular libraries' – which profess to communicate all sorts of knowledge so cheaply and easily, and which, in truth, very frequently do little or nothing, but confirm the vanity and self-conceit to which we are already too prone, by making us believe we know many things thoroughly, of which we know next to nothing – may ultimately take away from this age all reverence, and with it all capability of acquiring, or even seeking for, any deep or genuine knowledge? (508)

In a not so subtle dig at Henry Brougham's reforming vision for a literate stable society, diffusion becomes synonymous with the frenetic production of second-rate content and the ascendancy of an 'autodidact culture' fostered by commercial enterprises falsely branded as 'libraries'. The sins of vanity and self-conceit are encoded here with a deeper social anxiety about the atomistic individualism arising from such programmatic diffusions of knowledge. Nor were these anxieties lost on Brougham himself, who consistently called for caution, reminding his readers of the 'necessity of some considerable degree of restraint to the well-being of society – the impossibility of the supreme power being left in the hands of the whole people'.[28] Indeed, this alignment between Brougham and his critics is itself indicative of prevailing concerns about resurgent radicalism that characterised debates about popular education and literature throughout the 1820s and 1830s.[29]

Scott, given this context, was quick to deflate the expectations of readers searching for a rigorous antiquarian study of the history of superstition. Instead, his introductory chapter simulates the intimate conversational mode of a private correspondence with Lockhart: 'You have asked of me, dear friend, that I should assist the Family Library, with the history of a dark chapter in human nature, which the increasing civilisation of all well-instructed countries has now almost blotted out.'[30] Scott assumes his readers share his own well-instructed approach to the psychology of belief:

> My purpose is, after a general account to confine myself to narratives of remarkable cases, and to the observations which naturally arise out of them,

– in the confidence that such a plan is, at the present time of day, more likely to suit the pages of a popular miscellany, than an attempt to reduce the contents of many hundred tomes, from the largest to the smallest size, into an abridgement, which, however compressed, must remain greatly too large for the reader's powers of patience. (3)

What is required is an abridged form of edited highlights to be selectively consumed by impatient readers familiar with the model of miscellaneous reading popularised by anthologists, such as Vicesimus Knox. By 1790, according to Knox, 'the art of printing' had 'multiplied books to such a degree' that readers necessarily began reading 'in the classical sense of the word, LEGERE, that is, to *pick out* . . . the best part of books'.[31] In a similar spirit, Scott licenses the reader to pick out 'remarkable' and memorable cases that catch their eye as they scan through the volume in the limited hours modern life allows for such indulgences; cases in other words that lend themselves to memorisation and repetition. The aim was to inculcate his readers with his own 'conservative scepticism' towards spectral illusions and offer a physiological account of the perceptual ambiguities that he had used to such great effect in popular ghost stories, such as 'The Tapestried Chamber' and 'My Aunt Margaret's Mirror'.[32]

As Brewster was quick to recognise, there were significant parallels between Scott's sceptical physiological diagnosis of a diverse array of supernatural visitations experienced from classical times to the present, and his own interest in perceptual physiology and optical devices. Both Scott and Brewster were immersed in a broader cultural debate about the epistemological value of sight. Correspondingly, their work is informed by contemporary debates surrounding the declining hegemony of theological explanation and the widening dissemination of a new physiologically based optics that informed contemporary accounts of the relationship between perception and cognition.[33] Cruikshank's illustrations for the *Demonology* further amplify Scott's sceptical physiological approach to the psychology of belief. In illustrations such as 'The Corps de Ballet' (Figure 3.2) Cruikshank comically animates Scott's anecdote of an alcohol-addled libertine haunted by

a band of figures dressed in green, who performed in his drawing room a singular dance, to which he was compelled to bear witness, though he knew, to his great annoyance, that the whole *corps de ballet* existed only in his imagination. His physician immediately informed him that he has lived upon town too long and too fast not to require an exchange to a more healthy and natural course of life. (19)

On removing to his country house the suffering libertine experiences some relief, but his recovery is short-lived. Keen to establish himself

Figure 3.2 George Cruikshank, 'The Corps de Ballet'

more permanently he sends for the contents of his London town house:

> But alas! No sooner had the furniture of the London drawing room been placed in order in the gallery of the old manor-house, than the former delusion returned in full force! the green *figurantes*, whom the patient's depraved imagination had so long associated with these movables, came capering and frisking to accompany them, exclaiming with great glee, as if the sufferer should have rejoiced to see them, 'Here we all are – here we all are!' The visionary, if I recollect right, was so much shocked at their appearance, that he retired abroad, in despair that any part of Britain could shelter him from the daily persecution of this domestic ballet. (20)[34]

One of many 'remarkable' cases, this potentially diverting anecdote provides relief from Scott's laboured diagnosis of the expected derangement of sight and mind induced by habitual intoxication. It also offers Cruikshank a self-contained narrative to caricature. Pressed against the hearth, the tortured libertine cringes away from the domestic ballet that fills his drawing room. Leering and grimacing chairs jig around a table where discarded books lie open suggesting previously undisturbed nights of more rational leisurely reading.

Scott's informal recollections license a certain degree of embellishment in the interest of bringing the libertine's private torment to life, to give it the requisite touch of the real. As Joel Fineman has observed, the anecdote has a particular counter-historical potency, producing 'the effect of the real' or 'occurrence of contingency, by establishing an event as an event within and yet without the framing context of historical successivity'.[35] Evoking the intimate ambience of a fireside exchange of much-told supernatural tales, Scott prioritises instructive entertainment over empirical accuracy. His subsequent discussion of the psychological consequences of experimenting with mind-altering substances further accentuates the fallibility of human perception. Moving fluidly between enumerating symptoms of addiction and retelling abridged anecdotes from familiar popular sources, such as John Ferriar's *An Essay Towards the Study of Apparitions* (1813) and Samuel Hibbert's *Sketches of the Philosophy of Apparitions* (1825), Scott invites the reader to rethink their own acquiescence or resistance to commonly held beliefs and con-sensual truths.[36] Ferriar and Hibbert, like Scott and Brewster, argued that apparitions, illusions, or spectres were emanations of dreams and memories.

Scott's personal physician, Dr Abercrombie, was an equally rich source of diagnostic anecdotes and medical authority. Indeed Scott reproduced a case history of one of Abercrombie's current patients in the *Demonology*. The patient suffered from hallucinations inspired by the character of Duke D'Olivarez from the popular French novel, Alain-René Le Sage's *The Adventures of Gil Blas De Santillane* (1715–35). In the final chapter of the novel the Duke confesses to Gil Blas: 'In vain have I said to myself that it is no more than an illusion, an insubstantial phantom of my brain: the continual apparition infects my view, and dis-turbs my repose.'[37] Bizarrely, Abercrombie's wife succumbed to a similar hallucination after reading her husband's book *Inquiries Concerning the Intellectual Powers* (1830), where this case was recounted, as well as other books on similar topics, including Hibbert's.[38] Perplexed by his wife's ailment Abercrombie consulted David Brewster, who was consid-ered one of the foremost authorities on optical phenomena at the time. Brewster concluded that Mrs A, as he called her in his own account of the case in *Letters on Natural Magic*, was a victim of her own reading, a 'morbidly sensitive imagination' and a 'disordered state of the digestive organs'.[39]

Abercrombie first published his account of his wife's case in a series of anonymous communications to David Brewster published in the *Edinburgh Journal of Science*, which just to complete the anecdotal circle, includes a description of his wife's vision of an enshrouded figure in a looking glass which bears an uncanny resemblance to Scott's recently published supernatural tale 'My Aunt Margaret's Mirror'.[40] According to Abercrombie, his wife also turned to Scott's *Demonology* in her struggle to bring her hallucinations under control, leading him to conclude that her 'successive delusions' were merely derivative re-enactments of 'the usual circumstances of the ghost stories we have all heard repeated, with more or less authority for them, from our cradles upwards'.[41] Mrs A, it seemed, was an unsuspecting victim of the contents of the Family Library, but not quite in the way John Murray had envisaged. Rehashing this anecdote yet again in his *Letters on Natural Magic*, Brewster described how reading the story of her husband's delusional patient in Scott's *Demonology*, inspired Mrs A to summon 'up the requisite resolution to enable her to cross the space before the fireplace, and seat herself in the same chair with the figure', who promptly vanished (46).

Scott's version of Dr Abercrombie's patient's mortal struggle with a similar apparition to the Duke d'Olivarez in *The Adventures of Gil Blas de Santillane* relies on the same natural magical demystification. Abercrombie, according to Scott, observed: 'Of the idea . . . that he was haunted by an apparition, to the actual existence of which he gave no credit, but died, nevertheless, because he was overcome and heartbroken by its imaginary presence.'[42] His subsequent examination of his patient creates the frame for Scott's narration of a procession of apparitions beginning with a large cat that appears and disappears at will, not unlike Carroll's Cheshire Cat, and culminating with a skeleton, which Cruikshank illustrates with comic relish.

After establishing that the skeletal apparition is always present to his patient's imagination, consistently appearing at the foot of his bed, Dr Abercrombie urged his patient to act as his own wife had done and rise from his sickbed, place himself where he believed the apparition stood and thus 'convince' himself 'of the illusion' (32). When his patient is unable to act on this advice the good doctor does so in his stead, resulting in the following scene that Cruikshank's comic eye transformed into a diverting illustrative opportunity:

> 'Well,' said the Doctor, 'we will try the experiment otherwise.' Accordingly, he rose from his chair by the bedside, and placing himself between the two half-drawn curtains at the foot of the bed, indicated as the place occupied by the apparition, asked if the spectre was still visible? 'Not entirely so,' replied the patient, 'because your person is betwixt him and me; but I observe his skull peering above your shoulder.'
>
> It is alleged the man of science started on the instant, despite philosophy, on receiving an answer ascertaining, with such minuteness, that the ideal spectre was close to his own person. He resorted to other means of investigation and cure, but with equally indifferent success. The patient sunk into deeper and deeper dejection and died in the same distress of mind in which he had spent the latter months of his life. (33)

Figure 3.3 George Cruikshank, 'The Spectre Skeleton'

Cruikshank took a less reverential approach to Brewster, satirising Abercrombie's suggestibility, rather than his rationalising intellect (Figure 3.3). The doctor's lips are primly pursed in Cruikshank's image, his eyebrows quizzically arched and his stance embodies the momentary lapse of reason that prompts him to believe his patient's claims. Like a figure in a popular spectre drama, the skeleton emerges from the shadows, temporarily illuminated by the doctor's superstition.

Brewster, like Scott, insisted upon a radical divide between the empirically verifiable and the intuitively knowable. He shared Scott's concern that the traditional claims of religion over the domain of the invisible and unknowable were being diminishingly characterised as superstitious survivals in a rational scientific age. But he was ultimately more interested in expanding the technical and scientific aspects of Scott's physiological diagnosis of the optical spectra that plagued the human sensorium. Consequently *Letters on Natural Magic* was driven by a desire to historically narrate and reveal the epistemological significance of new visual technologies from the illusionistic sophistry of the ancient world to the self-reflective optics of industrial modernity.

Casting himself as a leading figure in an explicitly nationalistic secular priesthood, Brewster outlined his vision of a modern scientific culture in his presidential address to the British Association for the Advancement of Science in 1850:

> Truth secular cannot be separated from truth divine; and if a priesthood has in all ages been ordained to teach and exemplify the one, and to maintain, in ages of darkness and corruption, the vestal fire upon the sacred altar, shall not an intellectual priesthood be organized to . . . make the dull eye of man sensitive to the planet which twinkles from afar, as well as to the luminary which shines from above – and to incorporate with our inner life those wonders of the external world which appeal with equal power to the affections and to the reason of immortal natures?[43]

This speech is symptomatic of the idiosyncratic fusion of messianism and commercial pragmatism that shaped Brewster's career. Inspired by Charles Babbage's *Reflections on the Decline of Science in England* (1830), Brewster had initially envisaged the British Association for the Advancement of Science as a proactive body with the collective power to fight for government funding of the sciences. It is this fear of decline that inspires the over-reaching claims for science in the above extract, as well as the civilising drive of *Letters on Natural Magic*, which was published at the height of Brewster's activity as the association's chief 'propagandist and projector'.[44]

Brewster's first letter redirects Scott's genealogical history of superstition towards an historical defence of the importance of the 'marvellous expedients' offered by optical technologies from classical times to the present. According to Brewster, while ancient cultures may have lacked the technological wonders of the microscope, the telescope or the modern phantasmagoria, they were drawn, like the contemporary readership of Murray's Family Library series, to 'the power of bringing the remotest objects within the very grasp of the observer, and of swelling into gigantic magnitude the almost invisible bodies of the material world'.[45] Enlisting the revelatory rhetoric of natural magic, Brewster differentiates his work from Scott's by stressing the technological illumination of the hidden secrets of the material world, including the physiology of the eye and mind.[46] He also explicitly links his work to a tradition of secular magic and experimental science that enlisted a range of illusions and tricks to debunk superstitions and expose erroneous beliefs.

Continuous with the tradition of natural magical writing, Brewster's letters provide detailed accounts of natural marvels, rare mechanical devices and optical apparatus written in an anecdotal epistolary style interspersed with conversational asides to Scott. Brewster also sustains Scott's focus on the 'minute and popular details' of 'singular illusions of sense . . . where the efforts and the creations of the mind predominate over the direct perceptions of external nature' (6). If anything, he contracts the focus still further, from the theatrical antics exemplified by Scott's alcohol-addled libertine to the closely observed interactions of the eye and mind of the reader with technologically generated images of various kinds. Correspondingly, Brewster encouraged his readers to experiment on their own bodies and with everyday phenomena in their domestic environment, suggesting ways in which they could master their mental reflexes and, in the process, understand and train their minds to respond rationally and scientifically to seemingly inexplicable phenomena.

Brewster's account of illusions produced by the diminution of peripheral vision when the mind is 'occupied with any engrossing topic of speculation or of grief', for example, includes an easy experiment in which the reader is instructed to place two pieces of white paper three to four inches apart on a green cloth and then fix their eye on one piece at a distance of twelve to eighteen inches, causing the other piece of paper to disappear and then reappear once the eye's fixed attention is broken (15). This simple experiment then becomes the basis of the first of Brewster's demystifying accounts of the physiological basis of claimed ghost sightings as a common symptom of the persistence of vision. According to Brewster, when one finds oneself in a dimly lit room the 'imperfect view which we obtain' forces the eye to focus on objects in its environment with greater than usual intensity:

> The eye is actually thrown into a state of the most painful agitation, the object will swell and contract, and partly disappear, and it will again become visible when the eye had recovered from the delirium in which it has been thrown. (15)

This effect is heightened in a darkened room, where partially obscured white objects that flicker in and out of the eye's peripheral vision take on 'the semblance of a living form' (17) in the minds of the 'timid or credulous' (16):

> In these observations we have supposed that the spectator bears along with him no fears or prejudices, and is a faithful interpreter of the phenomena presented to his senses; but if he is himself a believer in apparitions, and unwilling to receive an ocular demonstration of their reality, it is not difficult to conceive the picture which will be drawn when external objects are distorted and caricatured by the imperfect indications of his senses, and coloured with all the vivid hues of the imagination. (17)

As a contrast to this credulity, Brewster then recounts an anecdote about Locke and Newton conversing about their experiments with ocular spectra, generated by staring into the sun for a sustained period of time, before moving into a darkened room where they would experience the illusion of a projected image or 'phantasm' (23–4). Succumbing to such 'imperfect indications' of the senses as the grounds for belief as this scene demonstrates, is antithetical to the rational, civilised mind of Brewster's ideal reader, who it is assumed will reproduce their own domestic versions of this exemplary style of experimental sociability in their family library, nursery or parlour.[47]

Brewster further exemplifies the persistence of vision that engaged Locke and Newton with the first of many accounts of the instrumental simulation of the dynamics of perceptual cognition by an easily acquired philosophical toy, Dr Paris' 'pretty little instrument, called the *Thaumatrope*, or the *Wonder-turner*' (27). The thaumatrope was a simple device consisting of a circular disc with an image on either side. When twirled by a connected string the images combined to create the illusion of movement. In yet another example of the mutually reinforcing network of popular science publication in this period, Brewster's account virtually repeats Paris' novelistic account of the thaumatrope's potential applications as a primitive narrative device or language game in *Philosophy in Sport Made Science in Earnest, Being an Attempt to Illustrate the First Principles of Natural Philosophy by the Aid of Popular Toys and Sports* (1827).

In *Philosophy in Sport* the thaumatrope is presented as a gift to a wealthy middle-class family and soon becomes a catalyst for a parental discussion of how it might help teach their children to read. The family gather around as the father, Mr Seymour, reads out the accompanying instructions:

> This philosophical toy is founded upon the well-known optical principle, that an impression, made on the retina of the eye, lasts for a short interval, after the object which has produced it has been withdrawn. During the rapid whirling of the card, the figures on each of its sides are presented with such a quick transition that they both appear at the same instant, and thus occasion a very striking magical effect. On each of these cards a device is introduced, with an appropriate motto, or epigram; the point of which is answered, or explained, by the change which the figure assumes during the rapid whirling of the card.[48]

Paris also included the following Swift-inspired detour on the thaumatrope as a means of mechanising the creative process, which Mr Seymour reads out to his bemused family:

> It is well known that the Laputan philosopher invented a piece of machinery, by which works could be composed by a mechanical operation; . . . the author of the present invention claims for himself the exclusive merit of having first constructed a hand-mill, by which epigrams may be *turned* with as much ease as tunes are played on the hand-organ . . . (3:10)

This inspires Mrs Seymour to speculate on the application of this magical new invention to the more worthy task of 'impressing classical subjects upon the memory of young persons': 'Why can we not . . . thus represent the Metamorphoses of Ovid; or, what you say . . . to converting the fleet of Aeneas into sea-nymphs, as Virgil has it?' (3:10).

Brewster's version of Paris' narrative also dwells on the thaumatrope's diverting illustrative versions of familiar figures, including Harlequin and Columbine, who appear in projected form on the frontispiece of Brewster's *Treatise on Optics* and were also a popular subject of early moveable books. This, in turn, leads to more expansive speculations on the thaumatrope's animating powers:

> As the revolving card is virtually transparent, so that bodies beyond it can be seen through it, the power of the illusion might be greatly extended by introducing into the picture other figures, either animate or inanimate. The setting sun, for example, might be introduced into a landscape; part of the flame of a fire might be seen to issue from the crater of a volcano, and cattle grazing in a field might make part of the revolutionary landscape. For such purposes, however, the form of the instrument would require to be completely changed, and the rotation should be effected round a standing axis by wheels and pinions, and a screen placed in front of the revolving plane with open compartments or apertures, through which the principle figures would appear. (28)

Brewster's proto-cinematic rhetoric is typical of the futuristic tone of much of his writing on visual and acoustic media. Similar speculations about the potential to transform and animate the projected image characterise his accounts of the magic lantern and photography, the kaleidoscope and the stereoscope.

To return to the opening address to Scott in *Letters on Natural Magic*, Brewster continually reiterates that these present technological marvels are simply the realisation of a long history of interactions between imagination and science. The ancients may not have had access to 'the transformations of the modern phantasmagoria', but their 'primitive' theatrical illusions augured the technological advances of the present age. Given this proselytising vision of scientific progress, it is hardly surprising that Brewster's *Letters* were taken up by a new generation of writers. John Henry Pepper, was one of the more popular of this new generation, who made explicit and numerous references to Brewster's work and inventions in his writing and magic lantern shows.

Pepper's *The Boy's Playbook of Science* was popular with critics and readers alike. It went through multiple editions and revisions, until it finally went out of print just prior to the First World War, along with many Victorian children's titles, as the resistance to high-Victorian didacticism intensified. In contrast to Murray's Family Library, Routledge, Pepper's publisher, captured the family reading market in the second half of the nineteenth century, revising and reprinting popular scientific classics designed to inspire the enthusiasm of a new generation of readers with triumphal histories of scientific progress and enlightenment. Pepper, however, had little interest in educating girls. His focus was the moral improvement of boys. Given the popularity of his work, this meant that Pepper played a significant role in the increasingly explicit gendering of physical science, while promoting scientific education as a national character-building enterprise, as James Secord observes:

> Readers of the *Boy's Playbook of Science* were not asked to memorise experiments nor to follow careers as scientists and engineers; instead, what mattered was mental preparation for the challenges of the modern world of competitive global capitalism . . . Science helped to build character and prepare for 'The Battle of Life', to serve nation and empire.[49]

Pepper's alignment of science and empire also echoed David Brewster's *Letters on Natural Magic*, explicitly positioning English technological invention as the culmination of a global history of mechanical innovation and ingenuity. Pepper contended that:

> Those mechanical wonders, which in one century enriched only the conjuror who used them, contributed in another to augment the wealth of the nation; and those automatic toys, which once amused the vulgar, are now employed in extending the power and promoting the civilization of the species.[50]

Far removed from their vulgar origins as the playthings of an indiscriminate crowd, recalling Brewster's grim characterisation of the crazed reception of his kaleidoscope, Pepper envisages a civilised future shaped by a new rationalised order of visual experience predicated on an infinitely reproducible technological image. Given how amenable to commercialisation these 'automatic devices' were, this was not an unrealisable dream. By the mid-nineteenth century unprecedented numbers of people had access to a self-consciously modern scientific conception of the relationship between eye and mind as a consequence of the rapid circulation of devices such as the kaleidoscope, the thaumatrope and the dissolving effects of the lantern and stereoscope. Faced with a far more complex multi-functioning media network of moving images and proliferating print, the primitive illusions of natural magic no longer sufficed. Unsurprisingly, this was also the ideal media environment for Pepper to achieve his entrepreneurial and institutional ambitions, which he did in the spectral form of 'Dr Pepper's Ghost', one of the most popular magic lantern spectacles of the period and the subject of the following chapter.

Notes

1. Cited in Gordon, *The Home Life of Sir David Brewster*, pp. 96–7.
2. Brewster, *Treatise on the Kaleidoscope*, p. 7.
3. Brewster, *The Kaleidoscope. Its History, Theory and Construction with its Application to the Fine and Useful Arts*, p. 42.
4. Percy Bysshe Shelley to James Hogg, 21 December 1818: 'Your Kalleidoscopes [sic] spread like the pestilence at Livorno. A few weeks after I sent your description to a young English mechanist of that town, I heard that the whole population were given up to Kalleidoscopism. It was like the fever which seized the Abderites who wondered about the streets repeating some verses of Euripides.' *The Letters of Percy Bysshe Shelley*, vol. 2, pp. 68–9.
5. Brewster, *The Stereoscope: its History, Theory and Construction, with its Application to the Fine and Useful Arts, and to Education etc.* Morrison-Low provides a full bibliography of Brewster's publications, including details of the multiple editions of his books, in Morrison-Low and Christie (eds), *'Martyr of Science': Sir David Brewster 1781–1868.*
6. 'Literature of the Day: – The New Magazine', *The Metropolitan Journal of Literature. Science, and the Fine Arts* (May to August 1831), p. 19.
7. Klancher, *The Making of English Reading Audiences 1780–1832*, p. 9
8. Klancher, *The Making of English Reading Audiences*, p. 131.
9. Christensen, *Lord Byron's Strength: Romantic Writing and Commercial Society*, p. 77.
10. More detail of Brewster's inventions and career as a scientific writer can be found in Morrison-Low and Christie (eds), *'Martyr of Science'.*
11. 'The Caleidoscope and the Tetrascope', *The Literary Journal* (17 May 1818), p. 122.
12. Brewster, *The Kaleidoscope*, p. 84.
13. Brewster wrote in his diary, as reproduced in his daughter's biography, after meeting Brontë in 1851: 'One of the most interesting acquaintances I have made since I came here, I made yesterday. It was that of Miss Brontë, the authoress of *Jane Eyre* and *Shirley*, a little, pleasing-looking woman of about forty, modest and agreeable. I went through the Exhibition with her yesterday.' Gordon, *Home Life of Sir David Brewster*, p. 223.
14. Brewster, *The Kaleidoscope*, p. 160.
15. In addition to the many accounts of these popular spectacles, Castle describes the cultural and imaginative reverberations of Philipstal and Robertson's Phantasmagoria in 'Phantasmagoria and the Metaphorics of Modern Reverie', Chapter 9 of *The Female Thermometer: Eighteenth-Century Culture and the Invention of the Uncanny.*
16. Dr Pepper's Lecture was entitled 'Sir David Brewster and The Kaleidoscope', advertised in the *Illustrated London News* (31 March 1866), p. 306. On 6 July 1874 a projecting device patented as the Kaleidograph was also exhibited in the Great Hall of the Polytechnic. See the Polytechnic Programmes Collections, University of Westminster.
17. John Limbird's pictorial miscellany was twopence an issue, an affordable price for artisans and the top echelons of the working classes, although as Anderson notes the *Mirror's* 80,000 audience was predominantly

drawn from the upper and middle classes. See *The Printed Image and the Transformation of Popular Culture 1790–1860*, p. 46.

18. Of the 20,385 copies of Scott's *Letters on Demonology and Witchcraft* printed by Murray, 13,592 were sold. Bennett reproduces the sales records of the Family Library in 'John Murray's Family Library and the Cheapening of Books in Early Nineteenth-Century Britain', *Studies in Bibliography* 29 (1976), pp. 162–7.

19. Thomas Tegg (1776–1846) in the largest purchase of his career paid 8,000 pounds for 355,000 volumes of the library. He did not acquire the copyrights, which may explain the absence of the inserted Cruikshank illustrations from his reprinted copies. His son William Tegg (1816–95) inherited a substantial portion of his father's stock on his death and used it as a basis for his own bookselling business. He also wrote under the pseudonym Peter Parley and produced popular children's books.

20. Cohn, *A Bibliographical Catalogue of the Printed Works Illustrated by George Cruikshank*, p. 179.

21. Cruikshank, *Twelve Sketches Illustrative of Sir Walter Scott's Demonology and Witchcraft*. According to Richard Vogler it is not clear which volume was published first. Vogler, *Graphic Works of George Cruikshank*, p. 143.

22. Sutherland, *The Life of Walter Scott: A Critical Biography*, p. 336.

23. Scott, *The Journal of Sir Walter Scott*, p. 681. Murray paid Scott 600 pounds for his efforts.

24. Scott, *The Journal of Sir Walter Scott*, p. 690. The capitalisation of Damn is Scott's own.

25. Lockhart, *Memoirs of Sir Walter Scott*, vol. 5, p. 263.

26. 'Family Library, Vol. XVI, – *Letters on Demonology and Witchcraft, addressed to J. G. Lockhart, Esq.* By Sir Walter Scott, Bart. London, 1830. Murray (Unpublished)', *Athenaeum* 151 (September 1830), p. 577.

27. 'Letters on Demonology and Witchcraft. By Sir Walter Scott, Bart – London, 1830', *Fraser's Magazine* (December 1830), p. 508.

28. Brougham, 'Discourse of the Objects, Pleasures, and Advantages of Political Science', *Works of Henry Lord Brougham*, vol. 7, pp. 397–8.

29. Klancher analyses these anxieties in *Making of English Reading Audiences*, pp. 98–134.

30. Scott, *Letters on Demonology and Witchcraft. Addressed to J. G. Lockhart*, p. 2.

31. Knox, *Winter Evenings, or, Lucubrations on Life and Letters*, vol. 2, p. 10.

32. Duncan also identifies the 'privatising aesthetic of conservative scepticism' at the core of *Waverley* in *Modern Romance and Transformations of the Novel: The Gothic, Scott, Dickens*, p. 8. See also Smajić's close reading of 'The Tapestried Chamber' in 'The Trouble with Ghost-Seeing: Vision, Ideology, and Genre in the Victorian Ghost Story', 1107–35.

33. Crary offers a polemical account of the cultural implications of this intensification of interest in perceptual aberration in *Techniques of the Observer: On Vision and Modernity in the Nineteenth Century*.

34. Scott's original spellings, including the elision of drawing room are reproduced in this passage.

35. Fineman, 'The History of the Anecdote', in *The New Historicism*, p. 61.

36. Scott's references are to Dr Samuel Hibbert, *Sketches of the Philosophy*

of *Apparitions* and John Ferriar, MD, *An Essay Towards the Study of Apparitions*.

37. Le Sage, *The Adventures of Gil Blas de Santillane* [1715–35], vol. 4, p. 261.
38. Abercrombie, *Inquiries Concerning the Intellectual Powers and the Investigation of Truth*.
39. Brewster, *Letters on Natural Magic, addressed to Sir Walter Scott*, p. 47.
40. Brewster recounts this scene and refers to the publication of Abercrombie's anonymous communications in *Letters on Natural Magic*, pp. 42–3. Brewster describes Mrs A witnessing an apparition in her looking glass 'enveloped in grave-clothes, closely pinned, as is usual with corpses' (44).
41. Abercrombie, 'Correspondence', *Edinburgh Journal of Science*, New Series no. 4, (1830), p. 218, 219. The other numbers in the series are no. 6 (1830), p. 244 and no. 8 (1830), p. 261. Brewster cites this reference in *Letters on Natural Magic*, p. 46.
42. Scott, *Letters on Demonology*, p. 29.
43. Cited in Gordon, *Home Life of Sir David Brewster*, p. 209.
44. Morrell, 'Brewster and the early British Association for the Advancement of Science', in *'Martyr of Science'*, p. 26.
45. Brewster, *Letters on Natural Magic*, p. 5.
46. This is consistent with the natural magical tradition seminally outlined by Giambattista della Porta in *Natural Magick* (1558): 'that Magick is nothing else but the survey of the whole course of Nature. For, whilst we consider the Heavens, the Stars, the Elements, how they are moved, and how they are changed, by this means we find out the hidden secrets of living creatures, of plants, of metals, and of their generation and corruption; so that this whole Science seems merely to depend upon the view of Nature.' Della Porta, *Natural Magick*, p. 2.
47. Secord identifies the importance of conversation to the aims and practice of nineteenth-century science in 'How Scientific conversation Became Shop Talk', in *Science in the Marketplace*, pp. 23–59.
48. Paris, *Philosophy in Sport Made Science in Earnest, Being an Attempt to Illustrate the First Principles of Natural Philosophy by the Aid of Popular Toys and Sports*, vol. 3, p. 6.
49. Secord, 'Portraits of Science: Quick and Magical Shaper of Science', *Science* 297:5587, (6 September 2002), p. 1649.
50. Pepper, *The Boy's Playbook of Science*, p. 286.

Chapter 4

Reading Habits and Magic Lanterns: Dickens and Dr Pepper's Ghost

Reflecting on the mechanical diversions of Polytechnic Institutions in general Dickens observed, 'we think of a people formed *entirely* in their hours of leisure' by such places as 'an uncomfortable community'.[1] Minds forged by the repetitive movements of 'cranks and cogwheels' could never replace the habitual sympathies acquired from more imaginative childhood amusements. Indeed there is something fundamentally untrustworthy, Dickens suspects, in this transformation of minds into machines:

> We would be more disposed to trust him if he had been brought into occasional contact with a 'Maid and a Magpie'; if he had made one or two diversions into the 'Forest of Bondy'; or had even gone the length of a Christmas Pantomime. There is a range of imagination in most of us, which no amount of steam-engines will satisfy; and which The-great-exhibition-of-the-works-of-industry-of-all-nations, itself, will probably leave unappeased. The lower we go, the more natural it is that the best-relished provision for this should be found in dramatic entertainments; as at once the most obvious, the least troublesome, and the most real, of all escapes out of the literal world. (13)

The risqué burlesque of *The Maid and the Magpie*,[2] a play about thieving magpies, the orchestrated chaos of Christmas Pantomime, or trouble-free escapes into the 'Forest of Bondy' offered by the popular melodrama, *Le Chien de Montargis*,[3] provide more comfortable collective experiences than the utilitarian functionalism of the Polytechnic's mechanical attractions. While equally ritualised and repetitive, formulaic theatrical amusements, Dickens argues, answer the 'innate love' that the 'common People' have for drama, which 'nothing will ever root out' (13).

As the above passage suggests, the 'lower we go' the more important drama's indifference to the literacy of its audience became. Although, as Juliet John argues, 'all modes of drama' infuse Dickens's humanising ambitions for his writing as a potent social medium forged in reaction to the reifying force of industrialisation.[4] Joe Whelks, a working class archetype, who makes several appearances in *Household Words* and *All the Year Round*, embodies the potential 'mental improvement' to be gleaned from dramatic forms of any kind, high or low:

> Joe Whelks, of the New Cut Lambeth, is not much of a reader, has no great store of books, no very commodious room to read in, no very decided inclination to read, and no power at all of presenting vividly before his mind's eye what he reads about. But, put Joe in the gallery of the Victoria theatre; . . . tell him a story . . . by the help of live men and women dressed up, confiding to him their innermost secrets, in voices audible half a mile off, and Joe will unravel a story through all its entanglements, and sit there as long after midnight as you have anything left to show him.[5]

Joe may be functionally literate, but his powers of imagination cannot escape the discomfort of the literal world. In isolation, his 'mind's eye' has no animating powers, but immersed in the social dynamism of the theatre he automatically responds to the visceral pleasures of its immediacy. Surrendering to reverie, his mind wanders freely through the entanglements of the plot, indifferent to the constraints of time and space.

This chapter examines the assumptions about the training of the popular imagination that underlie Dickens's famous account of 'The Amusements of the People' in the context of one of the most iconic popular amusements of the mid-Victorian period, Dr Pepper's Ghost. Pepper's spectre show first appeared at the Royal Polytechnic Institute on Regent Street in the Christmas Season of 1862. It was advertised as an inspired adaptation of an idea taken from one of Dickens's Christmas books, *The Haunted Man; or the Ghost's Bargain* (1848), on a handbill that made no distinction between mechanical and imaginative attractions. What I want to argue here is that despite Dickens's efforts to distinguish the potentially transformative humanising power of popular theatre from the mechanical attractions of the Polytechnics, the assumed automatism that underlies his concept of the imagination as a form of involuntary response was echoed in Pepper's rationale for introducing imaginative content into the Royal Polytechnic programme when he took over management in the early 1850s. Pepper hoped that his working class audiences would come to associate his spectacular magic lantern performances with the unfettered wonder Joe Whelks experiences when his mind's eye moves from the lifeless black and white experience of isolated reading to the colourful dynamism of live theatre.

Inspired by the natural magical tradition of David Brewster, Pepper, like Dickens, was committed to defining the habits of his audience; a mutual commitment which positions the literary and technological enterprises of both men within an established philosophical and psychological debate on 'habit as a guiding psychological mechanism of social structure', to quote Athena Vrettos.[6] This debate about the complex social implications of habitual behaviour dated back to the associationist philosophy of John Locke, David Hume, David Hartley and Dugald Stewart, and was sustained in the middle to late nineteenth century by George Henry Lewes, John Stuart Mill, James Sully, William Carpenter, Alexander Bain and William James (399). Training the mind to think in repetitive patterns was seen as the basis of all learning. Theories of habit also conceptualised the mind as 'a closed system', as Vrettos argues, 'driven to repetitive, automatic behaviours in order to conserve energy for more difficult tasks' (400). The involuntary energy of the imagination, despite its transformative potential was a 'special function' of this closed system of habituated behaviours, according to the explicitly psychological aesthetics of E. S. Dallas, who knew Dickens, and was also one of his more subtle and demanding critics.[7] Dallas argued in *The Gay Science* that the 'imagination or fantasy is not a special faculty but that it is a special function. It is a name given to the automatic action of the mind' (194). Expanding on this mode of automatic functionality Dallas speculated:

> Now for the most part this automatic action takes place unawares; and when we come to analyse the movements of thought we find that to be quite sure of our steps we are obliged very much to identify what is involuntary with what is unconscious. We are seldom quite sure that our wills have had nought to do in producing certain actions, unless these actions have come about without our knowledge. (195)

This extract captures the tension between volition and automatism that characterises Victorian writing on the involuntary dimensions of thought more generally. As William Carpenter explained in his account of the machinery of unconscious cerebration, the 'train of thought, which we volitionally set going in the Cerebrum in the first instance, continues to work by itself after our attention has been fixed upon some other object of thought'.[8] To return to what happens in Joe Whelks's mind's eye, while the choice to go to the theatre rather than read a book is his, the vivid associative imagery the performance generates in his mind continues with no 'exertion on his part' – he has no 'consciousness of any continued activity', to adapt Carpenter (784).

Pepper's Polytechnic

John Henry Pepper lectured at the Royal Polytechnic Institution from 1848 and took over its management from 1854 until 1872, a period in which he became known as 'one of the premier showmen of science'.[9] Established in 1838, the Royal Polytechnic was known for its diverse attractions. It consisted of a 'Great Hall', filled with the kind of mechanical and technological attractions that Dickens dismissed as 'cranks and cogwheels', and a 'Lecture Theatre', where Pepper and other lecturers entertained audiences with spectacular displays of scientific wonders, including optical illusions demonstrated by the Polytechnic's numerous magic lanterns. In the Great Hall, one could see a diver submerged in a diving bell, look through an oxyhydrogen microscope, witness large electrical machines in action, examine scientific instruments, including kaleidoscopes and stereoscopes, and observe experiments conducted in a purpose-built laboratory. A marvellous hybrid, the Polytechnic was the consummate scientific 'miscellaneous exhibition', as a contemporary guide to the city categorised it, competing for market share with other exhibition spaces of the period, such as the Egyptian Hall, Madame Tussaud's, and Wyld's Model of the Globe.[10]

Pepper, however, had greater ambitions than presenting a diverting miscellany of scientific wonders. After becoming manager in 1854, he started to introduce theatrical entertainments. He began with readings from Shakespeare, but this soon extended to plays and pantomimes. The success of the panoramic and dioramic devices of the spectacular theatre of Edmund Kean and others, as I have discussed previously, provided a contemporary model for how one could combine novel visual media with the 'comforting' collective forms of melodrama and Shakespearean adaptations. Drawing on the popular devices of musical theatre, the ever-changing programme included adaptations of *A Christmas Carol*, the 'Gabriel Grubb' sequence from *The Pickwick Papers*, *The Cricket on the Hearth*, Tennyson's *Elaine*, as well dramatic readings from *The Merchant of Venice*, *Hamlet*, and *Romeo and Juliet*, and popular songs interspersed with spectacular scientific demonstrations.[11] Victorian audiences responded positively to these well-advertised additions to the programme, although critics were quick to remark on their hybrid scientific theatrics. *Punch* satirised Pepper's attempt to marry science and imagination, noting that 'the proprietors of the Polytechnic and Panopticon are about to introduce dramatic readings and singsongs as part of their attractions', and suggesting the staging of new plays set in a laboratory where 'scenes of thrilling interest might easily be got up with the voltaic battery'.[12]

Andrew Halliday's satirical account of 'Mr Whelks combining instruction with amusement' in *All the Year Round* was even more sceptical of the Polytechnic's miscellaneous fusion of instruction and entertainment. Confused and harried, the hapless Mr Whelks 'was allowed exactly a quarter of an hour to make himself acquainted' with all the 'wonders of nature' in the Polytechnic's Great Hall, ranging from geological models, to drawing room fireworks, the cosmorama, impressions made by a new 'foliographic machine', to china and glass mending, before being ushered into the main lecture hall to hear an optical lecture on the 'wonderful discoveries of Sir David Brewster'.[13] This lecture combined projections of kaleidoscopic effects with an account of Brewster's life before concluding with 'a startling and wonderful optical illusion, entitled "Shakespeare and his Creations, Hamlet, Launce [sic], and Macbeth"', which Halliday parodically describes:

> With regard to Shakespeare, the lecturer ventured to say, by way of introduction, that he was the glass of fashion and the mould of form, 'the observed of all observers,' and that, 'take him for all in all, we ne'er should look upon his like again.' Further, he declared that 'to take him inventorially would be to dizzy the brain' with the overwhelming details of his greatness; so we were invited to take him with an optical illusion, a few recitations from his works, and a little smothered music. (611)

In contrast to Dickens's characterisation of Joe Whelks's theatrical reverie, Halliday conveys Mr Whelks's experience at the Polytechnic as disrupted and fragmented by didactic intrusions and miscellaneous diversions. Prevented from the potentially dizzying effects of immersing himself in the uninterrupted pleasure of any one of Shakespeare's plays, Mr Whelks finds himself unable to sit still for very long.

Moving back out into the exhibition space he observes the legendary Diving Bell before being summoned once more into a smaller theatre to be 'amused' with 'A New Vocal, Instrumental, Descriptive, and Dioramic Entertainment, founded upon Sir Walter Scott's beautiful poem of the Lady of the Lake' (612):

> The magic lantern, once more the leading star of the performance. Sir Walter Scott, and the clever artist who is engaged to read and illustrate his work, both being condemned to wait upon and feed the magic lantern. The recital of the poem must keep time with the manipulation of the slides, compelling James Fitzjames, lyrically to go through the whole of his adventures at a gallop, and in the dark, the whole concluding with 'two spectral or ghost scenes,' one of them representing Fitzjames and Roderick Dhu before they arrived at a ghostly condition of existence, fighting their celebrated combat. (613)

Subservient to the technology of the magic lantern, Shakespeare and Scott are consumed by the relentless machinery of mass production. In contrast to the way the magic lantern circulated as a metaphor for the imaginative process in Dickens's work, in Halliday's satire the lantern usurps literature's place as the privileged medium. The consequences of this unnatural inversion, according to Halliday, are predictably banal, reducing imaginative works to automatised stereotypes served up to mechanical minds trained to respond in equally automated ways.

This was a far remove from the positive invocation of the lantern to describe the magical transformations of the modern observer's mind as a 'wizard chamber of dissolving views' in an essay on the stereoscope's effects in *Household Words*.[14] Or Dickens's reliance on magic lantern allusions in his description of the stimulation he drew from the perpetually moving spectacle of the London streets, in a letter penned while he was in Switzerland writing *Dombey and Son* in the summer of 1846: 'I can't express how much I want [the London] streets . . . The toil and labour of writing without that magic lantern [before me] is IMMENSE!'[15] As Joss Marsh has observed, in addition to Dickens's evident relish for optical metaphors such as these, his work became the 'dominant literary source for later Victorian magic-lantern storytelling'.[16] Despite the strict limitations of copyright, lanternists were quick to exploit Dickens's allusions to the lantern's dissolving effects in tales such as *A Christmas Carol* (1848) and the *Gabriel Grubb* episode from *The Pickwick Papers* (1836). The latter was adapted to spectacular effect for a production at the Royal Polytechnic in 1875 that Marsh contends 'became a lodestar for later-nineteenth century lantern storytelling'.[17] Such a claim, however, overlooks the seminal place of Pepper's Dickensian ghost in the Victorian popular imagination, and its complex implications for the shaping of the 'machine minds' of the mass culture both Pepper and Dickens struggled to engage.

Dickens's Haunted Man

The first illustrated edition of *The Haunted Man and The Ghost's Bargain* introduced the central character, Redlaw, a reclusive chemist plagued by his past, through a sequence of lantern-like visual frames. These begin with John Tenniel's double frontispiece depicting Redlaw sitting and gazing into a fire while his spectral double mirrors his posture unseen to all but the reader (Figure 4.1). On the facing page, Redlaw's path to heaven or perdition is symbolised by an angel and an enshrouded figure holding an innocent child between them (Figure 4.2). Pointing towards darkness, the child augurs the corruption of innocence that will follow in the wake of Redlaw's surrender to the dark forces that haunt his mind. Both these scenes focus, as Pepper's illusion would do, on the climactic moment when Redlaw's spectral double appears to

Figure 4.1 John Tenniel, 'The Haunted Man'

Figure 4.2 John Tenniel, Title Page, Charles Dickens, *The Haunted Man and The Ghost's Bargain*

grant his wish that his memory be erased, a wish accompanied by a curse that condemns all those who come in contact with him to the same fate. Confronted by the brutal consequences of his desire, Redlaw ultimately repents, and his punitive ghost lifts the curse.

Tenniel's third plate, which illustrates the first page of the first chapter, portrays a child reading in the foreground of another fireside scene, holding a book up to capture the illumination of the flames (Figure 4.3). While the child reads, smoky shadows take shape, combining fantastic oriental and supernatural figures with the distorted forms of familiar domestic bodies and objects.

The accompanying text frames this reading scene with a series of reflections on the collective habits and involuntary responses that drive long-held superstitions:

EVERYBODY said so.
Far be it from me to assert that what everybody says must be true. Everybody is, often, as likely to be wrong as right. In the general experience, everybody has been wrong so often, and it has taken, in most instances, such a weary while to find out how wrong, that the authority is proved to be fallible.[18]

Figure 4.3 John Tenniel, Chapter 1, Charles Dickens, *The Haunted Man and The Ghost's Bargain*

Questioning the dubious authority of collective wisdom, this passage serves as a natural magical caveat for the appearance of Redlaw's ghost: a fictional pre-emption of Pepper's equally sceptical illustration of the idea of the haunted man.

Redlaw, like Pepper, is also a celebrity lecturer known 'far and wide' for his ability to mediate scientific ideas to 'a crowd of aspiring ears and eyes' (328). But, as the gossipy narrator quickly reveals, private torment shadows Redlaw's public success:

> Who that had seen him in his inner chamber, part library and part labora-tory, . . . – who that had seen him there, upon a winter night, alone, sur-rounded by his drugs and instruments and books; the shadow of his shaded lamp a monstrous beetle on the wall, motionless among a crowd of spectral shapes raised there by the flickering of the fire upon the quaint objects around him; some of these phantoms (the reflection of glass vessels that held liquids), trembling at heart like things that knew his power to uncombine them, and to give back their component parts to fire and vapour; – who that had seen him then, his work done, and he pondering in his chair before the rusted grate and red flame, moving his thin mouth as if in speech, but silent as the dead, would not have said that the man seemed haunted and the chamber too? (328)

Redlaw's considerable intellectual powers to illuminate and inspire have turned inward, taking the form of a self-destructive melancholia that threatens to 'uncombine' his own psyche, just as the chemical elements may be induced to uncombine and 'give back their component parts to fire and vapour'. He is consumed with his memories to the point that he is no longer able to distinguish between the external world and the vivid images that haunt his mind. In his delusional state, everyday objects take on uncanny defamiliarising forms, dark doubles of their prosaic func-tions as tools of his trade.

Redlaw also fails to recognise the civilising function of memory that the tale's moral rests upon, an existential blindness that implicitly challenges one of the central assumptions of Victorian psychology, according to Sally Shuttleworth, that 'memory, with its assurance of a continuous identity through time, functions as the grounding for social and personal morality'.[19] Memory is precisely what has driven Redlaw mad, disabling his capacity to control his waking and sleeping thoughts. This association of memory with the disruptive affects of melancholy, in turn, aligns with a more pervasive suspicion in the work of Dickens's contemporaries that the idea of a continuous self might be an involuntarily generated and necessarily selective illusion. What the respected physician Henry Holland labelled 'double-consciousness', and Lewes and Carpenter would speak of as 'streams of consciousness' or 'unconscious cerebration', proposed that conscious memories were only one of many streams of unconscious thought.[20]

According to Carpenter's *Principles of Mental Physiology* (1853), the conditions of authorship were an ideal catalyst for the emergence of suppressed memories:

> When the Imagination has been exercised in a sustained and determinate manner, – as in the composition of a work of fiction, – its ideal creations may be reproduced with the force of actual experiences; and the sense of personal identity may be projected backwards (so to speak) into the characters which the Author has 'evolved out of the depths of his own consciousness,' – as Dickens states to have continually been the case with himself. (455)

Carpenter likens this to the reproduction of ideas or events in dreams so real that they inspire the dreamer to ask, 'Did this really happen to me, or did I dream it?'[21]

Dickens's interest in the involuntary illusions generated by minds under the influence of extreme emotion pervades his fiction and journalism. He also collected anecdotes of ghost sightings as evidence of the relationship between perceptual physiology and the psychology of belief. Over a decade after the publication of *The Haunted Man* Dickens wrote to the enthusiastic spiritualist William Howitt:

> I have always had a strong interest in the subject, and never knowingly lose an opportunity of pursuing it. But I think the testimony which I cannot cross-examine sufficiently loose to justify me in requiring to see and hear the modern witnesses with my own senses, and then to be reasonably sure that they were not suffering under a disordered condition of the nerves or senses, which is known to be a common disease of many phases.
>   Don't suppose that I am so bold and arrogant as to settle what can and what cannot be after death. The truth is not so at all.[22]

Dickens was equally interested in training his readers to distinguish between credulous delusion and verifiable spectral phenomena, circulating fictional as well as eye-witness accounts of ghost sightings in *Household Words* and *All the Year Round*.[23] He also reviewed prominent supernatural publications such as Catherine Crowe's *The Night-Side of Nature; or Ghosts and Ghost Seers* (1848), which he criticised for claiming too much based on 'imperfect grounds of proof' when ghosts are most commonly seen 'even on Mrs Crowe's own showing, in that imperfect state of perception, between sleeping and waking . . .'[24] Crowe deliberately resisted the influential natural magical scepticism synonymous with David Brewster, in contrast to Dickens, who turned to both Samuel Hibbert's *Sketches of the Philosophy of Apparitions* (1825) and Brewster's *Letters on Natural Magic* in 1845, while treating

Augusta de la Rue's nervous ailments and spectral hallucinations with mesmeric techniques. Louise Henson argues that Dickens even echoed Brewster's language and approach to the case of Mrs A, which I discussed in the previous chapter, in his account of the case of Augusta de la Rue, which in turn became one of many narrative resources for Dickens's fictional versions of altered states of mind, dreams states and hallucinatory experiences.[25]

Dickens's debt to natural magical descriptive devices is vividly demonstrated by the atmospheric evocation of the conditions commonly associated with ghost sightings in *The Haunted Man*:

> When twilight everywhere released the shadows, prisoned up all day, that now closed in and gathered swarms of ghosts. When they stood lowering, in corners of rooms, and frowned out from behind half-opened doors. When they had full possession of unoccupied apartments. When they danced upon the floors, and walls, and ceilings of inhabited chambers, while the fire was low, and withdrew like ebbing waters when it sprung into a blaze. When they fantastically mocked the shapes of household objects, making the nurse an ogress, the rocking horse a monster, the wondering child, half-scared and half-amused, a stranger to itself, – the very tongs upon the hearth, a straddling giant with his arms akimbo, evidently smelling the blood of Englishmen, and wanted to grind people's bones to make his bread.
>
> When these shadows brought into the minds of older people, other thoughts, and showed them different images. When they stole from their retreats, in the likenesses of forms and faces from the past, from the grave, from the deep, deep gulf, where the things that might have been, and never were, are always wandering.
>
> When he sat, as already mentioned gazing at the fire. When, as it rose and fell, the shadows went and came. When he took no heed of them, with his bodily eyes; but let them come or let them go, looked fixedly at the fire. You should have seen him then. (331)

Recalling the phantasmagoric effects of a child's magic lantern, the shadows come to life on the fire-lit walls of countless homes across England and beyond. Nothing is clearly visible. Familiar 'household objects' inhabit a liminal space where the eye strains to hold on to what it should be seeing.

Everyday phenomena, however, go unseen by Redlaw's 'bodily eyes', further intensifying his dissociative tendencies, rather than fostering a civilising sense of identification and sociability. It is this profound alienation from the present that summons the ghost:

> As the gloom and shadow thickened behind him, in that place where it had been gathering so darkly, it took by slow degrees, – or out of it there came, by some unreal, unsubstantial process – not to be traced by any human sense, – an awful likeness of himself!

Ghastly and cold, colourless in its leaden face and hands, but with his features, and his bright eyes, and his grizzled hair, and dressed in the gloomy shadow of his dress, it came into his terrible appearance of existence, motionless, without sound. As *he* leaned his arm upon the elbow of his chair, ruminating before the fire, *it* leaned upon the chair-back, close above him, with its appalling copy of his face looking where his face looked, and bearing the expression his face bore.

This, then, was the Something that had passed and gone already. This was the dread companion of the haunted man! (341–2)[26]

The spectre is an externalisation of what are later described as the 'banished recollections' underlying the manifest 'inter-twisted chain of feelings and associations' haunting Redlaw's thoughts (346). Emanating from the darkest recesses of his mind, the spectre materialises that part of Redlaw's psyche that eludes the reach of his will and ultimately forces him to recognise the distortive moral effects of his narcissistic dwelling on past wrongs.

John Leech's illustration of the appearance of Redlaw's spectre, which echoes but varies slightly from Tenniel's frontispiece, reinforces the phenomenon of double-consciousness that Dickens describes (Figure 4.4). The spectre rests his head on his hand and gazes into the fire, mirroring Redlaw's melancholic reverie. The only difference between them is the spectre's bemused expression signalling that he is a separate consciousness beyond the will of the mind he haunts. Dickens reveals the meaning of this smile on the facing page, where he describes Redlaw and his ghost struggling over the same memories, the former alternating between resistance and mesmerised submission as the ghost repeats the history of Redlaw's treacherous betrayal by a friend who stole the woman he loved and, in the process, broke the heart of his now dead sister. This traumatic dialogue culminates in Redlaw's unravelling as past and present are radically severed by the 'bloodless hand' of his double – an act of psychological violence that elicits a natural magical reading that leaves multiple senses of the ghost in play (343). As the narrator concludes at the end of the tale:

Some people have said since, that he only thought what has been herein set down; others, that he read it in the fire, one winter night about twilight time; others, that the Ghost was but the representation of his own gloomy thoughts . . . (441)

Given these natural magical resonances it is hardly surprising that Pepper would find inspiration in the epistemological questions raised by Dickens's text. Not the least of these remains unanswered by Pepper throughout his theatrical rendition of *The Haunted Man*: what

Figure 4.4 John Leech, 'Redlaw's Spectre'

ontological status does the ghost have? Like Brewster, Pepper finds the answer to this question in the literal demonstration of the way eye and mind can be tricked by the technical manipulation of a projected image. In the process Pepper created one of the most famous pre-cinematic adaptations of Dickens's work: histories of early cinema frequently note that Pepper's Ghosts inspired the Lumière brothers to choose the Polytechnic for the first English exhibition of their cinematograph.[27] Initially inspired by *The Haunted Man*, Pepper and his collaborator, Henry Dircks, drew upon a very similar archive of natural magical and scientific literature – including Hibbert's *Sketches of the Philosophy of Apparitions*, Brewster's *Letters on Natural Magic* and Samuel Warren's *Diary of a Late Physician* (1832–8), all of which explored the relationship between illusion and 'the recollected images of the mind', to quote Hibbert (iii). The surviving accounts of the genesis and reception of the illusion by Pepper and Dircks also reveal that they were pragmatic selective readers who combined fanlike admiration of Dickens's ghost stories with savvy technological entrepreneurialism.

Pepper's Idea of the Haunted Man

Pepper's lecture script framed Dickens's story with an anti-spiritualist lecture that taught the audience about optical illusions more generally. The main illusion, as the title suggested, was inspired by the idea of Dickens's *The Haunted Man*. This consisted of a simple but spectacular three-dimensional spectre that appeared to walk through solid objects before fading away (Figure 4.5). It was produced by a custom-designed magic lantern concealed beneath the stage that projected a strong light onto an actor positioned before a sheet of glass that extended from pit to ceiling between the audience and the stage. A moving image of the concealed actor would then appear superimposed on a second actor onstage above, so that when the latter enacted Redlaw's feverish desire for amnesia, his spectral double came to life.

Henry Dircks provided a minimal contemporary description of what audiences would have seen:

> A student is seen sitting at a table spread over with books, papers and instruments. After a while he rises and *walks about* the chamber. In this there is nothing remarkable. But the audience is perplexed by a different circumstance: they see a man rising from his seat and see him walking about, but they also see that *he still sits immovably in his chair* – so that evidently there are two persons instead of one, for, although alike in dress, stature, and person, their actions are different. They cross and recross; they alternately take the same seat; while one reads, the other is perhaps walking; and yet

Figure 4.5 Pepper's three-dimensional spectre

they appear very sullen and sulky, for they take no notice of each other, until one, after pushing down a pile of books, passes off by walking through the furniture and walls.[28]

This vignette contracts Dickens's plot into a single illusionistic scenario dependant on the framing lecture for dramatic context. Like Tenniel and Leech, Pepper and Dircks present the illusion as a symptom of Redlaw's dissociative reverie. Surrounded by scholarly paraphernalia he remains mesmerised '*immovably in his chair*' while his ghostly double wanders the stage. Dircks's mention of the 'sullen and sulky' demeanour of both man and ghost suggests that their illusion echoed Leech's emphasis on Redlaw's misanthropic pose. The ambiguity surrounding the mutual awareness of man and ghost also indicates that Pepper understood Redlaw's spectre as a perceptual aberration induced by a diseased memory. This is consistent with both the reported anti-spiritualist emphasis of Pepper's lecture and Dickens's recurring refrain throughout the tale: to 'keep one's memory green' (411).

In his account of the illusion *The True History of the Ghost; and all About Metempsychosis* (1890) Pepper compares his lecture to George Cruikshank's sceptical pamphlet *A Discovery Concerning Ghosts, with a Rap at the Spirit Rappers* (1863). In his typical self-aggrandising style, Pepper overstated the performance's impact, claiming that he needed to be escorted home after the show, so sensational was it:

> Like Cruikshank, I vigorously denounced the traders in spirits, founding my arguments on the belief that God was too merciful to us to add to the troubles of the world the fear and trembling brought about by pretended communication with the invisible world.[29]

Pepper also provides a detailed description of the first scene of the illusion – Redlaw's Laboratory – in the process of authenticating his connection with Dickens:

> The ghost illusion was first shown in what was called the small theatre of the Royal Polytechnic, but as the audience increased so rapidly it was removed by the following Easter and shown on a grander scale in the large theatre of the Institution, and where the dissolving views were usually exhibited.
>   The late Mr O'Connor, of the Haymarket, painted the first scene used, representing the laboratory of 'The Haunted Man,' which Christmas Story the late Charles Dickens, by his special written permission, allowed me to use for the illustration of the Ghost illusion. The ghost scene ran for fifteen months, and helped realise, in a very short time, the sum of twelve thousand pounds, not counting what I received for granting licenses to use the Ghost, and also the sums realised during many successive years as new ghost stories were brought out. (12)

Pepper's selection of the laboratory scene reinforces the natural magical subtext of Dickens's tale. The success of his reading is contingent on the public's appetite for novel visual effects. The long afterlife of the ghost illusion in various theatrical and later fairground attractions is also foreshadowed here, including Randall Williams's popular walk-up version of the ghost show in the 1890s and consequent 'Grand Phantascopical Exhibition' at the World's Fair in Islington in 1896, which, notably, included the first fairground cinema show.

Both Pepper and Dircks wanted to train their audiences to simultaneously recognise and indulge in the collective pleasures of ghost story-telling. And according to contemporary accounts, their intentions were successfully realised; the *Illustrated London News* enthusiastically reported that Pepper's 'Strange Lecture' caused 'phantoms to appear at will, such as to produce the fullest impression of their reality [while] at the same time a real body will pass through them'.[30] Pepper's lecture undoubtedly compounded the thrill of this initial visual impact. Like many other Polytechnic lecturers, Pepper was somewhat of a celebrity in the 1860s.[31] Even Dircks begrudgingly acknowledged the role Pepper's notoriety played in the success of the ghost, although he was quick to stress that the true reason behind the appeal to 'the public mind' was its affinity with a collective archive of dreams, 'fancies', spectre dramas and ghost stories:

> An invention of so large a scale being expensive to adopt, could have no success unless it captivated the public mind. And, in this respect, considering its imperfections to the present time of its exhibition, 'The Ghost' has never failed to draw crowded, admiring audiences. It was the absolute realisation of all that ever had been dreamt, or ever had occupied frenzied fancies, or formed the staple conceits of dramatists and romancers. (23)

Dircks then goes on to explain the manner in which viewers of the illusion might draw upon recollections of their past experiences to process the spectacle. He continues:

> We first see and then exercise our mental faculties. In forming judgements we bring to bear on the subject all our experience, reading, study, and power of investigation. If the offered mystery has its equal in some jugglery we have seen, then doubt steps in; or, if we have seen a scientific experiment closely allied to alleged mystery, doubt again interposes; and so on, step by step, we compare the unknown subject with what is known bearing any collateral quality. (23)

According to this logic, an illusion, no matter how elaborately conceived and executed, will only succeed if it can be associatively linked to a previous experience.

Dircks makes a distinction between illusions that form part of an avowed narrative sequence and illusions designed to produce cognitive or perceptual aberrations. In the case of the latter, the spectator must calibrate involuntary wonder with the rational demystification of the unknown. This process echoes John W. Herschel's ascription of illusion to a flaw in memory rather than perception:

> Though we are never deceived in the sensible impression made by external objects on us, yet in forming our judgements of them we are greatly at the mercy of circumstances, which either modify the impression actually received, or combine them with adjuncts which have become habitually associated with different judgements.[32]

Memory is profoundly unreliable and subjective according to Herschel, much like Dickens's portrayal of Redlaw's selective recall and the distortions of present perceptions it produces. Developing further on this theme, Hermann von Helmholtz called the sequencing of events that Herschel's explanation implies the 'grammatical relations' or syntax into which the mind translates a series of images or visual events.[33] Read through this theoretical optics, Pepper's illusion can be seen as a manifestation of the active formation of the perceptual syntax Helmholtz describes, training audiences to recognise and normalise mysterious or anomalous visual stimuli.

In his account of this interplay between memory and illusion, Dircks acknowledges Brewster's insistence on the need for a habituated retrospective demystification of psychologically induced apparitions, such as in the following passage from *Letters on Natural Magic*:

> When a spectre haunts the couch of the sick, or follows the susceptible vision of the invalid, a consciousness of indisposition divests the apparition of much of its terror, while its invisibility to surrounding friends soon stamps it with the impress of a false perception. The spectre of the conjurer too, however, skilfully they may be raised, quickly lose their supernatural character; and even the most ignorant beholder regards the modern magician as but an ordinary man, who borrows from the sciences the best working implements of his art. But when, in the midst of solitude, and in situations where the mind is undisturbed by sublunary cares, we see our own image delineated in the air, and mimicking in gigantic perspective the tiny movements of humanity; – when we see troops in military array performing their evolutions on the very face of an almost inaccessible precipice . . . when distant objects, concealed by the roundness of the earth, and beyond the cognisance of the telescope, are actually transferred over the intervening convexity and presented in distinct and magnified outline to our accurate examination; – when such varied and striking phantasms are seen also by all around us, and therefore appear in the character of real phenomena of nature, our impressions of supernatural agency can only be removed by a distinct and satisfactory knowledge of the causes which gave them birth.[34]

This passage parallels Dickens's tale, both in its emphasis on the interplay between voluntary and involuntary thought processes and in the obvious relish Brewster takes in describing the various causes and effects of visual phenomena. Brewster never doubts that illusions, no matter how extraordinary, have rational causes. And yet, underlying this confidence, there is a persistent emphasis on the fragility of the individual mind, its susceptibility, especially in moments of intense isolation, to see its 'own image delineated in the air' in the manner of Redlaw's ghost, 'mimicking in gigantic perspective the tiny movements of humanity'.

Pepper, even more than Dircks, was influenced by Brewster's demystifying ethos. In *The Boy's Playbook of Science* (1860) Pepper reveals the mysteries of the technology behind the Polytechnic illusions in a discussion of 'Light, Optics and Optical Instruments' illustrated by an engraving of 'The Interior of the Optical Box at the Polytechnic – looking towards the screen'.[35] This instructive behind-the-scenes glimpse allowed Polytechnic audiences to unravel the mystery of Pepper's Ghost. More generally, Pepper's explanation of his own spectacular illusion suggests that an emerging and rapidly expanding visual vernacular fostered sceptical curiosity and a self-consciously interactive engagement with a range of visual and narrative media. It is in this spirit that Pepper also turned to Dickens, whose popular readings established such a powerful recent precedent for the performative translation of familiar literary texts into spectacular events of collective identification and recollection. To quote the contemporary eyewitness account of Dickens's admiring friend Charles Kent:

> Densely packed from floor to ceiling, these audiences were habitually wont to hang in breathless expectation upon every inflection of the author-reader's voice, upon every glance of his eye, – the words he was about to speak being so thoroughly well remembered by the majority before their utterance that, often, the rippling of a smile over a thousand faces simultaneously anticipated the laughter which an instant afterwards greeted the words themselves when they were articulated.[36]

Kent provides a vivid image of an audience who literally knew their Dickens by heart, who were so familiar with the twists and turns of plot, character and description that they pre-emptively responded with knowing pleasure. This was precisely the habituated identification that Pepper and Dircks attempted to reproduce by weaving their own illusions into one of Dickens's familiar narratives in a format designed to hold their audience's interest, which was a perpetual problem at the Polytechnic. As Cecil Hepworth remarked, most pre-cinematic spectacles failed because they did not integrate their visual effects into a compelling narrative with the imaginative power to keep viewers engaged beyond the first moment of wonder and delight.[37]

Eager to avoid this possibility, Pepper reworked his original script in 1863 to include more extensive readings from *The Haunted Man*, and the run of the show was extended well beyond the Christmas season. In the initial Christmas programme for December 1862, the performance was divided into three main segments. The first segment showcased a version of Cinderella, illustrated by dissolving views, dioramic and shadow effects. This was followed by

> the remarkable illustration of Mr Charles Dickens's idea of 'THE HAUNTED MAN,' in a new and curious illusion, devised by Henry Dircks, Esq., and other singular Experiments will be included in the new Philosophical Entertainment by Professor J. H. PEPPER entitled A STRANGE LECTURE.[38]

Finally, Valentine Vox, the 'Celebrated Ventriloquist' closed the show. This format was substantially altered after 1 June 1863, during the Whitsun Holiday Entertainments. From this point on, the programme and advertising bills began with Pepper's illusion, which included an extended reading from Dickens's tale:

> Great Additions to and New Experiments in Professor Pepper's Lecture of Optical Illusions. Professor Pepper will (by the kind permission of the Author) read and illustrate a portion of Mr Charles Dickens's Tale of THE HAUNTED MAN AND THE GHOST will actually appear to walk across the New Platform arranged in the Large Theatre.[39]

Perhaps Pepper hoped to create his own illusionistic version of Dickens's extraordinarily popular public readings.[40] If this was his intention, he met with more success than Dickens himself, who tried and failed to adapt *The Haunted Man* into a reading script.[41]

The contemporaneous account of Dickens's readings of *A Christmas Carol* by the American freelance journalist, Kate Field, provides a further rationale for Pepper's spectacular translation of *The Haunted Man* into a multimedia event.[42] In *Pen Photographs of Charles Dickens's Readings. Taken from Life* Field describes Dickens reading the Christmas dinner scene with Scrooge and the Cratchits as a 'charming cabinet picture' and the transition between scenes as kaleidoscopic: 'One turn of the kaleidoscope and we stand before the body of the plundered unknown man; another, and there sit the Cratchits weeping over Tiny Tim's death . . .'[43] Field's emphasis on both the arresting power of individual narrative frames and the kaleidoscopic transitions that provide continuity between them, also forms part of an enduring argument about the social potency of Dickens's translation of his narratives into events that take on a life of their own. Grahame Smith's reading of Dickens's work as intrinsically proto-cinematic agrees with Field's stress on the visual dynamism of the readings.[44] Smith suggestively aligns Dickens's narratives with proto-cinematic visual media in their appeal to 'the human desire for reciprocity' (21), the desire to 'see ourselves in the company of others, surrounded by the minutiae of daily existence' (21). Following André Bazin's dismissal of the distinction between the psychological affects generated by the cinematic image, the theatre and the novel, Smith embraces the 'fearless rejection of the separation of forms' as the guiding ethos of his argument that Dickens's writing provides a 'blueprint of a dream of cinema' (47).

Early reviewers of Pepper's Ghost shared Kate Field's interest in the visual animation of the literary text. Claiming enthusiastically that Pepper's show was the most wonderful series of 'optical illusions ever placed before the public', a critic in *The Times* in December 1862 remarked that:

> The spectres and illusions are thrown upon the stage in such a perfect embodiment of real substance, that it is not till the *Haunted Man* walks through their apparently solid forms that the audience can believe in there being optical illusions at all. Even then it is almost difficult to imagine that the whole is not a wonderful trick, for people cling to the old saying, that seeing is believing, and if ever mere optical delusions assumed a perfect and tangible form they do so in this strange lecture. Why did not the medium and spirit rappers get hold of this invention before it was made public? The illusions might fail to convince, but at least they would have left all seekers after spiritual revelations in a sore state of puzzle and uncertainty, as they most certainly do now at the Polytechnic.[45]

This review captures the excitement inspired by the revelatory powers of Pepper's and Dircks's invention. The reviewer playfully considers the broader cultural implications of the idea of a new technology with the power to give uncanny visual form to a perennial epistemological question – the role the eye plays in the psychology of belief.

A clearer picture of the Polytechnic audience, puzzled and uncertain, also emerges from this account. Unlike the dupes of spiritualist charlatans, their eyes have been trained according to the Polytechnic ethos, which, conforming to Henry Brougham's principles for the diffusion of useful knowledge, privileged logic over belief.[46] To quote an early Polytechnic publication that outlined the Institute's foundational vision for the education of eye and mind:

> The education of the eye is, undeniably, the most important object in elementary instruction. A child will pass many years before he can be made thoroughly to understand, by *unassisted* description ... the powers of

Galvanism, the properties of Electricity, the mysteries of Chemistry, the laws of Mechanics, the theory of Light, the developments of the microscope, the wonders of Optics, the construction of Ships, with various other matters in Science and Art, are made palpable by exhibition; and thus instruction is rapidly and pleasurably communicated in awakening curiosity, excitement, and attention, and by such means leaving a durable impression.[47]

Read in this context the 'sore state of puzzle and uncertainty' suffered by Pepper's audiences noted by the previous reviewer would have been quickly resolved by durably impressed reasoning. They also would have been comforted, to adapt Dickens's rhetoric from the extract with which this chapter began, by familiar episodes from one of his own popular Christmas tales. As Dircks confirmed in his account, Polytechnic audiences may have known 'more about optics than some very clever men even 100 years ago', but they also knew their Dickens (31). To quote Dircks's account of his initial pitch to the Polytechnic managers:

Among a long list of pieces which I had arranged in 1858, I usually directed attention to one which I proposed, calling it 'Charles Dickens, Esq.'s Haunted Man,' from his well-known Christmas piece of that name, conceiving that it would command a double interest. (65)

Dickens's psychological framing of the illusions produced by a diseased memory unmoored from social responsibility effectively haunts Pepper's and Dircks's remediation of his tale, serving as a familiar basis for the creation of a new form of visual entertainment and narrative temporality. Pepper, in turn, shared Dickens's interest in the power of unconscious habituated responses, reflecting their mutual implication in a more general discussion about the ameliorative benefits of habit on character, to quote Samuel Smiles influential *Self-Help* (1859):

Here it may be observed how greatly the character may be strengthened and supported by the cultivation of good habits. Man, it has been said, is a bundle of habits; and habit is second nature . . . Wherever formed, habit acts involuntarily, and with out effort; and it is only when you oppose it, that you find how powerful it has become.[48]

Both Dickens and Pepper were keenly aware of this ethos, and, accordingly, trained their respective audiences to think across a range of visual and textual media in a manner that can be traced back to the demystifying descriptive techniques of Brewster, Cruikshank and Scott. Correspondingly, the success of Pepper's illusion, and the Institute more generally, relied upon experimental techniques of visualisation that synthesised new knowledge with common knowledge – the latter functioning in a Humean sense as the necessary condition for co-ordinated social interaction – to create a collective moment of instructive curiosity under Pepper's watchful eye.[49]

Pepper's illustration of Dickens's idea of *The Haunted Man*, like Cruikshank's illustrations of Scott, effectively compressed a series of narrative actions into 'an order of *poses* or privileged instants', a compression which Gilles Deleuze identifies with the dialectical forms and regulated transitions of pre-cinematic realisations of forms or ideas.[50] Deleuze opposes this to the post-dialectical 'mechanical succession of instants' of modern science that is more concerned with producing 'an intelligible synthesis of movement' between 'any-instant-whatever', a lineage that he traces, via Bergson, from Kepler through to modern cinema (4). However, the seminal Dickens-inspired montage of Sergei Eisenstein disrupts Deleuze's smooth historical transitions and equally intransigent demarcations of what is and is not proto-cinematic. Strategically omitting Eisenstein's account of the literary derivation of his cinematic technique, Deleuze insists: 'If Eisenstein picks out remarkable instants, this does not prevent him deriving from them an immanent analysis of movement, and not a transcendental synthesis. The remarkable or singular instant remains any-instant-whatever among others' (6).

By contrast, Eisenstein portrays himself as an avid reader of Dickens as a child, hungrily consuming and unconsciously internalising his compositional techniques:

> All of us read him in childhood, gulped him down greedily, without realising that much of his irresistibility lay not only in his capture of detail in the childhood of his heroes, but also in that spontaneous, childlike skill for story-telling, equally typical for Dickens and for the American cinema, which so surely plays upon the infantile traits in its audience. We were even less concerned with the technique of Dickens's composition: for us this was non-existent – but captivated by the effects of this technique, we feverishly followed his characters from page to page, watching his characters now being rubbed from view at the most critical moment, then seeing them return afresh between the separate links of the parallel secondary plot.[51]

Eisenstein further aligns his own assimilation of the descriptive machinery of Dickens's novels with that of David Wark Griffith, citing the latter's avowal of Dickens's influence on his idea for a new editing technique which inserted a break in the narrative, shifting from one parallel narrative to another: 'I went home, re-read one of Dickens's novels, and came back the next day to tell them they could either make use of my idea or dismiss me.'[52] But Dickens's structural proximity to the cinematic techniques of exposition and viewpoint is only one facet of his legacy, according to Eisenstein, the other is the social dimension of his appeal to the sentiment and passions of a mass readership exemplified by the popularity of Dickens's public readings: a passionate collective identification which returns Eisenstein to the formal structure of Dickens's syntax in search of clues to unlock the mystery of its affective power.

Eisenstein's ensuing segmentation of the twenty-first chapter of *Oliver Twist* into a montage structure, in which each numbered passage indicates a new compositional set-up, echoes a long tradition of visual habits of reading which can be traced back to eighteenth-century theories of spectatorship (214).[53] As Luisa Calè has observed, Eisenstein's invocation of sympathy when arguing for the Dickensian genealogy of the cinematic close-up, recalls Adam Smith's account of spectatorship as a mechanism of social cohesion effected by the binding power of sympathy. Smith argued that mutual understanding and individual regulation resulted from examining 'our own conduct as we imagine any other fair and impartial spectator would imagine it'.[54] The 'civilising work of the aesthetic sphere', as Calè argues, 'exercises the mind in the production of mental images and in projecting and practising the position of the spectator' (7–8).

Lewis Carroll, the focus of the next chapter, was also compelled by the question of how one produced a new mode of imaginative experience that extended the limits of traditional reading habits by mimicking the projections of an immersed spectator – a fascination that was matched by the technological inventiveness of Pepper's fellow lanternist, George Buckland. Buckland, with Carroll's consent, transformed Alice's dream into a sensational dissolving view adaptation in the main Lecture Theatre of the Royal Polytechnic, a transformative process that unwittingly mirrored Carroll's profound desire to communicate with his child readers unfettered by the constraints of the printed page.

Notes

1. Charles Dickens, 'The Amusements of the People', *Household Words* 1 (30 March 1850), p. 13.
2. One contemporary version of *The Maid and the Magpie* was a popular risqué burlesque, which Dickens himself attended at The Strand, although as David Pascoe notes there was a range of plays performed about thieving magpies in the first half of the century, in addition to popular chapbook and balladic adaptations. Sherson discusses the performance attended by Dickens and Dickens's correspondence with John Foster regarding its 'impudent' content in *London's Lost Theatres of the Nineteenth Century*, pp. 220–1; David Pascoe notes that the first theatrical version of this story was S. J. Arnold's *The Maid and the Magpie, or Which is the Thief* (1815);

and the most contemporary C. Stansfield Jones, *The Maid and the Magpie* (1848). Both were adaptations of the successful French melodrama *La Pie Voleuse; ou la Servante du Palaiseau* (1815) by Jean-Marie-Théodore Baudouin d'Aubigny and Louis-Charles Caigniez. See Dickens, *Selected Journalism, 1850–1870*, p. 638.

3. The full title of the story that appeared on the London stage for the first time in 1814 was *Le Chien de Montargis* adapted from the popular French writer René-Charles Guilbert de Pixérécourt. It tells the tale of the devoted dog of Aubrey de Montdidier, who revealed his master's assassin, defeated him in open combat and compelled him to confess his crime.

4. John, *Dickens and Mass Culture*, p. 41.

5. Dickens, 'The Amusements of the People', p. 13.

6. Vrettos, 'Defining Habits: Dickens and the Psychology of Repetition', *Victorian Studies* (Spring 1999/2000), p. 399.

7. Dallas, *The Gay Science*, vol. 1, p. 194.

8. Carpenter, *Principles of Human Physiology, with Their Chief Applications to Psychology, Pathology, Therapeutics, Hygiene, and Forensic Medicine* (London: Churchill, 1853), p. 784.

9. Lightman, 'Lecturing in the Spatial Economy of Science', in *Science in the Marketplace: Nineteenth-Century Sites and Experiences*, p. 114.

10. *London as it is To-Day: Where to Go, and What to See*, p. 268.

11. Brooker, 'Paganini's Ghost: Musical Resources of the Royal Polytechnic Institution', in *Realms of Light: Uses and Perceptions of the Magic Lantern from the Seventeenth to the Twenty-First Century*, pp. 146–54.

12. 'Philosophical Drama', *Punch* 27 (1854), p. 179.

13. Halliday, 'Mr Whelks Combining Instruction with Amusement', *All the Year Round* 15:376 (7 July 1866), pp. 610, 611.

14. Morley and Wills, 'The Stereoscope', *Household Words* (10 September 1853), p. 42.

15. Letter cited in Kaplan, *Dickens: A Biography*, p. 208.

16. Marsh, '"Dickensian Dissolving Views": The Magic Lantern, Visual Story-Telling, and the Victorian Technological Imagination', *Comparative Critical Studies* 6:3 (October 2009), p. 336.

17. Marsh, 'Dickensian Dissolving Views', p. 336. Guida refers to these adaptations in *A Christmas Carol and Its Adaptations*, p. 50.

18. The first edition of the tale was illustrated by John Tenniel, John Leech, et al., and was published under the following title: Charles Dickens, *The Haunted Man and the Ghost's Bargain A Fancy for Christmas Time*. References in this chapter are to Dickens, *Christmas Books: A Reprint of the First Editions, with the illustrations, and an introduction, biographical and bibliographical, by Charles Dickens the Younger*, p. 327.

19. Shuttleworth, '"The malady of thought." Embodied memory in Victorian psychology and the novel', in *Memory and Memorials 1789–1914*, p. 47.

20. Holland, *Chapters on Mental Physiology*, p. 9; Lewes, *The Physiology of Common Life*, vol. 2, pp. 62–5; Carpenter, *Principles of Mental Physiology*, p. 436.

21. Carpenter, *Principles of Mental Physiology*, pp. 455–6. Ryan has recently extended the implications of such claims for the Victorian novel more generally in *Thinking without Thinking in the Victorian Novel*.

22. Charles Dickens to William Howitt, 6 September 1859, *The Letters of Charles Dickens*, vol. 9, pp. 116–17.
23. Henry Morley, 'New Discoveries in Ghosts', *Household Words* 4 (1852), pp. 403–6; 'A Physician's Ghosts', *All the Year Round* 1 (1859), pp. 346–50; 'A Physician's Dreams', *All the Year Round* 2 (1859), pp. 109–13, 135–40; Henry Morley and W. H. Wills, 'The Ghost of the Cock Lane Ghost', *Household Words* 6 (1853), pp. 217–23.
24. *Examiner* (26 February 1848), reprinted in Collins, 'Dickens on Ghosts: An Uncollected Article', *Dickensian* 59 (1963), pp. 5–14, 8–9.
25. Henson discusses this treatment in the context of Dickens's ghost stories in 'Investigations and fictions: Charles Dickens and ghosts', *The Victorian Supernatural*, p. 47.
26. The italics in this passage are Dickens's.
27. Mannoni, *The Great Art of Light and Shadow: Archaeology of the Cinema*. See Chapter 11.
28. Dircks, *The Ghost! As Produced in the Spectre Drama, popularly illustrating the marvellous optical illusions obtained by the apparatus called the Dircksian Phantasmagoria*, p. 65. The italics are Dircks's.
29. Pepper, *The True History of the Ghost; and all About Metempsychosis*, p. 28.
30. 'The Polytechnic', *Illustrated London News* 42:1 (3 January 1863), p. 19.
31. Pepper's obituarist Edmund H. Wilkie remarked upon his fluent, engaging lecturing style that combined conversational fluency with carefully scripted erudition. Wilkie, 'Professor Pepper – A Memoir', *The Optical Magic Lantern Journal and Photographic Enlarger* II (June 1900), p. 72.
32. Herschel, *A Preliminary Discourse on the Study of Natural Philosophy* [1851], p. 83.
33. Helmholtz, *Treatise on Physiological Optics* [1867], vol. 3, p. 23.
34. Brewster, *Letters on Natural Magic, addressed to Sir Walter Scott*, pp. 147–8.
35. Pepper, *The Boy's Playbook of Science*, p. 255.
36. Kent, *Charles Dickens as a Reader*, p. 20.
37. Hepworth, *Came the Dawn: Memories of a Film Pioneer*, p. 205. Hepworth's father, T. C. Hepworth was a contemporary of Pepper's who also lectured on *The Footprints of Dickens*. Hepworth recalls the wonderful appearance of the Ghost and its influence on early cinematic practice, including his own films. Dickens also influenced his own film work; Hepworth's production company made an adaptation of *Oliver Twist* in 1912.
38. *The London Polytechnic Institution Programme* (December 1861–January 1864), British Library Collection.
39. *London Polytechnic Institution Programme*. By 31 August 1863 the whole performance was more of a hybrid of earlier and later versions but still included a reading from Dickens: 'Professor Pepper's adaptation of Mr Dircks's Original and most startling GHOST ILLUSION! In three scenes. First scene: Reading from Dickens's "HAUNTED MAN" and appearance of the GHOST and SPECTRE of the sister. Second scene: THE ARTIST'S STUDIO. The Ghostly visitor in the form of a Rival Artist. THE GHOST DRINKING A GLASS OF WATER!! (*This Illusion must be seen to be*

believed.) The reading of the *LOVE LETTER*, and mysterious arrival of the Little Postman "CUPID"' (*London Polytechnic Institution Programme*). This is the format that continues into the next year's Christmas programming as well.

40. Contemporary accounts of the immersive affects of Dickens's public readings are given by a range of Dickens's contemporaries, including Field, who in *Pen Photographs of Charles Dickens's Readings* described the transitions between scenes and characters as kaleidoscopic transitions between illuminated cabinet pictures; Kent, *Charles Dickens as a Reader*; Dolby, *Charles Dickens as I Knew Him: The Story of the Reading Tours in Great Britain and America (1866–1870)*. Small provides an insightful analysis of the politics of affect in relation to Dickens's readings in 'A pulse of 124: Charles Dickens and a pathology of the mid-Victorian reading public', in *The Practice and Representation of Reading in England*, pp. 263–90.

41. Philip Collins provides a detailed account of Dickens's struggles with the reading script for *The Haunted Man* in *Charles Dickens: The Public Readings*, p. 103.

42. Dickens ultimately favoured Charles Kent's more extensive account and discouraged the publication of Field's version of the readings, despite Anthony Trollope's petitioning on Field's behalf and his own initial encouragement to publish in England.

43. Field, *Pen Photographs of Charles Dickens's Readings*, pp. 34, 35.

44. Smith, *Dickens and the Dream of Cinema*.

45. Rev., *The Times* (27 December 1862), cited in Dircks, *The Ghost!*, p. 6.

46. Brougham outlines this approach in *Practical Observations upon the Education of the People, Addressed to the Working Class and Their Employers*, pp. 1–10.

47. *The Royal Polytechnic Institution, for the advancement of the arts and practical science; Catalogue for 1845. New Edition* (London: Reynell and White at the Royal Polytechnic Institution, 1845), pp. 5–6.

48. Smiles, *Self-Help. With Illustrations of Conduct and Perseverance*, ed. Asa Briggs, p. 274.

49. Hume, *A Treatise on Human Nature* [1740], Book 3, Part 2, 5:8.

50. Deleuze, *Cinema 1: The Movement-Image*, p. 4.

51. Eisenstein, 'Dickens, Griffith, and the Film Today', *Film Form: Essays in Film Theory*, p. 201.

52. D. W. Griffith interview with A. B. Walkley in *The Times* (London), (26 April 1922), cited in Eisenstein, 'Dickens, Griffith, and the Film Today', p. 205. Notably Walkley contends that Griffith could have found a very similar technique in other long and crowded Victorian novels by Thackeray, Eliot, Trollope, Meredith or Hardy, as well as 'great artists' such as Tolstoy, Turgenev, and Balzac.

53. Calè traces this history in depth in *Fuseli's Milton Gallery: 'Turning Readers into Spectators'*.

54. Smith, *The Theory of Moral Sentiments*, p. 110. This reference to Smith is indebted to Calè's analysis of Eisenstein in the context of 'Galleries of Illustration'.

Chapter 5

Dissolving Views: Dreams of Reading Alice

The Mad Hatter and the Hare went 'mad together the day they murdered time', according to Gilles Deleuze.[1] The teleological momentum of common sense no longer anchors them in any chronological sequence, 'they now change places endlessly, they are always late and early, in both directions, but never on time' (79). The dream life of Alice herself mirrors this anachronistic disarray, always going in two directions at once, 'the becoming-mad' and the 'unforeseeable' (78). She loses hold of time, as well 'as the identity of things and the world' (77–8). Bereft of the means to decode and fix any truth from the surrounding nonsense, she is caught in a seemingly endless cycle of unanswered questions and questioning answers. Yet these riddling dialogues that seem at first to lead nowhere had, in fact, an implicit target – the unthinking learning by rote promoted by utilitarian mechanisms of modern education. Carroll was equally contemptuous of the heavy-handed truisms of Victorian didactic and moral literature. His concern was that forcing a child to memorise without comprehension conspired against understanding. The message would, in other words, get lost in the medium. As the mock turtle observes: 'What is the use of repeating all that stuff? . . . if you don't explain it as you go on?'[2]

This fear of the signal going unheard, or the message being lost or misunderstood, was an enduring one for Carroll. Nowhere is this more apparent than in Carroll's struggle to control the reception of *Alice's Adventures in Wonderland* (1865) and *Through the Looking-Glass* (1872). In his editorial prefaces to the multiple editions of both books, Carroll expressed an anticipatory desire to 'be there' to encode future responses to Alice, to push through the surface of print into the space of reading. This resonates with Gillian Rose's suggestive redescription of the future as the supreme anachronism, 'the time in which we may not be, and yet we must imagine we will have been'.[3] Carroll's increasingly directive prefatory framings of Alice articulate the pathos of this temporal conundrum, caught between the time 'one nominally inhabits and the actuality of any other' (126). Such editorial efforts were particularly salutary given the present-minded criticism of Carroll's reviewers, who turned their attention to the technology of mediation, the letter press, and Tenniel's illustrative rendering of character, and were correspondingly indifferent to the implicit meanings to be derived from Alice's phantasmagoric dream-life.

The following chapter reconsiders Carroll's multifaceted relationship to the way images of Alice were generated in his readers' minds, from her incarnation in the first imprint of *Alice's Adventures in Wonderland* in 1865 to George Buckland's dissolving view adaptation, staged at the Royal Polytechnic in 1876. As his private and published writings attest, the dynamics of literary mediation preoccupied and frustrated Carroll. His prefaces flirt with a technologically impossible immediacy, pressing against the material limits of the printed page in his earnest desire to communicate with his readers with a persistence that exemplifies Walter Benjamin's familiar theory that certain art forms and, correspondingly, artists aspire to effects that 'could be fully obtained only with a changed technical standard'.[4] It is striking therefore, that Carroll chose the medium of the dream as his organising motif for the Alice books, a state of consciousness which his contemporaries, such as Frances Power Cobbe, George Henry Lewes, William Carpenter, and James Sully, variously theorise as an infinite archive of remembered activities, including books read and images viewed, that momentarily emerge then dissolve in a timeless associative stream. Carroll, as a quick perusal of the catalogue of his library reveals, was very familiar with these ideas. He owned works by all of the above, in addition to an impressive range of other complimentary and conflicting psychological theories penned by key figures in the emerging science of mind, including Henry Holland, Herbert Spencer, Frederic W. H. Myers (one of the founding figures of the Society of Psychical Research which counted Carroll as one of its early members), as well as popular works by David Brewster and Frank Seafield's extensive anthology of dream-writing, *The Literature and Curiosities of Dreams* (1865).[5]

Much has been written on Carroll's use of the dream as an organising motif, particularly from a psychoanalytic perspective. Ronald Thomas, for example, reads the translation of the pictorial images of Alice's dream in *Alice's Adventures* into the currency of language, as a struggle towards self-possession:

> The whole adventure begins when Alice drifts off to sleep because the book that her sister was reading had no pictures and no conversation. Alice escapes

from the mastery of this text by 'falling' into images of her own dream and then arising to tell her own story. When Alice wakes to recount that story to her sister, she provokes the sister to dream the very same dream.[6]

Alice's sister dreams the same dream, but with one significant variation, it concludes with an image of a future Alice telling 'many a strange tale' of her past dream life to groups of entranced children, much as Carroll dreamed of doing with his own Alice books (111). Thomas reads this intimate scene of unconscious mediation between two minds as a triumph of dream work, in which a young woman 'converts her dream into a book about herself'.[7] Given, however, that Carroll, was well aware of contemporary Victorian dream theory, there is a less anachronistic way of reading this scene that aligns with Carroll's interest in immediate communication with his own readers. Rather than a moment of personal empowerment for Alice, this scene, as my stress on unconscious mediation suggests, could be read as an experiment with how particular stories, conveyed in particular ways, can enter into what George Henry Lewes seminally called, 'the general stream of consciousness', which he defined as both the process of the mind moving between conscious and unconscious, voluntary and involuntary states, and 'the general stream of Sensation which constitutes his [the reader's] feeling of existence – the consciousness of himself as a sensitive being'.[8]

While Carroll may have been antipathetic to the more radical implications of Lewes's physiological emphasis on the interdependence of body and mind, there is a significant parallel between their interest in the proximity between dreaming and waking life, and the corresponding sense of the dream as a generative resource of revelatory images. In dreams, as in reverie, Lewes argued, the mind does not pause to reflect on 'certain suggestions', letting 'one rapidly succeed another, like shadows chasing each other over a cornfield' (2:370). Combining experiential evidence with associationist ideas of how the mind works, Lewes concluded that the apparent 'coherence of dreams results from the succession of associated thoughts', which mirror the associative streams of conscious thought that fill the waking mind in a state of reverie 'uncontrolled by reference to external things' (2:370). Echoing the conventional portrayal of the dreamer as a passive observer watching what might be termed a proto-cinematic sequence of moving images projected on an internal screen, Lewes drew on his own experience to capture the dynamic flow of the dream:

Nothing *arrests* us; but every incongruity surprises us, at least as much in dreams as in reveries. I am distinctly conscious of this in my own experience. If when I dream that I am in a certain place, conversing with a certain person, I am also aware that the place suddenly becomes another place, and the person has a very different appearance, a slight surprise is felt as the difference is noted, but my dream is not arrested; I accept the new facts, and go on quite content with them, just as in reverie the mind passes instantaneously from London to India, and the persons vanish to give place to very different persons, without once interrupting the imaginary story.[9]

While 'fresh streams of association' may momentarily divert or interrupt the flow of the dream, the movement remains constant – nothing can interrupt the story, unless, as in Alice's case, the dreamer is sharply awakened by the querulous demands of an older sister.

The following chapter is divided into three sections that ultimately draw together Carroll's parallel engagements with the idea of unconscious networks between minds and the technological networks in which his dreams are transformed into literary commodities that then circulate in an increasingly uncontrollable modern media system. The first section deals with Carroll's literal struggle to mediate Alice to the 'child reader', beginning with George Buckland's dissolving view adaptation, and then moving back through the production and reception of the multiple print iterations of Alice. The second section analyses the way the dream motif intersects with Carroll's multi-medial exploration of generating moving images in the reader's mind. The third section then locates Carroll's dream story in a network of theories concerned with the dreaming mind's capacity to communicate beyond the grasp of conscious sense and the constraints of technological mediation.

Mediating Alice

Writing of the proto-filmic desire for moving images in literary forms Friedrich Kittler observes: 'Even the most poetic of words could not store bodies. The soul, the inner self, the individual: they all were only the effects of an illusion, neutralised through the hallucination of reading and widespread literacy.'[10] Carroll was, nevertheless, compelled by the idea of bringing Alice to life for his readers, an enthusiasm that was emphatically reciprocated by contemporary audiences. Attendances at a wide range of theatrical and early magic-lantern adaptations of *Alice's Adventures* were high, and predictably, given this exemplary commercial success, Cecil Hepworth's early film adaptation of *Alice in Wonderland* (1903), to which I will return in the concluding chapter of this study, reverentially mediated the spirit of Alice, adhering to Tenniel's illustrations and relying upon the audience's familiarity with the narrative.

Carroll's reviewers shared this interest in whether Carroll had successfully mediated the spirit of Alice. While they may have disagreed on questions of literary merit, their overriding concern was whether Tenniel and Carroll had succeeded in bringing Alice to life for their readers. Carroll was typically fastidious in his response to these reviews, collecting and archiving them, as he did the many variant editions of the Alice books published during his lifetime. Carroll's direct prefatory addresses to 'the child reader' also reflect this preoccupation with being heard by his target audience. Indicatively, in his Easter Greeting of 1876, which formed part of the editorial apparatus of subsequent editions, Carroll urged his readers to:

> Please fancy, if you can, that you are reading a real letter, from a real friend whom you have seen, and whose voice you can seem to yourself to hear wishing you, as I do now with all my heart, a Happy Easter.[11]

Metaphorically projecting his voice through the medium of print, Carroll conscripts the reader into the desire for unmediated interaction. Rhetorically enacting the double logic of remediation as Jay David Bolter and Richard Grusin elaborate it, Carroll both concedes and denies the technological mediation of his work.[12] Accordingly, he visualises Alice as both of and beyond the various media that multiplied her image, whether it be illustrations, letterpress, magic-lantern sequences, theatrical adaptations, or photographs. Alice exists instead, according to Carroll, in a continuous present where reader and character can meet in an illusory face-to-face encounter.

Carroll's avid consumption of new media is continuous with this desire for both instantaneity and duration. In addition to his well-known pursuit of photography, Carroll collected new technologies, such as Edison's electric pen and Remington's typewriter, and attended early exhibitions of Edison's phonograph in London, noting excitedly in his diary:

> It is a pity that we are not fifty years further on in the world's history, so as to get this wonderful invention in its *perfect* form. It is now in its infancy – the new wonder of the day, just as I remember Photography was about 1850.[13]

Carroll was equally engaged by the future of the cinematograph, although he would not live to see Cecil Hepworth's 1903 adaptation of *Alice in Wonderland*.[14] As the above diary entry indicates, it is the prospect of future perfection, of capturing an accurate recording of a voice or, indeed, of a body in motion, that compels him. In this sense Carroll is very much of his time. His response conforms to the fundamental rethinking of time, as both contingent and archivable, prompted by the advent of new technologies of representation, such as photography, phonography and the cinematograph.[15]

Carroll's fractious relationship with his illustrator John Tenniel also testifies to his preoccupation with questions of mediation, as does the close attention he paid to various theatrical productions of the Alice books. A less well-known, but indicative example of the latter can be found in his correspondence and diary entries regarding pre-cinematic magic-lantern adaptations of *Alice's Adventures in Wonderland*. In 1876 George Buckland, a popular lecturer at the Royal Polytechnic on Regent Street, presented a dissolving view adaptation of *Alice in Wonderland* entitled *Alice's Adventures; or, More Wonders in Wonderland*. The 'Entertainment' as Carroll described it in his diaries,

> lasted about one and a quarter hours. A good deal of it was dissolving views, extracts from the story being read, or sung to Mr Boyd's music; but the latter part had a real scene and five performers (Alice, Queen, Knave, Hatter, Rabbit) who acted in dumb show, the speeches being read by Mr Buckland.[16]

Given the extraordinary popularity of *Alice in Wonderland*, Buckland's entertainment quickly found an audience. As *The Times* theatrical notices predicted, Buckland's 'spectacular recital' was very popular and continued to be performed throughout the summer season and was reprised the following year.[17] Carroll attended three times, once in April and twice in June 1876. His repeat visits were primarily motivated by anxiety that the changes he had suggested to Buckland regarding the musical interpolations of the Cheshire Cat were implemented. By contrast, Buckland's textual abridgments and dissolving views seem to have been familiar and expected dimensions of the multi-medial performance.

The first mention of what would become *Alice's Adventures; or, More Wonders in Wonderland* appears in Carroll's correspondence with his publisher Alexander Macmillan. Carroll expresses concern that he could not grant permission for the Polytechnic adaptation because he 'had already given leave for them to be published as magic-lantern slides, which of course involved the right to *exhibit* the slides'.[18] Clearly this conflict of interest was resolved and Buckland's production became part of the complex assemblage of the commercial mediation of Alice. Nor is it surprising that Buckland's dissolving views would appeal to Carroll's penchant for eliding reading with projecting images of Alice. In his Christmas letter of 1871 addressed to 'all child-readers of "Alice's Adventures in Wonderland"' Carroll dwells on the 'thought of the many English firesides where happy faces have smiled her a welcome, and of the many English children to whom she has brought an hour of (I trust) innocent amusement'.[19] Alice must be 'welcomed' into the domestic space of his readers. Carroll projects himself into their space as well. He is there with them to orchestrate the ensuing innocent entertainment while artfully dismantling the didactic clichés of Victorian instructive literature. Reading Alice, Carroll insists, should be a playful, light interaction rather than a catechistic exchange of rational precepts of the kind Alice had internalised before her own fall into Wonderland. Correspondingly, Tenniel's illustrations and Buckland's dissolving views of Alice form part of a process of visual mediation that begins with Carroll's insistent desire to create a more porous surface between Alice and her readers, an intimate synchronous connection that would ideally dissolve the time lag between writing and reading.

The initial press notices and early responses to *Alice's Adventure's in Wonderland* listed in Carroll's diaries suggest that his reviewers shared his interest in technologies of mediation, an emphasis that was sustained by subsequent reviews of *Through the Looking Glass, and What Alice Found There*.[20] *The Times* reviewer barely mentions Carroll, other than to note that he produced the 'letter-press':

> Mr Tenniel ... has illustrated a little work – *Alice's Adventures in Wonderland*, with extraordinary grace. Look at the first chapter of this volume, and note the rabbit at the head of it. His umbrella is tucked under his arm and he is taking the watch out of his pocket to see what o'clock it is. The neatness of touch with which he is set living before us may be seen in a dozen other vignettes throughout the volume, the letter-press of which is by Mr. Lewis Carroll, and may best be described as an excellent piece of nonsense.[21]

The author is reduced here to one of a number of technical elements that bring the book to life for the reader as an intimate interactive space. Carroll merely produces the letters on the page that nonsensically connect one vignette with another. According to this reviewer, it is ultimately Tenniel's illustrations which bring the text closer 'spatially and humanly', to quote Benjamin's account of the desire to get hold of objects at close range that characterises the work of art in the age of mechanical reproduction.[22] Stressing the haptic affects of Tenniel's 'neatness of touch' as he literally sets the white rabbit down before the reader reinforces the material presence of the book, the way it looks and feels.

The notice in the *Athenaeum* was less positive in its characterisation of Carroll's manufactured dream story and its legibility to the juvenile reader:

> Who can, in cold blood, manufacture a dream, with all its loops and ties, and loose threads, and entanglements, and inconsistencies, and passages which lead to nothing, at the end of which Sleep's most diligent pilgrim never

arrives? Mr Carroll has laboured hard to heap together strange adventures, and heterogenous combinations; and we acknowledge the hard labour. Mr Tenniel, again, is square, and grim, and uncouth in his illustrations, howbeit clever, even sometimes to the verge of grandeur, as is the artist's habit. We fancy that any real child might be more puzzled than enchanted by this stiff, over-wrought story.[23]

Carroll appears as a calculating manufacturer of industrial fiction here, labouring hard to produce a coherent narrative commodity from the inchoate raw material of the dream. Tenniel's illustrations are begrudgingly acknowledged, but like Carroll's heaping together of 'strange adventures' and 'heterogeneous combinations', they fall short of genius and are ultimately mechanical in effect, 'square', 'grim' and 'uncouth'. The question of whether 'any real child' will understand or derive pleasure from Carroll's text is a recurring one in early reviews, such as *The Scotsman*, which Henry Kingsley, a friend of Carroll, dismissed as indicative of the paper's critical limitations.[24] It is nevertheless consistent with both *The Times* and the *Athenaeum* reviewers' stress on the text as a mechanical diversion:

> Nor is the story unreadable; but it is dull. There is no flow of animal spirits in its fun, which is forced and over-ingenious. Mr Carroll seems to have said to himself, 'Go to now, I shall write a child's book,' and forthwith he has done it; whereas true children's literature is really of the poetical order, and must be born, not made.[25]

More positive reviews typically engaged with Carroll's narrative rather than the relative merits of Tenniel's illustrations, but the preoccupation with the dynamics of mediation persisted. A reviewer in *Aunt Judy's Magazine*, a monthly children's magazine that published the work of Carroll and many other children's writers, warned that: 'Parents and guardians ... must not look to "Alice's Adventures" for knowledge in disguise.'[26] The reviewer in the *Sunderland Herald* went further noting an anti-didactic strain in Carroll's text,

> It has this advantage, that it has no moral, and that it does not teach anything ... We can confidently recommend this book as a present for any children who are in the habit of spending a part of each day in 'doing their lessons,' and who may therefore be fairly allowed a little unalloyed nonsense as a reward.[27]

Here the many unanswered questions that pervade *Alice's Adventures* constitute a happy escape into nonsensical distraction from the catechistic pedagogic devices of the Victorian classroom. Carroll's text licenses anti-telcological reverie, daydreaming and unsupervised play, the antithesis of the conventionally rigid controls on the attention spans of the juvenile mind. Priority is given to the therapeutic benefits of taking time out, of moving against the standardising rhythms of the modern classroom – the irony being that these reviews enlist Carroll's work as a therapeutic supplement to the systematic training of young minds that the Alice books satirised.[28] Notably, this didactic possibility also appealed to school inspectors during the 1860s and 1870s. They regularly included *Alice's Adventures* on lists of recommended recreational reading to manage the lagging attention spans of students weary of rote-learning the useful knowledge required by the school curriculum.[29]

More positive reviews of *Through the Looking-Glass* were also keen to associate reading Alice with the timelessness of therapeutic reverie, such as the following from *The Spectator*:

> The creations of Alice's second fairyland have a comparatively mature air. Without being a bit more like the outer world than before, they have an increased element of inner congruity in their nonsense. They seem this time to work by some obscure law, – a law of nonsense, of course, but discoverable by the corresponding faculty. (There is good philosophical authority for the Faculty of Nonsense; Ferrier [sic] talks of it somewhere.)[30]

The reference to Ferriar is consistent with this reviewer's interest in the psychological verification of Carroll's embrace of anachronic irrationality. In his much reprinted *An Essay Towards the Study of Apparitions* Ferriar urges his readers to relax their vigilant application of the machinery of rational explanation and embrace the inexplicable phenomena of dreams, hallucinations and apparitions of various kinds.[31] Wonderland, according to this reviewer, is a dreamscape far removed from practical considerations, explicable transitions and the chronological sequence of 'the outer world'. Organised like a random series of waking dreams, the text's 'changes of scene' move in and out of focus like a series of dissolving views, to quote a relatively contemporary account of this visual effect:

> The effect to the beholder is the gradual and imperceptible transition of the one scene into the other. If the reader will be so kind as to suppose that his two eyes represented the magic lanterns, and will close one eye first, and then gently lift the lid while he shuts down that of the other, he will obtain a perfect idea of the dissolving mechanism.[32]

Contrarily, the passage selected to exemplify the above reviewer's account of reading Alice suggests that existing on the cusp between illusion and reality more closely resembles a nightmarish threat to self than an ultimately normative indulgence in a waking dream. In this well-known scene Alice tearfully struggles to hold onto the shreds of rational explanation in the face of Tweedledee and Tweedledum's insistent dismantling of the divide between reality and illusion:

> 'He's dreaming now,' said Tweedledee: 'and what do you think he's dreaming about?'
>
> Alice said 'Nobody can guess that.'
>
> 'Why, about *You!*' Tweedledee exclaimed, clapping his hands triumphantly. 'And if he left off dreaming about you, where do you suppose you'd be?'
>
> 'Where I am now, of course,' said Alice.
>
> 'Not you!' Tweedledee retorted contemptuously. 'You'd be nowhere. Why, you're only a sort of thing in his dream!'
>
> . . .
>
> 'Well, its no use *your* talking about waking him,' said Tweedledum, 'when you're only one of the things in his dream. You know very well you're not real.'
>
> 'I *am* real!' said Alice, and began to cry.
>
> 'You won't make yourself a bit realer by crying,' Tweedledee remarked: 'there is nothing to cry about.'
>
> 'If I wasn't real,' Alice said – half-laughing through her tears, it all seemed so ridiculous – 'I shouldn't be able to cry.'
>
> 'I hope you don't suppose those are *real* tears?' Tweedledum interrupted in a tone of real contempt.
>
> 'I know they're talking nonsense,' Alice thought to herself: 'and it's foolish to cry about it.' (168)

The question of what Alice learns from such exchanges in both *Alice's Adventures* and *Through the Looking-Glass* continues to exercise critics. Jennifer Geer, for example, argues that the interplay between fantasy and didacticism in such scenes arrests Alice in a relentless and inescapable discursive feedback loop.[33]

A few pages after the above passage, Carroll breaks the frame with Alice's own conscious return to the scene of Tweedledum and Tweedledee's absurd inquisition, but her observation that 'she had never seen such a fuss made about anything in her life' is hardly enlightening (170). This obfuscatory reading backwards into Wonderland also recalls the final sequence of *Alice's Adventures* where Alice runs off carelessly remarking upon 'what a wonderful dream it had been', leaving her sister to retrospectively reduce the strange figures of Wonderland into the superficial affects of external sensory stimuli and thus return Alice to the developmental narrative of Victorian domestic ideology:

> Lastly, she pictured to herself how this same little sister of hers would, in the after-time, be herself a grown woman; and how she would keep, through all her riper years, the simple and loving heart of her childhood; and how she would gather about her other little children, and make *their* eyes bright and eager with many a strange tale, perhaps even with the dream of Wonderland

of long ago; and how she would feel with all their simple sorrows, and find a pleasure in all their simple joys, remembering her own child-life, and happy summer days. (111)[34]

Alice's 'after-time' is suffused with affective images of empathic maternal nurture and the passive mediation of 'simple' tales of wonder that serve as an antidote to the inexorable linearity and competition of the outside world. Action and curiosity are a thing of the past, a distant memory of an alternate reality. Carroll's stress on making 'eyes bright and eager' portrays reading Alice as an intimate interactive performance between storyteller and audience, with Alice herself functioning as an illuminative device giving life and sequence to the images that play across the surface of her mind. But, of course, this reading is easily undone by the fact that Alice escapes her sister's didactic interpretation of her dream. This version of the ending effectively has it both ways: critique masquerading as convention.

Mediating Dreams

Carroll consistently presents the reader with an image of Alice on the cusp of dissolving into another form, to quote the poem that concludes *Through The Looking-Glass*:

> Still she haunts me, phantomwise,
> Alice moving under skies (245)

Like Charles Kingsley's *Water Babies*, Carroll embraces the potential illumination that strategic omission offers, to quote Kingsley: 'It is not good for little boys to be told everything, and never be forced to use their wits.'[35] John Reichertz argues that this embrace of elusive form is continuous with Carroll's systematic inversion of the moral truisms of two traditional children's literary genres – the upside-down book and looking-glass tales and verse, such as the series *The Laughable Looking Glass for Little Folks*, published by one of the more prominent Victorian publishers of moveable and interactive books, Dean and Sons.[36] Notably the cover features a mother holding a baby up to a mirror, foreshadowing the ensuing comically didactic use of various mirror tropes featured within, as well as Carroll's own parodic use of the same scenario when Alice confronts her unruly kitten with its 'sulky' reflection in *Through the Looking-Glass*. Whether these playful anachronisms are incidental or intentional they are indicative of Carroll's satirically syncretic fusion of familiar didactic devices with the visual effects of popular illustrative media. Carroll coined a term to encapsulate this syncretic a-chronology in relation to the writing of *Sylvie and Bruno* – 'litter-ature', which consisted of the gathering together of fragments, 'random flashes of thought', sometimes traceable to 'books one was reading', sometimes 'struck out of the "flint" of one's own mind by the "steel" of a friend's chance remarks'.[37] The Alice books, according to Carroll's essay 'Alice on Stage', were 'made up almost wholly of bits and scrap, single ideas which came of themselves'.[38]

Isobel Armstrong's recent reading of Carroll's rhetorical play with various optical devices and tropes captures the technological encoding of this associative litter.[39] In *Through the Looking Glass*, the train guard runs his eye over the offending ticketless Alice 'first through a telescope, then through a microscope, and then through an opera-glass' before pronouncing 'You're travelling the wrong way' (150). Armstrong expands the referential scope of this scene:

> When Carroll's guard tries out different forms of prosthetic optical instruments, the farcical allusion is to the manifold types of lens available at the time, the monocular lens of the microscope, telescope, kaleidoscope, the binocular lens of the opera glass and stereoscope, all of which created different ways of seeing. (Three different Alices appear through the three instruments.) (317)

Tenniel's illustration reinforces this play with multiple versions of Alice. Obscured by shadow the guard leans into the carriage, his face covered by a pair of opera glasses pointed at the illuminated figure of Alice sitting demurely across from the gentleman dressed in white paper. The goat that participates in the subsequent dialogue is depicted in silhouette in the shadowy foreground of the image. The effect is of an image in the process of dissolving into something else. The goat seems to be disappearing as he speaks and the beetle who is meant to be there is impossible to detect amidst the dissolving lines of the illustration:

> A Goat, that was sitting next to the gentleman in white, shut his eye and said in a loud voice, 'She ought to know her way to the ticket-office, even if she doesn't know her alphabet!'
>
> There was a Beetle sitting next to the Goat (it was a very queer carriage-full of passengers altogether), and, as the rule seemed to be that they should all speak in turn, *he* went on with 'She'll have to go back from here as luggage!'
>
> Alice couldn't see who was sitting beyond the Beetle, but a hoarse voice spoke next. 'Change engines –' it said, and there it choked and was obliged to leave off.
>
> 'It sounds like a horse,' Alice thought to herself. And an extremely small voice, close to her ear, said 'You might make a joke on that – something about "horse" and "hoarse", you know.'

> Then a very gentle voice in the distance said, 'She must be labelled "lass with care", you know – ,' (150)

Expanding the scope of the visual analogy further still, Armstrong describes the spatial distortion generated by the attempt to visualise Carroll's description of Alice's struggle to bring her strange co-travellers into focus as analogous to the illusionistic experience of depth generated by the stereoscope:

> Scale retreats, the miniscule and gigantesque become incomparable: a goat and a beetle inhabit Alice's railway carriage on equal spatial terms ... Stereoscopic images 'rise up' from a surface, 'spring' into being, 'start forth', instantly start into all the roundness and solidity of life. (318)

Armstrong's stereoscopic analogy captures the animating compulsion of Carroll's incorporation of visual media of various kinds into his affective repertoire, but I would suggest that it is the material form of the page itself that draws the infinite regress of multiply generated Alices back into focus. Either way, the reader can never escape the technology of mediation. The self-conscious relay between image and text serves as a palpable reminder of the constructed nature of perception. Alice may not be able to trust what she sees, but underlying the cognitive dissonance this inspires is a reassuringly 'gentle' voice, seemingly of human derivation, given the scale of the font (in contrast to the type used for the voices of the looking-glass insects), ensuring her safe passage and the transience of the scene itself, which melts away as quickly as it appeared a few pages earlier. Carroll's loosely connected illuminated fragments and Tenniel's image are intentionally elusive and incomplete. They draw the reader back and forth across the page and in and out of visual fields and temporalities in search of answers in the process of mounting an implicit critique of the possibility of the transparent access to truth or knowledge that the technologies of useful knowledge – telescopes, microscopes, stereoscopes, binoculars, dissolving views – promised.

In typical Carroll-style double-sense, Wonderland is constructed as transcending the mechanical verities offered by the technological illumination on which it simultaneously depends. Likewise, Alice appears unchanged, despite her various struggles to derive sense and sequence from her encounters with the fractious inhabitants of Wonderland. As Susan Sherer observes, 'for a narrative that thematises motion, Alice's psychical growth remains disturbingly static'.[40] Ultimately she learns nothing from her adventures. Carroll's dizzying spatial transitions effectively slow down time, keeping Alice in a state of temporal arrest.[41] As the notoriously elusive dissolving Cheshire Cat points out in yet another satirically catechistic dialogue:

'Would you tell me, please, which way I ought to go from here?'
  'That depends a good deal on where you want to get to,' said the Cat.
  'I don't much care where —.' said Alice.
  'Then it doesn't matter which way you go,' said the Cat.
  '— so long as I get *somewhere*,' Alice added as an explanation.
  'Oh, you're sure to do that,' said the Cat, 'if you only walk long enough.'
(56)

According to Simon During, this scene and the subsequent appearance of the floating head of the Cheshire Cat were directly inspired by the ghost illusion produced by Dr Pepper at the Royal Polytechnic.[42] While there is no correspondence referencing this inspiration, other than Carroll's record of regular visits, this broader media context only serves to reinforce Carroll's complex engagement with the epistemological paradigms of rational recreation and useful knowledge with which the magic lantern and its optical effects were synonymous. Alice's inertia in the face of the Cheshire Cat's questioning emphasises the irrelevance of the teleological drive of will or desire to Carroll's plot. Just as it does not matter where or for how long Alice walks, it is equally irrelevant whether she is paying attention to the meaning of what she has experienced or not.

Distraction is simply claimed as the norm as Alice dreamily speculates on the likely reappearance of the Cheshire Cat before wandering off to see the March Hare. Disruptive narrative transitions, Carroll's visual experimentation with typographical inversions and scale, Tenniel's illustrative recapitulations, and recursive elliptical dialogue combine to impede linear progression by juxtaposing a series of temporally discrete visual moments. Correspondingly, the act of reading is characterised by periods of short duration that create just enough cognitive dissonance to draw the reader's eye backwards and forwards through the text again in the hope of putting all the pieces together in a legible sequence. Consistent with these oscillating movements, repeat reading is explicitly recommended in Carroll's various letters to his 'Child readers' (111). Even more conveniently, in his preface to yet another edition, repeat reading slips into repeat purchases as part of a characteristically detailed account of the literal machinery of book production. The preface informs potential consumers that 'fresh electrotypes have been taken from the wood-blocks . . . and the whole book has been set up afresh with new type', before somewhat defensively assuring that, if 'the artistic qualities of this re-issue fall short, in any particular, of those possessed of the original issue, it will not be for want of painstaking on the part of author, publisher, or printer.'[43]

Networked Minds

Although Carroll was a very peripheral member of the Society for Psychical Research, his name, which appears in the list of foundational members published in *Phantasms of the Living*, a seminal collaborative study of psychical phenomena penned by Frederic W. H. Myers, Edmund Gurney, and Frank Podmore, locates him in a vigorous intellectual network that shared his abiding interest in dreams and the mysteries of inspired communication between minds and within his own.[44] Often, harking back to the Romantic psychology of inspiration of William Wordsworth and Samuel Taylor Coleridge, Carroll described his writing process as an involuntary impulse or unconscious process that randomly materialises before his eyes:

> I jotted down, at odd moments, all sorts of odd ideas, and fragments of dialogue, that occurred to me – who knows how? – with a transitory suddenness that left me no choice but either to record them then and there, or to abandon them to oblivion . . . they had also a way of occurring of their own, *a propos* of nothing – specimens of that hopelessly illogical phenomenon, 'an effect without a cause.' Such, for example, was the last line of *The Hunting of the Snark*, which came into my head . . . quite suddenly, during a solitary walk; and such, again, have been passages, which occurred in *dreams*, and which I cannot trace to any antecedent cause whatever.[45]

Carroll also refers to 'thought–reading' in his correspondence, speculating in a letter to his friend James Langton Clarke that all 'seems to point to the existence of a natural force, allied to electricity and nerve-force, by which brain can act on brain'. On that day, he continues enthusiastically, such phenomena

> shall be classed among the known natural forces, and its laws tabulated, and when the scientific sceptics, who always shut their eyes, till the last moment, to any evidence that seems to point beyond materialism, will have to accept it as a proved fact.[46]

Carroll's electrical and neural metaphors in the above letter resonate with Alexander von Humboldt's suggestive name for telegraphy, 'wiring thoughts', with its assumed analogy between psychological and technological networks.[47] This implicit likeness complicates Carroll's drive to achieve a form of 'natural' or spiritual communication beyond the limits of the material. As Laura Otis argues, distinctions between organic and technological systems grew increasingly problematic in the nineteenth century. 'No mind', she contends, 'can be abstracted from the information system that feeds it' (3). Rather than 'passively receiving data', she continues, the mind actively 'controls the circuits that monitor its own environment' (3). Nerves, according to Otis, are a medial apparatus that performs the same functions as 'technological communications devices', and can, as a consequence, 'be studied with the same scientific methods' (3). Carroll, as the above letter's stress on 'tabulated' systematic knowledge of the mind's powers of communication suggests, agreed that the answer lay in the application of scientific methods to questions of mind and technology. He also, as the Alice books exemplify, invoked technological analogies to capture the phantasmagoric dynamism of dream-thought and the powers of imaginative process. Nevertheless, he retained, along with his fellow members of the Society for Psychical Research, a theological sense of mind that coexisted quite comfortably alongside his enthusiastic embrace of modern scientific method and mathematical theory.

Carroll shared Myers's belief that, while much had been revealed by physiological inquiries into 'the neural side of our mental processes, and the relation of cerebral phenomena to their accompanying emotion or thought', the human mind could not be reduced to a mechanical process.[48] Arguing against T. H. Huxley, Herbert Spencer and others, Myers insisted that human beings were not physiological automata. Our consciousness, he contended vigorously, is not 'a mere superadded phenomenon – a mere concomitant of some special intensity of cerebral action, with no basis beyond or apart from the molecular commotion of the brain' (1:xl). Carroll concurred, some Christian beliefs, such as the existence of God and Free Will, he suggested, 'are what could be called in Science "Axioms"'.[49] Carroll also shared Myers's interest in the mind's capacity to experience 'various psychical states, with varying degrees of consciousness', including an eerie state in which one may witness the appearance of supernatural beings and a trance-like or somnambulistic state in which the 'immaterial essence' of the unconscious person could migrate into other worlds or minds.[50] Carroll's rhetoric here echoes the contemporary parlance of hypnotism, which privileged insights into the nature of consciousness garnered from somnambulistic states. Such echoes exemplify how integral the discursive networks of psychical research became to his more mature speculations on the mind's capacity to move into the space of other worlds and minds, while also revealing the continuities between these later ideas of inter-psychical migration and his earlier conception of the communicative potential of his dream story of Alice moving beyond the materiality of print and entering into the streams of consciousness of the child reader.

Invoking the analogy of 'a partially illuminated body', Myers suggested that the privileging of physiology obscures the subtle traces of psychic residue that can be brought to light by hypnotically induced somnambulism (1:xli). Hypnotism provides the

> handle which turns the mechanism of our being . . . a mode of shifting the threshold of consciousness which is a dislocation as violent as madness, a submergence as pervasive as sleep, and yet is waking sanity; . . . The prime value of the hypnotic trance lies not in what it inhibits, but in what it reveals; not in the occlusion of the avenues of peripheral stimulus, but in the emergence of unnoted sensibilities, nay, perhaps even in the manifestation of new and centrally-initiated powers. (1:xliii)

Myers, like precursors such as Frances Power Cobbe and George Henry Lewes, identifies the revelation of the subliminal aspects of the self with the abeyance of will. The advantage of hypnotism was that it initiates an 'eclipse of normal consciousness which can be repeated at will', not unlike the infinite repetitions of mechanical reproduction that powered the circuitry of the late nineteenth-century literary culture in which Carroll's dreams of Alice circulated (1:xliii). Moreover, by simulating the unconscious liberty of the dream, the machinery of hypnosis revealed an image of the subliminal layers of the mind, which like a photographic record supplants and corrects the fallacies and artificial displacements of normal memory. Ideally, when confronted with the 'latent and delicate capacities of which his ordinary conscious self' has hitherto been oblivious, hypnotic subjects could shape the disparate elements of their personality into a coherent biography; a therapeutic forensic process which teaches, to invoke Myers's moralising rhetoric, that by 'self-reverence, self-knowledge, self control man may become the ruler of his own spirit and the fashioner of his own fate'.[51]

There are considerable parallels between Myers's underlying stress on coherence and control and the therapeutic narrative of psychoanalysis, which is hardly surprising given Freud's acknowledged debt to English dream theory.[52] Myers, like Freud, prioritises the reformation of a coherent self through a process of working through the unconscious layers of dream-life. Where Myers diverges from Freud, however, is in his passionate adherence to the transcendence of matter, which is also the point at which Myers's work converges with Carroll's vision of both alternative states of mind and the transcendent communicative power of Alice to move her readers to project themselves into the unfettered reverie of Wonderland. Both Myers and Carroll shared a very particular Victorian sense of networked minds, which has far more in common with mid-century dream theory, than Freud's seminal dream work.

Frances Power Cobbe, writing on 'Dreams, Illustrations of Involuntary Cerebration' in 1871, described 'the network of the dream' as a series of waves or rhythms connecting streams of consciousness and chains:

> Dreams are to our waking thoughts much like echoes to music; but their reverberations are so partial, so varied, so complex, that it is almost in vain we seek among the notes of consciousness for the echoes of the dream. If we could by any means ascertain on what principle our dreams for a given night are arranged, and why one idea more than another furnishes their cue, it would be comparatively easy to follow out the chain of associations by which they unroll themselves afterwards; and to note the singular ease and delicacy whereby subordinate topics, recently wafted across our minds, are seized and woven into the network of the dream.[53]

Acoustic metaphors here transform the mind into a resonant space filled with the competing strains of conscious and unconscious memory randomly assimilated by the dream into associative chains and networks.

Cobbe was a prominent Victorian feminist, who shared Carroll's passionate belief in anti-vivisectionism.[54] Her writing on dreams drew, albeit disputatiously, on the work of her friend and correspondent William Carpenter, whose *Principles of Mental Physiology*, which Carroll owned, would become a standard textbook in the latter decades of the nineteenth century.[55] Cobbe's enduring significance, however, lies in her role as a generalist, synthesiser and mediator of ideas, who moved freely between high and popular journalism and across genres and discourses. More particularly in the context of Carroll's interest in the dream as a transcendent medium, Cobbe pointedly differentiated her account of unconscious cerebration and dream phenomena from Carpenter's on theological grounds. She insisted in her typically forthright style on theistic notions of free will and moral responsibility. For this reason, her work captures the complex interplay between theological and scientific explanations of dreams and illuminatingly parallels Carroll's analogous calibration of spiritual and material concepts of mind and media.

William Carpenter seminally defined unconscious cerebration as encompassing any cognitive process that took place while the will was suspended. He concluded that a large part of our intellectual activity, ranging from the imaginative to the rational, was essentially automatic, a reflex or habitual response. Keenly aware of the accusations of materialism such conclusions might attract, Carpenter was quick to normalise such a proposition as continuous with a long Metaphysical tradition extending back to Liebnitz, which had sought to explain the ways the mind achieves quite elaborate intellectual results '*without any consciousness* on our own parts'.[56] Carpenter argued that it was hardly controversial to suggest that 'the Mind may undergo modifications, sometimes of very considerable importance, without being itself conscious of the process, until its *results* present themselves to the consciousness, in the new ideas, or new combinations of ideas, which the process has evolved' (515).

Carpenter's first example of this phenomenon involves the way the mind struggles and fails to consciously recollect a name, phrase or occurrence, only to find a short time later, or after awakening from a profound sleep, that the elusive memory flashes into consciousness. While implicitly drawing on Henry Holland, to whom he dedicates the volume – Holland argued that memory worked like a photograph, to quote Jenny Bourne Taylor's nice formulation, 'impressed on the brain to be developed after a lapse of time'[57] – Carpenter chose to cite Frances Power Cobbe's essay on unconscious cerebration to clarify his argument about the latent associative streams that provide the means of comprehending the self as a temporally continuous entity. Carpenter admired Cobbe's 'graphic sketches' (526) of everyday exempla of unconscious activity, as he called them, such as forgetting a particular word or line of poetry only to remember it hours later: 'as if we were possessed of an obedient secretary or librarian, whom we could order to hunt up a missing document, or turn out a word in a dictionary, while we amused ourselves with something else'.[58] He also cited Cobbe's evocations of the unconscious dimensions of reading and writing, when the words form on the page automatically while the mind is absorbed in thought, or when one reads aloud automatically 'taking in the appearance and proper sound of each word', while 'all the time we are not thinking of these matters . . . but of the argument of the author; or picturing the scene he describes' (526).

Speaking and thinking, or reading and writing as if in a dream are, according to both Carpenter and Cobbe, continuous with sustained processes of thought – particularly creative thought – as the mind moves between waking and sleeping states. Carpenter, for example, cites Elizabeth Gaskell on Charlotte Brontë's pre-emptive manipulation of her sleeping mind to unblock her imagination:

> Whenever she had to describe anything which had not fallen within her own experience, it was her habit 'to think of it intently many and many a night before falling to sleep, wondering what it was like, or how it would be'; till at length, sometimes after the progress of her story had been arrested at this one point for weeks, she wakened up in the morning with all clear before her, as if she had in reality gone through the experience, and then could describe it word for word as it had happened.[59]

Cobbe concurred with Carpenter's account of the creative cognition facilitated by sleep, transforming her illustrative figure of the secretary or librarian expeditiously hunting up the missing documents that elude our waking thoughts into a novelist or painter who creates 'the nightly miracles of unconscious cerebration':

> But our Familiar is a great deal more than a walking dictionary, a housemaid, a *valet de place*, or a barrel-organ man. He is a novelist who can spin more romances than Dumas, a dramatist who composes more plays than ever did Lope de Vega, a painter who excels equally well in figures, landscapes, cattle, sea-pieces, smiling bits of *genre* and the most terrific conceptions of horror and torture. Of course, like other artists, he can only reproduce, develop, combine what he has actually experienced or read or heard of. But the enormous versatility and inexhaustible profusion with which he furnishes us with fresh pictures for our galleries, and new stories every night from his lending library, would be deemed the greatest of miracles, were it not the commonest of facts. (27)

Cobbe relishes the idea of the dream as a space of unfettered invention, where even the most prosaic mind can reproduce phantasmagoric versions of childhood memories with the creative inspiration of a Dumas, Brontë or Coleridge.

Carroll's Alice enacts a similar transformation of the banal systematic knowledge of conscious thought into the unconscious creative chaos of the dream. As Alice falls deeper and deeper in to Wonderland, numbers, names and places are unmoored from their stable reference points. Out of sequence and out of place, she can no longer remember where to put them. 'I'll try if I know all the things I used to know', her dream self decides, 'Let me see: four times five is twelve, and four times six is thirteen, and four times seven is – oh dear! I shall never get to twenty at that rate!' (19). Comforting herself that 'the Multiplication-Table doesn't signify' in this world, she moves on to geography, 'London is the capital of Paris, and Paris is the capital of Rome, and Rome – no, *that's* all wrong, I'm certain!' (19). As the grounds of her conscious self dissolve into thin air, like a Cheshire Cat Alice asks: 'Who am I, then?' – a question that Carroll leaves unanswered, because it is ultimately secondary to the versatile profusion and combinatory power of the images that the dream generates in both her and the reader's mind (19).

One of the vital features of the dream, one which Cobbe, Carpenter, Lewes and Myers emphasised, was that everyone dreams, transforming the minutiae of their lives into potentially phantasmagoric tableaux. Deferring to Henry Holland on this matter, Carpenter concluded that sleep could not be 'distinctly differentiated' from waking activity, consisting instead of 'a gradational series of states, intermediate between

that of complete possession of the mental faculties, and that of complete
suspension of all psychical action' (578–9). Like Cobbe, whom he cites
in this context, Carpenter characterises the dream state as one in which
volition and moral judgement are suspended, while everyday thoughts
and experiences are sustained:

> We have in dreams, as Miss Cobbe remarks … a manifestation of that
> 'myth-making' tendency of the human mind, which is continually 'transmut-
> ing sentiments into ideas.' Even during the waking state, our minds are ever
> at work of this sort, 'giving to airy nothing' (or at least to what is merely a
> subjective feeling) 'a local habitation and a name.' The automatic action of
> the Brain during sleep proceeds on the same track. Our sentiments of love,
> hate, fear, anxiety, are each one of them the fertile source of a whole series of
> illustrative dreams … (585)

Carpenter and Cobbe's agreed interpretation of dreams as symptoms
of the 'myth-making' tendency of the human mind refers to the distortive effects of the dream as an illustrative embellishment, 'like those of
M. Doré to the page of life which we have turned the day before'.[60]

Carpenter concurred with Cobbe that while dreams may involve
intense cerebral activity, it is of an entirely automatic kind with only
a tenuous connection to 'the consciousness of the Ego': 'There can be
no doubt that the materials of our dreams are often furnished by the
"traces" left upon the brain by occurrences long since past, which
have completely faded-out of the *conscious* memory' (587). It would
be a mistake however, according to Cobbe, to accord these memory
traces with too much significance, given that this interplay between
conscious and unconscious memory mirrors the ordinary activities of
unconscious cerebration – such as walking, reading, writing, sewing,
playing and rudimentary comprehension. Indeed the close affinity
between the unconscious aspects of waking life and dream states serves
as a catalyst for Cobbe's polemical concluding argument for the necessary balance between material or physiological and spiritual aspects
required to define the self as something more than mechanical matter.
Distinguishing her observations from 'a certain loose and popular way
of speaking' that 'our brains are ourselves', Cobbe clarifies that the brain
generates dreams, like the heart beats, involuntarily, both are, therefore,
'organs of our frame, but not of our Selves' (36).

Unleashed from the constraints of will, 'the myth-creating power
of the human mind' takes control, Cobbe argues in her 'Dreams as
Illustrations', transforming past thoughts, sentiments, as well as present
sensations into 'ingenious fables explanatory of the phenomena around
us' (513). She suggests against the tendency of her contemporaries to
ascribe myth creation to the superstitious irrationality of primitive

cultures, suggesting instead that the 'instinct' to mythologise exerts a profound influence over the ways in which the conscious self dramatises otherwise unexceptional events, selectively embellishing and generalising the significance of certain memories over others (513):

> At the very least half our dreams (unless I greatly err) are nothing else than myths formed by unconscious cerebration on the same approved principles, whereby Greece and India and Scandinavia gave to us the stories which we were once pleased to set apart as 'mythology' proper. Have we not here, then, evidence that there is a real law of the human mind causing us constantly to compose ingenious fables explanatory of the phenomena around us . . . (513)

Cobbe's characterisation of this myth-making tendency as a social instinct is indicative not only of her alignment with Carpenter, but also Henry Holland, Alexander Bain, George Henry Lewes and Herbert Spencer, all of whom, in their very different ways were concerned with the ways in which acquired habits of thought and feeling evolved over time. Spencer in both 1855 and 1870 editions of the *Principles of Psychology*, which Carroll also owned, defined memory as an organised instinct, and correspondingly, instinct as a form of incipient memory that needed to be understood on both phylogenetic and ontogenetic levels.[61] Henry Holland, whose *Chapters on Mental Philosophy* also graced Carroll's shelves, shared Bain and Carpenter's interest in the relationship between will, habit-formation and instinctive or reflexive cerebration. Holland variously described mental experience as a paradoxical 'series of acts and states', or a 'wide and mixed current, in which, various sensations, thoughts, emotions and volitions' coalesce or coexist, drawing either consciously or unconsciously on the knowledge of a 'thousand memories of the past'.[62]

These 'wide and mixed' currents, as Holland termed them, networked minds through neural circuitry and offer an alternative model of communication that aligns with Carroll's ambitions for the medial powers of Alice's dream. Circulating in an infinitely phantasmagoric feedback loop, images of Alice exceeded even Carroll's desires, moving from his own fastidiously conceived dissolving views through an endless series of incarnations in multiple minds and media. Carroll's desire to communicate through Alice, in this sense, is both of its time and prescient of a definitely modern literary desire for communication. Claiming such a 'desire for communication' as a specific historical facet of literary modernism, Mark Goble has argued that this desire emerges 'not just as a response to the power of media technologies in the twentieth century, but as a way of insisting that this power is already modernism's own'.[63] I. A. Richards, Goble suggests, typifies these claims for the communicative power of a certain kind of literary modernism. 'Communication', I. A. Richards wrote in 1926,

> takes place when one mind so acts upon its environment that another mind is influenced, and in that other mind an experience occurs which is like the experience in the first mind, and is caused in part by that experience.[64]

Yet, as this chapter has demonstrated, this desire is not unique to literary modernism. A very similar drive to communicate informs Carroll's insistence on the literary imagination as the ultimate transcendent medium in an increasingly complex media landscape.

The following chapter sustains this focus on the desire for communication. Conforming to the pattern of this and the previous chapters, the ensuing chapter reads the work of late nineteenth-century writers, such as George Sims, whose series *The Social Kaleidoscope*, transformed scenes of London life into a disorientating series of flicker effects, alongside the work of psychologists, such as James Sully, who were contemporaneously examining the ways in which the modern mind could filter out the sensual and technological inundation of urban life. Sims, like many of his contemporaries, found an endless source of inspiration in the idea of a technologically reproducible moving image. Moving from kaleidoscopic to cinematographic analogies, his work provides a vital bridge between the dissolving views of the mid-nineteenth-century media landscape and the moving images that Cecil Hepworth and Robert Paul would ultimately transform into their seminal early cinematic adaptations of Carroll and Dickens's literary classics.

Notes

1. Deleuze, *The Logic of Sense*, pp. 181–5.
2. Carroll, *Alice's Adventures in Wonderland and Through the Looking-Glass and what Alice found there*, p. 94. Further references will be in the body of the text.
3. Rose, *Mourning Becomes the Law: Philosophy and Representation*, p. 126.
4. Benjamin, 'The Work of Art in the Age of Mechanical Reproduction', in *Illuminations*, p. 237.
5. These works are listed in *Lewis Carroll's Library: A Facsimile Edition of the catalogue of the auction sale following C. L. Dodgson's death in 1898, with facsimiles of three subsequent booksellers' catalogues offering books from Dodgson's library*. In the interests of consistency I use Lewis Carroll throughout rather than alternating between Charles Dodgson and Lewis Carroll depending on whether authorship refers to private correspondence, published texts or academic works.

6. Thomas, *Dreams of Authority: Freud and the Fictions of the Unconscious*, p. 57.
7. Thomas, *Dreams of Authority*, p. 57.
8. Lewes, *The Physiology of Common Life*, vol. 2, pp. 63, 66.
9. Lewes, vol. 2, *The Physiology of Common Life*, p. 371. The italics are Lewes's.
10. Kittler, *Gramophone, Film, Typewriter*, p. 151.
11. Reprinted in Carroll, *Alice's Adventures in Wonderland and Through the Looking-Glass*, p. 248.
12. Bolter and Grusin, *Remediation: Understanding New Media*, p. 5.
13. Lewis Carroll, diary entry for 11 August 1890, cited in Cohen, *Lewis Carroll: A Biography*, p. 289. The italics are Carroll's.
14. Cohen, *Lewis Carroll: A Biography*, p. 283.
15. Doane, *The Emergence of Cinematic Time: Modernity, Contingency, The Archive*, p. 4.
16. Lewis Carroll, 18 April 1876, *The Diaries of Lewis Carroll*, vol. 1, p. 352.
17. 'Theatres', *The Times* (17 June 1876), p. 587. Another positive notice appeared in *The Times* (17 August 1876), p. 175.
18. Lewis Carroll to Alexander Macmillan, 1 March 1876, *Lewis Carroll and the House of Macmillan*, p. 122. The italics are Carroll's. Carroll mentions that an 'application was made in January 1875 by W. L. Breare, Sun Lane, Burley-in-Wharfdale, Leeds' in his 1 March 1876 letter to Alexander Macmillan and follows up in a letter to Macmillan dated 17 March 1876, but it appears after some chasing up by Macmillan that this particular lantern slide set did not eventuate.
19. Carroll, 'To all Child-readers of "Alice's Adventures in Wonderland"'. This was printed separately as a miniature pamphlet in December 1871 and inserted in the first edition of *Through the Looking-Glass* (December 1871) and in the 1872 edition of *Alice in Wonderland*. It is reprinted in Carroll, *Alice's Adventures in Wonderland and Through the Looking-Glass*, p. 278. Further references to this pamphlet will be in the body of the text.
20. Carroll listed the press notices for *Alice's Adventures in Wonderland* opposite the diary entry for 2 October 1864; see also Cripps's survey of these notices in '*Alice* and the Reviewers', pp. 33–48.
21. Rev., *The Times* (26 December 1865), p. 5.
22. Benjamin, 'The Work of Art in the Age of Mechanical Reproduction' in *Illuminations*, p. 217.
23. '*Alice's Adventures in Wonderland*. By Lewis Carroll', *Athenaeum* (16 December 1865), p. 844.
24. Henry Kingsley noted the review in a letter to his brother Charles Kingsley: 'The literary ability of *The Scotsman* I really *cannot* rank high with regard to works of fiction and fancy: who could trust a paper which said that the letter-press of *Alice's Adventures* was pointless balderdash!' This letter is cited in Ellis, *Henry Kingsley, 1830–1876*, p. 75.
25. '*Alice's Adventures in Wonderland*', *The Scotsman* (22 December 1866), p. 5.
26. Cited in Cripps, '*Alice* and the Reviewers', p. 37. *Aunt Judy's Magazine* (May 1866–October 1885) was a monthly magazine edited by Mrs Alfred Gatty.

27. Rev., *The Sunderland Herald* (25 May 1866), p. 2.
28. Dames provides an extensive account of licensed reverie as integral to the training of young minds in the context of industrialised reading practices in *The Physiology of the Novel: Reading, Neural Science, and the Form of Victorian Fiction*, pp. 1–22.
29. Ellis, *Books in Victorian Elementary Schools*, p. 24.
30. 'Through the Looking Glass', *The Spectator* (30 December 1871), p. 1608.
31. Ferriar, MD, *An Essay Towards the Study of Apparitions*.
32. 'Optical Magic of Our Age', *Chambers's Edinburgh Journal* 278 (April 1849), p. 260.
33. Geer, '"All sorts of pitfalls and surprises": Competing Views of Idealized Girlhood in Lewis Carroll's *Alice* Books', *Children's Literature* 31 (2003), pp. 1–24.
34. Hancher reads the concluding scene of *Alice's Adventures* in the context of contemporary Victorian dream theory in 'Alice's Audiences', in *Romanticism and Children's Literature in Nineteenth-Century England*, pp. 190–207.
35. Kingsley, *The Water-Babies: A Fairy Tale for a Land Baby*, p. 190.
36. Newman and Friswell, *The Laughable Looking Glass for Little Folks*.
37. Carroll, Preface to *Sylvie and Bruno* (1889), p. 239.
38. Carroll, 'Alice on Stage', *The Theatre* 9:52 (April 1887), p. 181.
39. Armstrong, *Victorian Glassworlds*, p. 317.
40. Sherer, 'Secrecy and Autonomy in Lewis Carroll', *Philosophy and Literature* 20:1 (1996), p. 1.
41. The sexual connotations of this compulsion to arrest the growth of the pre-pubescent Alice have been discussed extensively. An exemplary recent study of this dynamic is Mavor's *Pleasures Taken: Performances of Sexuality and Loss in Victorian Photographs*.
42. During, *Modern Enchantments: The Cultural Power of Secular Magic*, p. 305.
43. Carroll, 'Preface to the Eighty-Sixth Thousand of the 6/- Edition', (Christmas 1896), reprinted in *Alice's Adventures in Wonderland and Through the Looking-Glass*, n. p.
44. Gurney, Myers, and Podmore, *Phantasms of the Living*, vol. 1, p. xii.
45. Carroll, Preface to *Sylvie and Bruno* (1889), pp. 239–40. The italics are Carroll's.
46. Letter to James Langton Clark, 4 December 1882, cited in Cohen, *Lewis Carroll: A Biography*, p. 369.
47. Cited in Otis, *Networking: Communicating with Bodies and Machines in the Nineteenth Century*, p. 1.
48. Gurney, Myers, and Podmore, *Phantasms of the Living*, vol. 1, p. xl.
49. Carroll, Letter to an Agnostic, 31 May 1897, cited in Cohen, *Lewis Carroll: A Biography*, p. 371.
50. Cited in Cohen, *Lewis Carroll: A Biography*, p. 369.
51. Myers, 'The subliminal consciousness: Chap 2, The mechanism of suggestion', *Proceedings of the Society for Psychical Research* 1 (1892), p. 355.
52. I have written about this elsewhere in Groth and Lusty, *Dreams and Modernity: A Cultural History*.
53. Cobbe, 'Dreams, as Illustrations of Unconscious Cerebration', p. 512.

This essay was also reprinted, along with 'Unconscious Cerebration. A Psychological Study', in Cobbe's *Darwinism in Morals and Other Essays*.

54. Caine provides a detailed account of Cobbe's seminal contribution to the history of Victorian feminism in *Victorian Feminists*, Chapter 4.

55. Carpenter, *Principles of Mental Physiology* [1874]. This was an expanded version of Carpenter's earlier studies of human physiology from the early 1850s which had established his reputation as a key theorist of unconscious cerebration.

56. Carpenter, *Principles of Mental Physiology*, p. 515. The italics in the above citations are Carpenter's.

57. Taylor, 'Forms and fallacies of memory in nineteenth-century psychology: Henry Holland, William Carpenter and Frances Power Cobbe', *Endeavour* 23:2 (1999), pp. 60–4.

58. Cobbe, 'Unconscious Cerebration. A Psychological Study', p. 25.

59. Elizabeth Gaskell, *Life*, p. 425; cited in Carpenter *Principles of Mental Physiology*, p. 535.

60. Cobbe, 'Unconscious Cerebration. A Psychological Study', p. 28.

61. Spencer, *Principles of Psychology*, pp. 554–64.

62. Holland, *Chapters on Mental Physiology*, pp. 48–50.

63. Goble, *Beautiful Circuits: Modernism and the Mediated Life*, p. 3.

64. Richards, 'A Theory of Communication', in *Principles of Literary Criticism* [1926], p. 177.

Chapter 6

Flickering Effects: George Robert Sims and the Psychology of the Moving Image

In the preface to his two-volume series on London Life, *The Social Kaleidoscope* (1881), the well-known late nineteenth-century social reformer and journalist George Robert Sims clarified his interest in the descriptive possibilities of kaleidoscopic vision:

> My purpose in these pages is not to strain metaphor, or to deal figuratively with important social subjects, but rather to describe truthfully and fearlessly the figure or shape of humanity which each turn of the Social Kaleidoscope offers for observation. Nay more than this. It will be my endeavour to trace it from the moment when the component parts are hurrying together, and to follow it down to the period when the atoms have disparted and the figure is destroyed.[1]

Rather than turning to photography, as so many of his contemporaries who were documenting urban life in the 1880s were doing, Sims found in the endless transformations of the kaleidoscope the ideal analogy for the perpetually moving scenes of London life. Like Charles Baudelaire's 'lover of Universal life', Sims embraced the kaleidoscope as a model of receptive consciousness, transforming an optical recreation commonly associated with derivative illusion into a revelatory device that illuminated the intimate details of everyday life in motion.[2]

The kaleidoscopic conceit was also conveniently expansive, freeing Sims from the demands of realistic description by literally shifting the focus to the dynamics of perception itself. How one saw the moving scenes of London was as important as the revelation of various social truths. Accordingly, *The Social Kaleidoscope* was composed of a series of vignettes that moved from sordid domestic interiors, to gin palaces and music halls, to street scenes and prison cells. In the process Sims' visually labile narration draws the reader into a disquieting convergence of diverse impressions with the aim of exposing the social inequities and injustices that threatened to fracture the progressive vision of urban reformers such as himself. Modern life demanded new ways of sensitising the eye to previously invisible aspects of urban life, Sims argued, a way of seeing that moved beyond the disinterested aestheticism of Baudelaire. Directing his audience to view the intimate details that flickered across their visual field as they walked down the street, Sims re-enacted the most ordinary of activities, from purchasing a new suit, ordering a drink at a local tavern, to lingering in front of a shop window.

Given Sims' predilection for essayistic bricolage, a popular child's toy invented in 1815 by David Brewster was the ideal descriptive device. Simple and accessible, the kaleidoscope's endless transformations captured the tension between chaos and order that Sims' journalism evoked:

> The kaleidoscope is an optical instrument which, by an arrangement of reflecting surfaces, presents to the eye a variety of colours and symmetrical forms. Turning it now this way and now that, the fragments of variously-coloured glass which it contains fall into a succession of peculiar figures, and we have a series of perfectly dissimilar pictures, the component parts of which are in every way the same. Substitute for the fragments of colour glass the many-hued virtues and vices, passions and peculiarities of mankind, and at every twist of the Social Kaleidoscope we get a glimpse of human nature in a varied aspect. While the arrangement of reflecting surfaces does for the glass atoms, the arrangement of surrounding circumstances forms for the attributes of humanity. It gives them a special form and a dominant colour, and unites them in a series of perfectly dissimilar pictures.[3]

Sims' idea of kaleidoscopic vision both registers the impact of the disorientation of modern life, and establishes a perceptual model that equates visual kinesis with stimulating an instructive emotional response. Differential movements are essential to the activation of the reader's attention according to Sims, an assumption that aligns with the influential psychologist Alexander Bain's contemporaneous account of the way the eye generates varying emotional responses to the perception of movement: 'A quick movement excites a different feeling from one that is slow; and we thence acquire graduated sensations, corresponding to degrees of speed up to a certain limit of nicety.'[4] These graduated sensations include the degrees of pleasure that the brain may derive from the muscular movements stimulated by the perception of different types of moving objects. Bain's research proved seminal to understanding how the perception of movement translated from the eye to the mind. Indeed, as Lynda Nead argues, Bain and his successor James Sully's work was the catalyst for a new psychological account of visual perception that 'was full of movement, both within the beholder and beyond; absolute rest was an empirical impossibility'.[5]

In addition to these psychological resonances, Sims' kaleidoscopic effects also contributed to a well-established vernacular of the moving image that dated back to the early decades of the century, when David Brewster's invention was still a novelty. Brewster himself noted the wonder and controversy engendered by the seemingly infinite patterns his optical device generated:

> This system of endless changes is one of the most extraordinary properties of the Kaleidoscope. With a number of loose objects, it is impossible to reproduce any figure which we have admired. When it is once lost, centuries may elapse before the same combination returns.[6]

From the beginning, to describe an event or phenomenon as kaleidoscopic was to evoke the idea of a continuous shifting visual field that never allowed the eye to rest, as I have argued in an earlier chapter, a 'movement-image' that tested the limits of verisimilitude and reflected the existential flux of modern life in Regency London.[7]

This chapter will locate the two-volume series of vignettes that comprise Sims' *The Social Kaleidoscope* in the context of a broader cultural analysis of the pervasive use of a new technological rhetoric of moving images in nineteenth-century accounts of London life, ranging from Charles Dickens's reflections on the process of capturing the dynamism of the modern city to Albert Smith's popular *Gavarni in London: Sketches of Life and Character* (1849) and culminating with the print remediation of one of Robert Paul's first urban flickers, 'The Prince's Derby' in the pages of the *Strand Magazine* in 1896. In these accounts kaleidoscopic and, later cinematographic, images are enlisted to communicate a distinctively modern sense of the mediated nature of modern life. To evoke Friedrich Kittler, this collective compulsion to describe the experience of mediation seems to register a dawning awareness that 'Media determine our situation, which – in spite of or because of it – deserves a description.'[8] Indeed Kittler attributes particular significance to writers in the period 1880–1920, describing their astonished reflections on 'gramophones, films, and typewriters' as 'a ghostly image of our present as future': 'Those early and seemingly harmless machines capable of storing and therefore separating sounds, sights, and writing ushered in a technologising of information that, in retrospect, paved the way for tomorrow's self-recursive stream of numbers' (xl).

Sims and his contemporaries shared a fascination with the idea of a perceptual process that transcended the circumscription of a single body and mind and encompassed the psychological and technological complexity of modern urban experience. Their collective embrace of technological metaphors to convey a distinctively modern psychological understanding of how the mind and eye process information, and how language works to mediate that process, is also consistent with the emerging psychological theories of George Henry Lewes, Alexander Bain and James Sully. While conceding that pictorial art can never convey the 'perfect sense of solidity' produced by the stereoscope, Sully, for example, described how inferences drawn from everyday life allowed the eye to conceive 'relations of depth or relief and solidity':

> If for example, on a carpet, wall-paper, or dress, bright lines are laid on a dark colour as ground, we easily imagine that they are advancing. The reason of this seems to be that in our daily experience advancing surfaces catch and reflect the light, whereas retiring surfaces are in shadow.[9]

Grounding his theory of the contingency of the perceptual process and how integral illusions are to everyday experience with references to David Brewster's *Letters on Natural Magic*, Sully insisted that 'optical illusions due to the reflection and refraction of light', such as those produced by the kaleidoscope, 'are not peculiar to the individual, but arise in all minds under precisely similar external conditions' (37).

Sims shared Sully's interest in the constitutive role illusion played in everyday perception. For Sims the awareness of perceptual aberration or illusion only enhanced the observer's attentiveness to their own perpetually shifting relationship to their immediate environment. Sims placed a premium on observing bodies in motion and simulating the ways in which fleeting impressions briefly converge in the urban observer's mind. Drawn together by a dynamic interplay of emotion, perception and imagination, this visual process played with the possibilities of expanding the act of reading into a three dimensional encounter and, correspondingly, releasing the perceptual process from static models of vision.

Kaleidoscopic Views

Sims' avowed debt to Dickens locates his work on the familiar divide between novelistic and journalistic description. In *Sketches by Boz* (1836) Dickens explicitly invoked the kaleidoscope to capture the endlessly changing faces and passing scenes one encounters riding on an omnibus through the streets of London: 'sameness there can never be. The passengers change as often in the course of one journey as the figures in a kaleidoscope, and though not so glittering, are far more amusing'.[10] Dickens's use of the kaleidoscopic analogy here is consistent with his reliance on explicitly sensational language to capture the attention of his readers. Visual and narrative technologies modulate the rhythms of a new mode of urban description designed to sensitise the reader to the presence of fugitive details. Figures continuously move across his visual field, summoning associations before disappearing, only to be replaced by another face, body, or scene that inspires further speculation and amusement. This elision of visual and literary effect is one that both Dickens and his peers identified as a distinctive characteristic of his work. Close to death, Dickens encapsulated his writing thus: 'I don't invent it – really I do not – *but see it*, and write it down.'[11] The act of composing is synonymous with the act of perception here, figures projected before the mind's eye are simply recorded and sequenced in a mystified act of authorial transcription – a belief that Catherine Gallagher and Stephen Greenblatt identify as a symptom of the role played by the nineteenth-century novel more generally, and Dickens's work in particular, in the representation of society 'through a series of imaginary projections and counterprojections', rather than as a static unified entity.[12] As George Henry Lewes observed two years after Dickens's death:

> When he imagined a street, a house, a room, a figure, he saw it not in the vague schematic way of ordinary imagination, but in the sharp definition of actual perception, all the salient details obtruding themselves on his attention. He, seeing it thus vividly, made us also see it.[13]

This concept of making the reader see the details of actual streets, houses, rooms and figures through the vivid descriptive force of narrative technique implicitly blurs the ontological distinction between the illusion of the real and the reality it represents. Fiction's illusion of the real is just as, if not more, real than the streets, houses, rooms and figures it represents precisely because it makes the act of perception an integral part of the narrative sequence.

This stress on the dynamics of visual effect in representations of modern urban life, however, predates what Deborah Epstein Nord describes as Dickens's pre-cinematic desire to 'turn the camera on' and keep it running 'hoping to capture movement, above all, and to show how a variety of types occupy the same urban space'.[14] As I discussed in Chapter 1, Pierce Egan's *Life in London* (1821) enlisted a similar proto-cinematic rhetoric to extol the insights to be gleaned from what he called a camera obscura view of the city with 'the invaluable advantages of SEEING and not being seen'.[15] The reader is then invited to look through a variegated lens at the rich complexity of everyday London life, to focus on details and illuminated fragments. Likewise, Lady Blessington's *The Magic Lantern; or Sketches of Scenes in the Metropolis* (1823) animated the mores and rites of the denizens of London, beginning with the epigraph:

My Magic Lantern holds to view,
Of fools, a crowd; of wise, but few.

Each chapter then proceeds in a similar style to Sims' *Social Kaleidoscope*, offering a progression of 'transparencies' in which imagination and perception blend. Kaleidoscopic images also mobilised Albert Smith's description of the descent of the Adelaide Gallery from a place of instructive entertainment to a dance hall in his popular series, *Gavarni in London: Sketches of Life and Character* (1849). Smith begins his essay by instructing his reader to 'raise your own eyes from the floating lumps of crystal you are so intently watching, and let us point out to you the persons who pass in this droll kaleidoscope of London life'. A list of 'city types' follows ranging from white collar workers, aristocratic dandies, two guardsmen in search of pleasure, a dancing barrister, 'a tribe of young litterateurs, making the visit on the strength of the "orders" of the journals with which they are connected', an array of shop boys, university men and 'provincial visitors' who all converge into a 'singular mass' that 'keeps moving round and round; and then the music begins again'.[16]

Later in the same volume, Smith offers a more evocative rendition of Regent Street, combining kaleidoscopic effects with allusions to the scrolling movements of the moving panorama:

> It is the beginning of the evening in the City . . . The flaring dusty thoroughfare is swarming with flashing equipages, and pouring crowds of gay pedestrians. The ample wooden pavement is divided into two long lines of moving vehicles. How they sweep gaudily on – a changing, shifting panorama of glittering panels and glancing wheels, and sleek-pacing horses, and over-powering footmen, and delicious peeps into the dim cushioned interiors, where the eye loses itself in half-seen, half-missed visions of fair faces and rich tresses, and reclining forms dressed in cool muslins, or lost in the massive folds of costly shawls . . . How it swarms with that continuous procession of gaily-dressed women and men. How, as you glance along it, the multitude – the shifting, rushing, rolling multitude – becomes a dazzling, puzzling, confounding chaos of faces and forms . . . – all jumbled up together – all mixing and blending – and all forming one confounding, bewildering, bewitching whole – which, as you contemplate it, makes the eye dazzle and the brain ache![17]

Like Egan, Blessington, Dickens and Sims, Smith's description reveals his drive to generate the sensation of movement in the reader's mind – an ambition that he literally translated into a novel technological form in his popular panoramic retelling of his own ascent of Mont Blanc, which drew unprecedented crowds to the Egyptian Hall in the early 1850s.[18] Sims, however, diverged from Smith in his alignment of urban description and social reform, an emphasis that paralleled the entrepreneurial activism of the underground journalist, James Greenwood, whose 'Night in a Workhouse' (1866) combined virtuosic masquerade with potent exposé.[19] Greenwood's work catered perfectly to the popular taste for mixing entertainment with reform by first becoming, as Sims observed, 'The talk of the town, and presently the rage of the town.'[20]

Sims began his career writing a column for the *Weekly Dispatch* in the 1870s and supplementing his income with theatre and sports reviews. He also courted controversy by translating Honoré de Balzac, wrote plays and ballads devoted to the exigencies of London life, most notably *The Dragonet Ballads* (1879) and *Ballads of Babylon* (1880), as well as novels exploring similar themes beginning with *Rogues and Vagabonds* (1885). Sims' social reporting began in 1881 with the publication of three series of articles published in the *Sunday Dispatch* – 'The Social Kaleidoscope', 'Three Brass Balls', and 'The Theatre of Life'. These series, combined with the social focus of his ballads and theatre work, led to him serving on a committee investigating social conditions in Southwark in 1882, which resulted in the tours of the slums recorded in *How the Poor Live* (1883). A lightness of touch characterises this body of work, despite the grim urban phantasmagoria it often evokes. Sims consistently stresses the glance, the glimpse, moving scenes – a stress heightened by suggestive titles such as *Biographs of London. Life-Pictures of London's moving scenes* (1902) and the impressionistic episodic structure of his writing, including his expansive anecdotal auto- biography, *My Life: Sixty Years' Recollections of Bohemian London* (1917).[21] The latter moves back and forth following associative, rather than chronological sequences, reflecting Sims' interest in convergences of impressions and associations involuntarily registered, rather than programmatic visions – what could be termed a stream of conscious- ness that aligns with George Henry Lewes's account of the dynamics of reverie in *The Physiology of Common Life*:

> We may walk through crowded streets absorbed in thought, yet every obsta- cle is avoided, and our destination reached with unerring accuracy. It is prob- able that from time to time the brain interrupts its course of thought to glance at the houses, and assure us we are not on the wrong track.[22]

Like Lewes's reverie, Sims' narrative voice dwelt on details, contours and colours calculated to engage the eye, without interrupting the associative flow he hoped to generate in his reader's mind. As he notes himself in the context of *How the Poor Live*, he was never concerned with the disinterested accumulation of information. It is Dickens, rather than Henry Mayhew's seminal urban ethnography, that pro- vides the template for his mode of social observation. Indeed Sims was quite dismissive of Mayhew, whom he briefly recalled meeting in his autobiography.[23] According to Sims, his own social explorations 'into the dark continent that is within easy walking distance of the General Post Office' were more effective because they took the form of vivid visual vignettes, rather than painstaking interviews (212). In contrast to Mayhew, he claimed that he recorded moving scenes and characters, producing exemplary anecdotes rather than official histories. This strategy, he argued, was designed to make people move beyond the fashionable practice of slumming or the blinkered vision of 'telescopic philanthropy', to emotionally engage with the parlous state of civilisation and the necessary reforms required.[24]

Each scenario in Sims' social kaleidoscope is designed to stimulate emotional associations or reverie of the kind Lewes described – a softening focus that recalls Marx and Engels's characterisation of the 'philanthropic illusions' of the petite bourgeoisie in their seminal discussion of the 'camera obscura of ideology'.[25] But there is a critical vitality to Sims' interest in the mutability of perception and contingency that offsets his unabashed desire to make his middle-class readers feel at ease. This balance between illusion and critique is exemplified by the ninth figure that appears in Sims' *Social Kaleidoscope* – 'A Brown Check Suit'.[26] In this account, the life of a commodity – the eponymous brown suit – is tracked from its display in a West End tailor's shop window to its purchase by a portly consumer, Mr Lumsden. The plot thickens when Mr Lumsden needs alterations done. The suit then progresses into the back room of the tailor's shop and then into the world of exploitative sweatshops created to service the middle-class desire to create the appearance of wealth on a budget: 'Let us shift the kaleidoscope, and follow Mr Lumsden's brown check suit as it is dispersed in portions, to be re-united presently in one perfect and symmetrical whole' (48). A gaunt famished woman gets the waistcoat, a dissipated young man the trousers, and a thin woman nursing her ailing husband and child in the back streets of Spitalfields gets the coat. The scene then shifts to Mr Lumsden donning the suit for his son's birthday and promptly infecting the village children and his own family with scarlet fever carried all the way from the back streets of Spitalfields. Returning the alienated commodity to the infected hands of anonymous workers, Sims ties up this tragic tale with a typically problematic conclusion, demanding that his readers act to rid the city of exploitative work practices, whilst at the same time reinforcing class divides by exploiting middle-class fears of physical and moral contagion.

The fallibility of perception is also exposed in Sims' scathing portrait of 'The Christian Sufferer', which reanimates a familiar figure in late-Victorian journalism; the false beggar who preys on the middle-class taste for spectacularised poverty (1–5). In a sordid scene not unlike Conan Doyle's more familiar barbed tale of *The Man with the Twisted Lip*, begging is exposed as an easy means of duping those who fail to look beyond the surface. This vignette invites the reader to apply the stock devices of reading identity through a kaleidoscopic assemblage of visual cues – beginning with the face, then the body, gestures and the minutiae of the sufferer's shabby domestic environs. The setting is a back parlour in Barnsbury where two sisters entertain a stream of well-meaning visitors. One appears to suffer from a debilitating disease, and the other is her devoted nursemaid. But, as Sims is quick to point out, the appearance of genteel poverty is part of a carefully constructed performance that masks a long history of exploiting the virtues of others:

> All this, however, you are not yet expected to know. As the world sees them now – as you see them in the Social Kaleidoscope, they simply represent a helpless crippled woman, worn with bodily anguish, surrounded with religious consolation and a meek and amiable female attendant . . . But it is here that my task commences. Before circumstances formed that picture what was its central figure? . . . What is she now? When the atoms dispart, and the picture is broken up, what will she become? (2–5)

The short answer to these questions is – a con artist who has turned her ill fortune into profit:

> As she is now when you see her in the kaleidoscope she is simply posed for the visitors she expects. In her character of a wretched sufferer, who endures with Christian resignation the will of the Almighty, Janet Gurton is a London celebrity. She is a yearly recipient of so many 'grants', 'gifts', 'pensions', and 'allowances', that one of other falls due nearly every week of the year. She is splendidly advertised. (5)

Again Sims treads a fine line between cynicism and critique, playing to the sentiment and anxiety that underlay what he scathingly describes in *My Life* as the middle-class fashion for slumming.

Sims' kaleidoscopic technique works to similarly ambiguous effect in his portrayal of the figure of a murderer who hides behind the mask of 'A Good Fellow' – a bon vivant and frequenter of music halls:

> Bright and pleasing to the eye is the figure into which the atoms are flung with this turn of the kaleidoscope. The dingy lodgings, the crippled woman and the shabby surroundings at which we lately gazed vanish in an instant, and as the fragments form again, the gayest colours reign supreme in the picture. The picture is crowded, and the eye is dazzled at first by the hundred lights of the hall, the glare from the brilliantly-illuminated stage and the hurry and

bustle of the scene. It is a gala night at the Royal Delirium Music Hall, and enthusiasm has reached fever heat . . . Hundreds of typical faces flash white across the scene; hundreds of typical forms of humanity crowd around the marble tables, converging for the moment to one common centre, only to be scattered in a few short hours . . . Presently the eye gets accustomed to the mass of detail, and travels steadily round ring after ring of merry-makers till it reaches the central figure of the picture, and on him it rests. Look at him well, as he leans across the side bar with the ease of an accustomed visitor, and pays the showy barmaid a flippant compliment. (6–11)

Again Sims presents a variation on a type, an apparently prosperous city man has just returned from murdering his mistress, who had been blackmailing him to the point of financial ruin. After dwelling on the attractions of the Royal Delirium, Sims draws the events together whilst stressing the ambiguities that the case raises. He challenges his readers to move beyond moral judgement to consider the banality of murder, arguing that countless similar cases go unnoticed in the modern Babylon that London has become. Advice that Sims did not always take, par-ticularly in the case of the celebrity murderer of the period – Jack the Ripper. In *My Life* Sims delightedly informs his readers that his close resemblance to the Ripper led to a coffee stall keeper taking a copy of the six-penny edition of *The Social Kaleidoscope*, which had a portrait of Sims on the cover, to Scotland Yard claiming that he had uncovered the identity of 'the assassin'.[27]

A similar balance between sensation and critique inflects Sims' account of exploring the slums of Southwark in *How the Poor Live*. Grim dark streets and decayed buildings are vividly described, filtered through the haze of anxious smoking:

We smoked like furnaces the whole time, but we did not smoke cigars or silver-mounted briars. In order to avoid all suspicion of swank and to make the inhabitants feel more at home in our company, we smoked clay pipes and coloured them a beautiful black . . . [28]

The stress here is on 'passing' and the illusory trappings of appearance that can be so easily acquired and shed. Sims and his companion also assume a disguise, as Greenwood and many others had done before them. This serves two purposes: ensuring access to otherwise forbidden scenes of human misery and degradation, as well as creating the requi-site dramatic edge to enliven the story – a strategy that Sims saw as the antithesis of the bourgeois solidity of mid-Victorian journalism which he compared to 'mid-Victorian furniture, solid and heavy'.[29]

Another device Sims uses to resist this worthy solidity is moving quickly from one vivid visual vignette to the next. The eye and imagination of the reader is never allowed to rest on any one surface. Sims moves quickly from the decayed room of a young mother forced to prostitute herself, to the crowded boarding houses that summon the Dickensian spectres of Nancy and Bill Sykes, to the grim oozing walls of decaying tenements. These scenes inspire further digressions on the duty of the state to intervene to protect tenants from the avarice of corrupt landlords, the advantages of the 1870 Education Act, the hypocrisy of the Temperance League, the dangers of the good intentions of Oxbridge educated clergy and the magical potential of a well-funded public transport system capable of spiriting workers away from grim slums to leafy suburbs.

Throughout these grim forays Sims maintains a lightness of tone that he defends in the preface to *How the Poor Live* as a necessary device to hold the attention of his easily distracted petit bourgeois readers. The crowded alcohol-charged music halls and gin palaces are gently parodied, whilst being defended as necessary distractions from the horrors of everyday life in a world that even the furniture can no longer endure:

> I cannot help being struck in my wanderings . . . with the extraordinary resemblance of spaces . . . One room in this district is very like another. The family likeness of the chairs and tables is truly remarkable, especially in the matter of legs. Most chairs are born with four legs, but the chairs one meets with here are a two-legged race a four-legged chair is a *rara avis*, and when found should be made a note of. The tables too, are out of a type indigenous to the spot. The survival of the fittest does not obtain in these districts in the matter of tables. The most positively unfit are common, very common objects. What has become of the fittest I hesitate to conjecture. Possibly they have run away. I am quite sure that a table with legs would make use of them to escape from such surroundings.[30]

Perpetually in motion, London fractures and flickers before the eye of the observer. This is, according to Sims, a far more accurate representation of the reality of the complexities of London life. Faces, bodies, houses, shops, streets cannot be simply read. They must be viewed from multiple perspectives. There is also a sensuality and aestheticism in Sims' portrayal of the city that resonates with Dickens's delight in the kaleidoscopic array of figures that move before the eye on an omnibus and with Baudelaire's far more decadent surrender to the electric chaos of modernity. The resulting effect, in the case of both *The Social Kaleidoscope* and the vivid visual vignettes of *How the Poor Live*, was a distinctively Victorian fusion of empiricism and impressionism, illusion and earnest social description.

Everyday Flickers

In many ways Sims' insertion of the kaleidoscope between the viewer/ reader and the phenomena of everyday life exemplifies Maurice Blanchot's account of the distorting effects of the 'passage from street to newspaper, from the everyday in perpetual becoming to the everyday transcribed'.[31] According to Blanchot, this transcription modifies everything, transforming the elusive anonymous verities of the street into a series of inauthentic images that sensationalise the everyday in the interests of apprehension. In effect, the anecdotal storytelling-mode of journalistic description transforms the 'nothing happens' of the everyday into the illusory immediacy of the 'something is happening' of historical event (18). The everyday escapes this process, Blanchot argues, unperceived and unassimilable by the 'panoramic vision' of spectacular media effects:

> It is the unperceived; first in the sense that one has always looked past it; nor can it be introduced into a whole or 'reviewed', that is to say, enclosed within a panoramic vision; for, by another trait, the everyday is what we never see for a first time, but only see again, having always already seen it by an illusion that is, as it happens, constitutive of the everyday. (14)

Henri Lefebvre ascribes a similar selective vision to both film and literature – both claim to represent everyday life while only exposing its more spectacular aspects. Writing, according to Lefebvre, 'can only show an everyday life inscribed and prescribed; words are elusive and only that which is stipulated remains'.[32] Sims, however, was more sceptical than Blanchot or Lefebvre about the possibility of an everyday life that exceeded or eluded mediation. His characters are locked inside the technological circuitry of industrial modernity. They accordingly function as conduits of information about a life already determined by the modern media through which their images move.

Like Blanchot's irresponsible television audience, readers of Sims' evocatively entitled journalistic series, *The Social Kaleidoscope*, *Living Pictures* (1901) and *Biographs of London. Life-Pictures of London's Moving Scenes* were promised a view of real life taking place before their eyes. The foreword to *Biographs of London* makes this promise explicit:

> There are strange human dramas, harrowing human tragedies, enacted daily beneath the roofs of the Great City. The actors, shut in by the four walls that the playwright removes, play their parts unseen by the world without. The tale of the tragedy is heard in the market-place only when the terrible denouement has been reached.
> There are scenes passing daily around us, scenes in which comedy and tragedy alike have their share; and no hint of the developing plot reaches

the spectator, because he catches only a glimpse now and then of the human puppets who are working out the scheme of the author – the author whom men call by various names according to their lights, but whose working name is fate.

Because in the biograph we watch the human figures pass and repass and their lips are dumb, because in the 'scenes' which they work together to make they are often ignorant of one another's presence, I have called these pictures of Babylon 'Biographs' also. They are all taken from life. As they happened so you will see them reproduce themselves.

So much by way of note upon the programme, that you may read it when the lights go down, and in the darkened house the first of the series of 'Biographs of Babylon' is shown on your sheet.[33]

The mix of media in this passage simulates the early exhibition of short single-shot films as part of music hall programmes. Each so-called biograph pointedly reminds the reader of their mediated relation to the scenes 'taken from life' that automatically reproduce themselves as they see them.[34] Indeed part of the attraction is the technological realisation of the idea of life as a recordable and infinitely reproducible phenomenon.

Recording technologies like the biograph and cinematograph, as Michael North observes, provided a more powerful and extensive indexical sign that promised 'to bridge the gap between language and visible phenomena by making a language *of* visible phenomena, a language impossibly more flexible and more various than any of the written languages'.[35] Sims attempted to rhetorically harness this unprecedented indexical power to enhance his own powers of social observation. To quote another of Sims' editorial formulations of his cinematic style in the first number of the 1901 series *Living London*:

> We are to find a breathing, pulsing panorama of Living London. Panorama is hardly the word – cinematograph would be a better one, for it is not a London of bricks and mortar that will pass before our eyes, but a London of flesh and blood.[36]

Sims' work thus exemplifies the intrinsically hybrid reception of early films in the late 1890s. While acknowledging their unprecedented animation of the fugitive temporality of scenes taken from life, Sims understood early films in the context of familiar amusements, a typical response according to historians of early cinema.[37] These amusements include the long history of 'animating the everyday', as Lynda Nead has recently argued in her analysis of the cultural reception of the cinematograph at the turn of the nineteenth century.[38] Nead offers a timely critique of the 'lumpen analysis of modernity and the city' that results from the endless rehashing of George Simmel's influential account of metropolitan life as an unexpected onrush of impressions from which the modern city dweller reels in shock (110). She rightly suggests that the visual archive of earliest projected moving films of London life has far more in common with the stillness, amusement and interactions of the world of Henry Mayhew than the alienating discontinuities and accelerated pace of the cinematic modernity evoked by Simmel's critique.

Sims' mystification of the transcriptive automatism of film in his preface to *Biographs of London* was undoubtedly indebted to Mayhew's drive to literally transcribe the lives of his working-class subjects. But what ultimately engaged Sims was the interplay between contingency and structure that the animating mechanisms of the kaleidoscope and biograph generated. Mary Ann Doane has identified a similar 'curious merger of contingency and structure' as specific to early forms of cinematic temporality.[39] Following the distinction made by film historians such as Charles Musser and Tom Gunning, Doane argues that there is a crucial representational shift between the non-fictional actualities that were primarily associated with cinematic experience prior to 1907 and the ascendancy of narrative cinema in subsequent decades.[40] Doane agrees with Nead that the fascination with the contingent that drove the popularity of actualities drew on a pre-cinematic pictorial syntax (142). Given this continuity, Doane's elaboration of the syntax of early cinema provides a clarifying lens through which to read Sims' various efforts to animate prosaic scenes of urban life for the instructive entertainment of his readers. Doane argues that while early cinema presented itself as an unprecedented indexical record of the 'aleatory, stochastic, contingent' unpredictability of unfolding events, it still remained intrinsically limited by both the individual frame and the length of the reel (140–1). The technological limits of the form created a discrete temporal unit, a carefully constructed re-presentation of the contingent.

This tension between structure and contingency is fundamental to Sims' translation of the kaleidoscope, the biograph and the cinematograph into reading devices. Sims' *Social Kaleidoscope*, like Blessington's magic lantern before it, foreshadows the multiple functions of recording and projection, a combination that the cinematograph would later realise in the form of a camera, printer and projector in one. Sims directs his kaleidoscope towards the scene and begins recording with a turn of the lens. *Biographs of London* sustains this simulation of pictures 'taken from life'.[41] Sims reassures his audience that as 'they happened so you will see them reproduce themselves' and literally positions them in 'the darkened house' of the music-hall auditorium, programme in hand (vii). Sims' readers may have even recognised the specific music hall, given that the Palace Theatre on Cambridge Circus in London was the home

of the American Biograph. From March 1897 the Palace featured 70mm
biograph films that produced exceptionally large clear images.[42] The
Palace was particularly associated with the biograph shows of William
Kennedy-Laurie Dickson whose news films, including his popular cov-
erage of the Anglo-Boer War would draw large audiences throughout
1900.

Sims revels in the animated mechanical reproduction of familiar
scenes and types, although as the title indicates, *Biographs of London*
tends more towards the salacious and sensational than his earlier social
reportage. The sixth biograph in the sequence, 'The Side-Show Pianist'
typifies this shift, trading on the familiar theatrical artifice of a play
within a play or, in this case, a film within a film. The first frame reveals
the figure of Miss Barbara Dare providing musical accompaniment for a
sideshow performance of an entertainment of the 'cinematograph order,
"Italian Scenery and Italian Life"' (76). Fallen on hard times, the middle-
class Miss Dare has been forced to prostitute her musical talents. Her
bad luck draws her into an unsavoury milieu, exposing her to the unwel-
come advances of a sideshow employee, an ardent Italian who murders
her as she accompanies the film. As with Sims' *Social Kaleidoscope*,
the ultimate effect of this rhetorical simulation of the visual effects of
the biograph was to heighten the overt theatricality of the audience's
emotional identification with the murder plot. The allure of authenticity
paradoxically intensifies the artificiality of the re-presentation of images
supposedly taken from life. As Martin Jay has argued, the faithful
mimesis that the invention of the camera promised 'helped ultimately to
undermine confidence in the very sense it so extended'.[43]

Tom Gunning uses the concept of the view to 'highlight the way early
actuality films were structured around presenting something visually,
capturing and preserving a look or vantage point'.[44] Gunning argues
that the most characteristic quality of this 'view aesthetic' is 'the way it
mimes the act of looking and observing' (15). The camera is positioned
at the best possible vantage point to capture the scene as it unfolds.
Notwithstanding the fundamental distinction between the figural simulation and the literal filming of a view of London street life that either
pre-dated the act of filming or would have taken place with or without
the presence of the camera, both mediate versions of a uniquely cinematic temporality.[45] First exhibited as part of a standard musical-hall
variety programme at the Alhambra Theatre, Leicester Square, Robert
Paul's surviving actualities exemplify both the view aesthetic Gunning
identifies, as well as a generic continuity with the urban ethnography of Mayhew, Sims and precursors such as Egan, Blessington and
Dickens. Like the biograph, Paul's theatrograph was an adaptation of

the Edisonian kinetoscope, designed to film and project both short non-fiction actualities, as well as the first narrative films produced in Britain between 1896 and 1906.

Paul's single shot film, *Blackfriars Bridge* (1896) is typical of the visual density and local appeal of the actuality. Paul positions his camera to maximise the illusion of immediacy and experiential authenticity. Pedestrians and horse-drawn carriages and omnibuses move in and out of frame in a single shot sequence filmed from the side of one of London's most iconic bridges. Like so many early actualities, the viewer's gaze is returned by some of the pedestrians who either look straight into the lens as they approach, or look back as if to catch the eye of the camera as they pass by. Walking towards the camera a young man slowly becomes aware of the camera, looking directly into the lens as he quickly disappears from the frame. Another middle-class man in a bowler hat cranes back towards the camera as he crosses the bridge from the other direction. These moments of gradual apprehension are as much the subject of the film as the bustling traffic of Blackfriars Bridge. The indiscriminate spectacle of movement captured prevails, as multiple anonymous faces and bodies move with varying gaits and bearing through the same public space. This is the London of 'flesh and blood' that Sims associates with the cinematograph in *Living London* (3).

Blackfriars Bridge is one of Paul's earliest actualities. Only a year before, inspired by H. G. Wells's novella *The Time Machine* (1895), Paul had filed a patent application for a moving picture version of a similar idea. Borrowing the title and drawing inspiration from Wells, Paul's 'Time Machine', as he called it, was designed to simulate the actual sensation of being transported through time and space.[46] The patent specified an arrangement of moving platforms where the audience would sit while being moved backwards and forwards before a screen filled with still and moving pictures, creating the illusion of being carried back and forth between the future and the past.[47] By 21 February 1896 Paul published an account in the *English Mechanic* of his first successful screen projection of moving images using a 35mm film projector that significantly developed on the peep-show format of Edison's kinetoscope.[48] Serendipitously, Paul first exhibited his theatrograph at his old technical college in Finsbury on the same day, 20 February 1896, that saw the inaugural demonstration of the Cinématographe Lumière at the Royal Polytechnic on Regent Street. While there were some flaws, Paul's theatrograph would prove to be the prototype for the modern projector and the short topical films he produced, such as the *Prince's Derby* of 3 June 1896, are seminal precursors of the newsreel.[49] Paul would also go on to make one of the first narrative films, a comedy called *A Soldier's Courtship*, to which I will return in the next chapter. Screened on the roof of the Alhambra Theatre, where Paul's actualities were a fixture in the daily variety programme, the instant popularity of *A Soldier's Courtship* consequently inspired Paul to start the first film studio in England.

Blackfriars Bridge most likely appeared as one in a series of short films Paul exhibited at the Alhambra demonstrating 'The Animatographe, Photo-Electric Sensation of the Day', another variation on the theatro-graph.[50] Unlike later programmes that featured the individual titles of actualities, these early exhibitions, like Sims' proto-cinematic journalism, stressed the 'marvellous mechanism' itself as the attraction. The animatographe, for example, was the seventh in eleven attractions in the Alhambra Theatre, 'Theatre of Varieties' programme for the week commencing Monday 20 April 1896. It followed a random selection of juggling, Norwegian dancing, Madame Bulgasy – a Hungarian chanteuse and a ballet version of *Blue Beard*. The ensuing order of attractions included a new series of popular imitations by Miss Cissie Loftus, an orchestral selection from *The Mikado*, Mademoiselle Bertoldi the contortionist and a new ballet divertissement, 'The Gathering of the Clans', suggested by Scott's poem *Lochinvar*.

Like the opening nights of the cinema around the world in the 1890s, the audience for this heterogeneous fare was a relatively elite one, well used to the charms of sumptuous vaudeville palaces and the long tradition of witnessing the latest technological marvel. They would have recognised the 'types' walking across Blackfriars Bridge, from the well-attired couple with top hat and parasol glancing politely into Paul's lens, to the carriage and omnibus drivers who inhabit the same social space. They may have also noted the familiar format of the audio-visual spectacle orchestrated by Paul, which as the programme stresses, involved a mixture of words, images and possibly music given the context of the Alhambra. As Norman King observes, the execution of sound during this period 'produced effects in the cinema that recorded cinema could not, a sense of immediacy and participation'.[51]

Arresting Movements

A frame-by-frame analysis of Robert Paul's 'The Prince's Derby. Shown by Lightning Photography' in the *Strand Magazine* in July 1896, provides a fitting concluding point for this chapter's analysis of Sims' journalistic remediation of various technologies of the moving image and the late nineteenth-century media ecology in which they circulated.[52]

Illustrated by a series of seventeen still frames from Paul's film, this essay mediated the technical intricacies and visual sensations of the cinema to the readers of the *Strand*:

> Hundreds of photographs are taken with amazing rapidity – say, twenty a second – on an enormous length of transparent celluloid ribbon. These photos are subsequently shown magic-lantern fashion, also with extreme rapidity, the result being 'living pictures' which completely baffle description. (134)

The ensuing narrative reverses the pace of the film, literally bringing images to a standstill so that the events of the 'now famous race' can be 'placed under a microscope for our benefit' (135).

While the resulting historical reconstruction recounts the details of the finish as an exemplary exercise in photographic detection, it is the incidental events surrounding the race that capture the author's attention. The policeman running forward to control the crowd rushing across the course: 'One can see his head turning round as the great river of humanity overwhelms the racecourse' (135). Singling out the jubilant faces in the crowd: 'the last photo shows that the river has grown into a veritable sea of human beings, each wild with excitement and delight' (135). Other 'amazing living photographs' by Paul are also recommended, such as the arrival of the Paris express at Calais – 'a scene of bustle and excitement scenes from Westminster, too with its superb equipages, high-spirited horses, and passing crowds and omnibuses, fairly glows with life' (136). Or, alternatively, more everyday images, such as children playing on Hampstead Heath or a rough sea at Ramsgate are praised for their authentic animation of scenes taken from daily life. A blow-by-blow description of Paul's technical ingenuity and personal travails in capturing the Derby on film frames the remaining seventeen stills. Marvelling at Paul's ability to develop 'the great negative' so quickly, the essay concludes with an account of the first projection of the film at the Alhambra the evening after the race in front of 'an enormous audience' who 'witnessed the Prince's Derby all to themselves amidst wild enthusiasm, which all but drowned the strains of "God Bless the Prince of Wales", as played by the splendid orchestra' (140).

Paul's film is literally remediated in extracted form for the instructive entertainment of the readers of the *Strand Magazine*. While conceding the distinction between still and animated images, the author constructs a detailed reading of the film, its production and reception. The intention is to bring the film to life by drawing together 'behind the scenes' highlights with the drama of the actual filming of the race. Attention is drawn to both the novelty of the medium and its continuity with previous technologies such as the magic lantern and photography, while implicitly reinforcing the parallels between the moving image and modern reincarnations of illustrated print media, such as the *Strand*. The latter stress on ingenuity was hardly surprising given George Newnes's vision for the *Strand*, which combined the entrepreneurial targeting of an aspirational middle-class market for 'cheap, healthful literature' with the latest publishing technologies.[53] Illustration was integral to Newnes's appeal to a modern readership that identified itself as educated and urban. Illustrations were never merely adjuncts to the text, as Christopher Pittard has noted, they played a crucial role in understanding how the *Strand* 'policed its reading community'.[54] By 1896 moreover, the *Strand* was at the height of its popularity. As Arthur Conan Doyle observed while travelling abroad at the turn of the century: 'Foreigners used to recognise the English by their check suits. I think they will soon learn to do it by their *Strand Magazines*. Everybody on the Channel boat, except the man at the wheel, was clutching one.'[55]

Given the self-consciously visual modernity of the *Strand*, the reproduction of Paul's stills could be dismissed as fairly unremarkable. What is striking however, in the context of Sims' textual incorporation of the effects of the kaleidoscope and biograph, is the ready assimilation of the arrested moving image into familiar techniques for reading the everyday events of urban life. The idea of looking through the printed page, of literally animating images in the mind of the reader through a fusion of print and visual technologies, invests the relatively uninspired reproductions of Paul's stills with the promise of an unprecedented means of transcription and transmission. The action slows to reveal the machinery of the viewing apparatus, a process that fundamentally aligns the experience of the everyday with its technological mediation.

Paralleling this convergence of perceptual and technological media, the psychology of the 1890s reflected a similar preoccupation with the mind as a dynamic medium in which impression after impression created the illusion of continuity. Combining kaleidoscopic and telephonic analogies in his vivid description of the dynamic shifts in 'brain-tension', William James's avowedly modern concept of consciousness asserts the neural networks of the brain as the ultimate communicative medium:

> As the brain-tension shifts from one relative state of equilibrium to another, like the gyrations of a kaleidoscope, now rapid and now slow, is it likely that its faithful concomitant is heavier footed than itself, and that it cannot match each one of the organ's irradiations by a shifting inward iridescence of its own? But if it can do this, its inward iridescences must be infinite, for the brain-redistributions are in infinite variety. If so coarse a thing as a telephone-plate can be made to thrill for years and never reduplicate its

inward conditions, how much more must this be the case with the infinitely delicate brain?[56]

While differentiating the coarse materiality of the telephone from the delicate receptiveness and excitability of the brain, James's technological rhetoric nevertheless concedes a parallel. The mind's perpetual motion is illuminated by its 'likeness' to the kaleidoscope and the telephone in the very act of metaphoric differentiation.

Hugo Munsterberg, who was a colleague and friend of James in the 1890s, was a little more explicit in his interest in the affinities between mind and media, ultimately producing his seminal psychological study of film, *The Photoplay: A Psychological Study* in 1916. Reflecting on the long history of reciprocal engagements between popular optical devices and the emergence of a modern psychology of moving images in the nineteenth century, Munsterberg enumerated a list of precedents, beginning with the camera obscura, the dissolving views of the magic lantern, the flicker effects of the phenakistoscope, the thaumatrope, the stop-motion photography of Muybridge and Marey, Edison's kinetoscope, culminating with the simultaneous triumphs of the Lumières' cinematograph and Robert Paul's animatograph/theatrograph. Elaborating on the psychology of how film particularly activates the mind's attentive focus, however, Munsterberg relied on an analogy with the immersive experience of reading a favourite book – 'fully absorbed in our book, we do not hear at all what is said around us and we do not see the room; we forget everything'.[57] Drawing on theories of unconscious or involuntary attention, Munsterberg describes how the mind of the observer is likewise drawn into the vivid depths of the cinematic image:

> Here begins the art of the photoplay. That one nervous hand which fever-ishly grasps the deadly weapon can suddenly for the space of a breath or two become enlarged and be alone visible on the screen, while everything else has really faded into darkness. The act of attention which goes on in our mind has remodelled the surrounding itself. The detail which is being watched has sud-denly become the whole content of the performance, and everything which our mind wants to disregard has been suddenly banished from our sight and has disappeared. The events without have become obedient to the demands of our consciousness. In the language of the photoplay producers it is a 'close-up'. The close-up has objectified in our world of perception our mental act of attention and by it has furnished art with a means which far transcends the power of any theater stage. (86–7)

Mimicking the mind's involuntary attention to seemingly fugitive detail, film, like a good book, transcends the materiality of the apparatus of mechanical reproduction and becomes art.

Cecil Hepworth shared Munsterberg's faith in the aesthetic potential of film, as the following chapter will argue. Initially captivated by the wonders of the apparatus itself, Hepworth drew on his long association with the magic lantern as a story telling device to develop some of the first narrative films, including his adaptation of Lewis Carroll's *Alice's Adventures* (1903). Like Robert Paul, who was his friend and mentor, Hepworth soon realised that the key to the new medium's survival lay in a creative convergence of showmanship, collective memory and storytelling.

Notes

1. Sims, *The Social Kaleidoscope*, p. i.
2. Baudelaire, *The Painter of Modern Life*, p. 9.
3. Sims, *The Social Kaleidoscope*, pp. vii–viii.
4. Bain, *Senses and the Intellect*, p. 252
5. Nead, *The Haunted Gallery: Painting, Photography, Film c.1900*, p. 33.
6. Brewster, *The Kaleidoscope. Its History, Theory and Construction with its Application to the Fine and Useful Arts*, pp. 131–3.
7. Deleuze, *Cinema 1*, p. 5.
8. Kittler, *Gramophone, Film, Typewriter*, p. xxxix.
9. Sully, *Illusions – A Psychological Study*, p. 77.
10. Cited in Slater (ed.), *Dickens' Journalism: Sketches by Boz and other early papers 1833–1839*, p. 139.
11. Cited in Foster, *The Life of Charles Dickens*, p. 558.
12. Gallagher and Greenblatt, *Practicing New Historicism*, p. 178.
13. Cited in Foster, *The Life of Charles Dickens*, p. 557.
14. Epstein Nord, *Walking the Victorian Streets: Women, Representation and the City*, pp. 33–5.
15. Egan, *Life in London*, p. ii.
16. Smith, 'The Casino', in Albert Smith (ed.), *'Gavarni in London: Sketches of Life and Character,' with illustrative essays by Popular Writers*, p. 15.
17. Smith, 'The Lounger in Regent St', in *Gavarni in London*, p. 70.
18. Thorington, *Mont Blanc Sideshow. The Life and Times of Albert Smith*.
19. Koven, *Slumming: Sexual and Social Politics in Victorian London*, pp. 23–74.
20. Keating (ed.), *Into Unknown England, 1866–1913: selections from the social explorers*, p. 16.
21. Sims, *Biographs of London. Life-Pictures of London's Moving Scenes*; Sims, *My Life: Sixty Years' Recollections of Bohemian London*.
22. Lewes, *The Physiology of Common Life*, vol. 2, p. 268.
23. Sims recalled meeting Mayhew but dismisses his reliance on interviews, voluminous statistics and other forms of veridical transcription in *My Life*, p. 212.
24. Dickens, *Bleak House* [1853], p. 231.
25. Marx and Engels, *The German Ideology*, vol. 1, p. 120.

26. Sims, *The Social Kaleidoscope*, pp. 46–51.
27. Sims, *My Life*, p. 141
28. Sims, *How the Poor Live*, p. 13.
29. Sims, *My Life*, p. 132.
30. Sims, *How the Poor Live*, p. 14.
31. Blanchot, 'Everyday Speech', *Yale French Studies* 73 (1987), p. 18.
32. Lefebvre, *Everyday Life in the Modern World*, p. 8.
33. Sims, *Biographs of London: Life-pictures of London's Moving Scenes*, p. vii.
34. The biograph camera and mutoscope peep-show device were the inventions of William Kennedy Dickson who founded the American Biograph and Mutoscope Company in 1895. While in the employ of Thomas Edison, Dickson played an instrumental role in the invention of the Edison camera. Gordon Hendricks provides a detailed history of the biograph and Dicksons's acrimonious relationship with Edison in *Beginnings of the Biograph*.
35. North, *Camera Works: Photography and the Twentieth-Century Word*, p. 8. The italics are North's.
36. Sims (ed.), *Living London: Its Work and its Play, its Humour and its Pathos, its Sights and its Scenes*, vol. 1, p. 3.
37. Gunning's field-defining work on the 'cinema of attractions' is exemplified in the following seminal essays: 'An Aesthetic of Astonishment: Early Film and the (In)Credulous Spectator', in Williams (ed.), *Viewing Positions: Ways of Seeing Film*, pp. 114–33; 'Now You See It, Now You Don't': The Temporality of the Cinema of Attractions', *Velvet Light Trap* 32 (1993), pp. 3–12.
38. Nead, *The Haunted Gallery*, p. 122.
39. Doane, *The Emergence of Cinematic Time: Modernity, Contingency, the Archive*, p. 141.
40. Musser, 'Rethinking Early Cinema: Cinemas of Attraction and Narrativity', *Yale Journal of Criticism* 7:2 (1994), pp. 203–33; Gunning, 'The Non-Continuous Style of Early Film 1900–1906', in Holman (ed.), *Cinema 1900/1906: An Analytical Study*, pp. 219–30.
41. Sims, *Biographs of London*, p. vii.
42. Luke McKernan has written extensively on the history and reception of the biograph, see *Who's Who of Victorian Cinema: a worldwide survey*, which he edited with Stephen Herbert (London: BFI, 1996).
43. Jay, 'Photo-Unrealism: the Contribution of the Camera to the Crisis of Ocularcentrism', in Melville and Readings (eds), *Vision and Textuality*, p. 345.
44. Gunning, 'Before Documentary', in Hertogs and Klerk (eds), *Uncharted Territory: Essays on Early Nonfiction Film*, p. 14.
45. These observations are indebted to Gunning's discussion of the critical legacy of John Grierson's seminal use of the term documentary in 'Before Documentary', pp. 9–14.
46. Marcus notes that the influence was mutual, reading Wells's play with velocity and reverse motion as allusions to cinematic effects in 'Literature and Cinema', in Marcus and Nicholls (eds), *The Cambridge History of Twentieth Century Literature*, p. 338.

47. Fielding describes this format in 'Hale's Tours: Ultrarealism in the Pre-1910 Motion Picture', in Fell (ed.), *Film Before Griffith*, pp. 116–17.
48. For a detailed contextualisation of Paul's contribution the early history of cinema in England see Barnes and Maltby, *The Beginnings of Cinema in England, 1894–1901*, vol. 5.
49. *The Prince's Derby* was exhibited in two major London theatres within twenty-four hours of the event, on 3 June 1896.
50. Alhambra Theatre, 'Theatre of Varieties' Programme, Monday 20 April 1896. Museum of London Collection of Music Hall Programmes.
51. King, 'The Sound of Silents', *Screen* 25:3 (May–June 1984), p. 15.
52. 'The Prince's Derby. Shown by Lightning Photography', *Strand Magazine* 12 (July 1896), pp. 134–40.
53. Newnes, Editorial, *Strand Magazine* 1 (1891), p. 1.
54. Pittard, '"Cheap, Healthful Literature": *The Strand Magazine*, Fictions of Crime, and Purified Reading Communities', *Victorian Periodicals Review* 40:1 (Spring 2007), p. 9.
55. Cited in Pound, *The Strand Magazine 1891–1950*, p. 63.
56. James, *The Principles of Psychology*, vol. 1, p. 235.
57. Munsterberg, 'The Photoplay: A Psychological Study', in *Hugo Munsterberg on Film*, ed. Langdale, p. 85.

Chapter 7

Literary Projections and Residual Media: Cecil Hepworth and Robert Paul

In his autobiography, *Came the Dawn*, Cecil Hepworth describes the 'thrill of joy' he felt when he passed through the Great Hall at the Royal Polytechnic on Regent Street.[1] The 'magic of its atmosphere', however, paled in comparison with the attractions of the theatre that ran alongside the Great Hall (16). Consisting of a complicated mixture of ordinary theatre fixtures, a stage and painted scenery, the theatre included a projection room that spanned the whole width of the theatre at dress circle level and contained upwards of fifteen limelight magic lanterns of various sizes set up to project a mixture of large painted and photographic slides, as well as trick slides of revolving geometrical patterns that created the illusion of movement on the screen. There was also a curious device known as a 'Choreutoscope' that Hepworth notes anticipated the modern cinematograph:

> it had a cut-out stencil of a skeleton figure in about a dozen different positions which changed instantaneously from one to another. The interesting thing about it now is that the means of that quick movement was practically the same as the 'Maltese cross' movement of a modern film projector. If you can imagine a Maltese cross straightened out into a line closing and opening a very rapid shutter, you will understand the 'Choreutoscope,' which was showing crude pictures before anyone had a film to show. For it was in or about 1878 or 1879 when I saw it and it had been showing long before that. (17–18)

As this passage suggests, Hepworth stressed the continuities between old and new media in his various accounts of the origins of the cinema. This was, in part, due to his early immersion in the sphere of instructive entertainment at the Royal Polytechnic on Regent Street, where his father Thomas Craddock Hepworth presented magic-lantern illustrated lectures, alongside John Henry Pepper, George Buckland and many others, on miscellaneous subjects, including 'The Footprints of Charles Dickens', 'Electricity', 'Telephony', and the 'Phonograph'.[2]

Cecil Hepworth shared his father's interest in explaining the historical and technological intricacies of optical and media systems. In *Animated Photography. The ABC of the Cinematograph* (1897), Hepworth outlined the differences and analogies between the optical systems of the magic lantern and the cinematograph as part of an evolving narrative of how the mind of the spectator could experience the most convincing illusion of movement. Moving from the dissolving view to the intermittent movements of the cinematograph, Hepworth stresses that the 'change from one picture to the next must be so quickly accomplished that it is indiscernible to the eye, and each picture must drop absolutely into the same place as that but an instant before occupied by its predecessor'.[3] Correspondingly, the 'change from one picture to the next', given that it could not be achieved instantaneously, had to be 'covered by a period of darkness, otherwise, by the phenomenon known as "persistence of vision", the impression received by the retina while the picture is moving will remain over into the period of rest, and give a blurred appearance to the picture' (19). Persistence of vision, according to Hepworth, impeded the fluid and clear transition from one image to another. While, on the one hand, the afterimages generated by the persistence of vision made 'animated photographs possible', he argued, they also left a residual impression on the retina that stayed 'there through the succeeding picture', flooding it with a 'grey mist that blocks out all the brilliancy' (55).

Drawing on his own experiences as an exhibitor and performer, Hepworth's approach to the language of the cinema, as his clear instructive prose suggests, was applied and pragmatic. His interest in the dynamics of attention, memory and imagination were equally concerned with achieving the most expedient and entertaining technological affect. In the manner of precursors such as David Brewster and John Henry Pepper, his driving ambition was to articulate and contribute to a process of experimentation, reflection and education, that would ultimately produce, in his case, the most accessible and communicable form of cinematic language. Given this didactic emphasis, the material presence of the reader and the audience was integral to Hepworth's accounts of his multiple trials and errors as he slowly forged his way in the cinema business. While referring back to the transfixed audiences at the Royal Polytechnic, Hepworth also captured the chaotic interactive experience of early cinematic production and performance. Recalling his earliest exhibitions in *Came the Dawn* he observed the 'intense enthusiasm' audiences felt for 'these short, crude films':

> I showed the films forwards in the ordinary way and then showed some of them backwards. I stopped them in the middle and argued with them; called out to the little girl who was standing in the forefront of the picture to stand

aside which she immediately did. That required careful timing but was very effective. But with it all I very soon found I must have more films and better ones. (33)

The dual challenge was to train his audiences' eyes and minds to respond to the new medium of cinema by illuminating its parallels with old media, while promoting its novel attractions and potential.

The following chapter begins with an analysis of Hepworth's forging of his cinematic vision out of the literal fragments of Robert Paul's 'throw outs' that he purchased from Paul for around four shillings. These fragments from Paul's 'junk basket' became the basis not only of Hepworth's cinematic practice, but also of his technical approach to the language of cinema.[4] As the first section of this chapter demonstrates, Hepworth's technical lexicon assumes fundamental parallels between the machinery of the cinematograph and the influential psychology of the persistence of vision that dated back to David Brewster's account of kaleidoscopic vision, John Ayrton Paris's Thaumatrope and Joseph Plateau's seminal account of the visual effects of the Phenakistoscope. Plateau, describing the phenomenon of the afterimage in 1830 wrote:

> If several objects, progressively different in form and position, are presented to the eye for very short intervals and sufficiently close together, the impressions they make upon the retina will join together without being confused and one will believe one is seeing a single object gradually changing form and position.[5]

Hepworth was keenly aware of these experimental precursors; their efforts to externalise the machinery of perceptual cognition inspired his own experiments with the moving image. In the late 1890s Hepworth began to fuse disparate images culled from Paul and his own stock of lantern slides to create what he called 'story content', supplemented by lectures and music, which he then proceeded to take 'all over the country to halls where many in the audience had never seen a living photograph in their lives'.[6]

Robert Paul was also one of many inspirations for Hepworth's subsequent transition from the documentary actuality format pioneered by Paul himself, as well as the Lumières, to the more ambitious literary adaptation of Lewis Carroll's *Alice's Adventures* (1903). The popularity of Paul's pioneering venture into romantic comedy, *A Soldier's Courtship* (1896), appealed to Hepworth's interest in the function of narrative as a form of managing his audiences' attention spans. Paul's production company was also responsible for the first known adaptation of Charles Dickens's *A Christmas Carol*, entitled *Scrooge, or, Marley's Ghost* (1901), which like Pepper's truncated version of *The*

Haunted Man, made no effort to adapt the entire tale, choosing instead to experiment with a series of trick effects to bring the ghost-plagued Scrooge to life. Hepworth's adaptation of Carroll's novel, however, was more concerned with narrative than illusion. The resulting film reflects Hepworth's preoccupation with the visual effects of continuity, integrating image and text in a format that supplemented what he saw as the distracting flicker effects of the cinematograph with titles designed to trigger the audience's memory of Carroll's familiar tale.

To be sure, integrating viewing and reading in this way was intrinsic to the narrative structure of early film, as P. Adams Sitney notes, 'the cinematic experience during the silent period was one of an alternation of reading and looking at images in an illusionistic depth'.[7] Yet read in the context of Hepworth's resistance to the effects of the persistence of vision in his short study of *Animated Photography*, significant parallels begin to emerge with Hugo Munsterberg's early theory of memory as a cinematic supplement and the structure of Hepworth's version of *Alice's Adventures*. Synchronising with the machinery of the cinematograph, the audience's memory literally fills in the gaps between images. The moving image is, to quote Hugo Munsterberg, 'superadded by the action of the mind'.[8] The final section of this chapter reveals the continuities between Hepworth's screen practice and Munsterberg's psychological approach to film. Munsterberg drew on an extensive nineteenth-century psychological network, not the least of which was the work of his teacher, the eminent German psychologist Wilhelm Wundt, and William James, the latter of whom facilitated his transition to Harvard, thus indirectly creating the space for his subsequent studies of American cultural life. For Munsterberg, the difference between art and science was that the former isolated and internalised, whereas the latter focused on connection and empirical externality. Resonating with Munsterberg's stress on the analogy between film and mind, the memory of reading *Alice's Adventures* that Hepworth channels through his film was intended to elide the space between the images projected on the screen and the nostalgic stream of images generated in the minds of the audience by Carroll's words and Tenniel's popular illustrations. In the process of remembering Carroll's text the audience would fail to register, or so Hepworth hoped, 'the distressing flicker' between one frame and the next.[9]

Robert Paul's 'throw outs'

In 1896 Hepworth went with his father to see Robert Paul's 'Living Photographs', a 'little side show' which involved projecting films made by Edison for his Kinetoscope through a translucent screen.[10] Inspired, Hepworth pushed through the crowd, introduced himself to Paul and secured an invitation to visit his office. In a scene worthy of a Dickens novel, Hepworth described the frenetic industry he found there:

> I went there and found that his work-room was at the very top of a tall building and I stumbled up the narrow staircase, trying not to tread upon the dozen or more sleeping Polish and Armenian Jews who had been waiting there for days and nights for delivery of 'Animatographs,' as Paul's machines were called. And there was Paul himself, perspiring freely and cranking away at his big clumsy machines in the hopeless endeavor to run them in and make them usable by the weaker brethren outside. (29)

This vision of strenuous mechanical reproduction in which the film-maker functions as worker, capitalist and artist catalysed Hepworth's cinematic and commercial ambitions. It was an emancipatory moment in which all the elements of his past life came together, as he reminds the reader: 'Remember my early life: photography – limelight-lantern shows-lectures. The next stop was obvious and inevitable' (31).

Scanning the workshop, Hepworth discovered a junk basket of cheap films that each ran for 40 second intervals and began the process of combining his magic-lantern slides and Paul's discarded footage into continuous narratives that he could then supplement in performance with commentary and musical accompaniment:

> I remember one little series which always went down very well indeed. It was called *The Storm* and consisted of half a dozen slides and one forty-foot film . . . The sequence opened with a calm and peaceful picture of sea and sky. Soft and gentle music (Schumann, I think). That changes to another seascape, though the clouds looked a little more interesting, and the music quickened a bit. At each change the inevitability of a coming gale became more insistent and the music more threatening; until the storm broke with an exciting film of dashing waves bursting into the entrance of a cave, with wild music (by Jensen I think). (32)

Hepworth's concept of the film experience made no distinction between commerce and aesthetic affect. He revelled in the alternative public sphere that the cinematic experience made possible in the minds of his audience, to invoke Alexander Kluge, while still drawing on existing literary-derived structures to create a semblance of coherence out of the waste and detritus of Paul's workshop and the residual medium of his own magic-lantern slides.[11] The result was an unapologetic composite of found objects, new and old media driven by the dual logic of communication and commerce. Confounding conventional narratives of technological progress, Hepworth's various media assemblages resembled a series of refashioned cultural afterimages generated from the storage dimensions of both film and photography.

As Charles Acland has noted of the intrinsically residual nature of modern media, 'The detritus of capital and commodity serve the dual purpose of announcing their own historicity and residing as a standing reserve, as Heidegger might have put it, for conversion into subsequent artifacts, memories, and stories.'[12] Underlying Acland's theorisation of residual media, as he acknowledges, is Raymond Williams' seminal articulation of the sustained and transformative potential of residual forms. Williams argued:

> The residual, by definition, has been effectively formed in the past, but it is still active in the cultural process, not only and often not at all as an element of the past, but as an effective element of the present.[13]

Transformation, rather than progressive obsolescence drives cultural formation, an accumulative dynamic that Hepworth was quick to channel into new versions of familiar artifacts, memories and stories that he pragmatically sourced from multiple media, both old and new, residual and emergent. In his memoir he speaks without distinction of the challenges and pleasures of transforming Paul's found footage, Carroll and Tenniel's redolent mediations of Alice, a novel by Dickens, or his own father's discarded magic-lantern scripts, into novel versions of existing archives of images.

Hepworth described himself in *Animated Photography* as a 'cinematographic experimenter' in the context of outlining a series of experiments to reduce the flicker effects that he felt threatened the naturalistic appearance of his films (54). One of these experiments involved using a translucent rather than a solid shutter on the cinematograph allowing 'a large quantity of light to reach the screen in the intervals between pictures, and thus do away with the flicker' (55). The problem with this tactic was that 'the dispersion of the light is such that it illuminates the whole room in a series of flashes, which, blending into another by "persistence of vision," give the effect of a lantern show in a room that is not properly darkened' (55). Flicker effects, compounded by the afterimages generated by the persistence of vision, distractingly illuminated the close proximity between the dynamic mobility of the cinematic image and the dissolving views of the old magic lantern. The potentially dynamic synthesis of old and new threatened to lapse back into familiar patterns, defeated by the reciprocal limitations of physiology and technology. The mechanisms of the eye and camera must synchronise, Hepworth argued, if the cinematic medium was to outlast the exigencies of the marketplace.

Hepworth's frustrations with the limiting effects of 'the persistence of vision', an optical concept which he invokes in inverted commas throughout *Animated Photography*, yet fails to ascribe to any particular scientific authority, assumes that his readers will be familiar with the term. This was a reasonable assumption, despite the fact that it was not the only available explanation for the illusion of motion at this time. Nevertheless, as Mary Ann Doane has argued, in contrast to these alternative explanations, the persistence of vision was 'fully imbricated with insistent concerns in the nineteenth and early twentieth centuries about representation, inscription, temporality, and the archive'.[14] As I discussed in Chapter 3 in the context of David Brewster's *Letters on Natural Magic*, the persistence of vision and the more scientific concept of the afterimage were part of a popular discourse on optics that emerged alongside inventions such as the kaleidoscope and the thaumotrope. Writing of the scientific origins of the thaumatrope, Brewster informed his readers:

> It was found by the French philosopher, M. D'Arcet, that the impression of light continued on the retina about the eighth part of a second after the luminous body was withdrawn, and upon this principle Dr Paris has constructed the pretty little instrument called the *Thaumatrope*, or the *Wonderturner*.[15]

In these early accounts of the afterimage the surface of the retina functions like a screen passively and transiently registering the flickering effects of each image just long enough to create the illusion of continuity between one scene and another, as Brewster exemplifies in the following experiment:

> It is a curious circumstance, that when the image of an object is impressed upon the retina only for a few moments, the picture which is left is exactly the same colour as the object. If we look, for example, at a window at some distance from the eye, and then transfer the eye quickly to the wall, we shall see it distinctly, but momentarily, with *light* panes and *dark* bars; but in a space of time incalculably short, this picture is succeeded by a spectral impression of the window, which will consist of *black* panes and *white* bars. (26)

This visual effect, however, was complicated, as James Sully later observed in his account of the psychological implications of such optical phenomena, by the fact that the observer rarely attends with such precision to the relative duration or variation of these impressions. Drawing on Brewster and the physiological psychology of Wilhelm Wundt, Munsterberg's teacher, Sully argued that these illusions were the material affects of the intermittent movements of attention and memory. Sully suggested an individual observer's capacity to recognise the meaning of an image was contingent on the intervention of memory:

Thus, when travelling in Italy, the visual impression answering to a ruined temple or a bareheaded friar is construed much more rapidly than it would be elsewhere, because of the attitude of mind due to the surrounding circumstances. In all such cases the process of pre-perception connected with a given impression is effected more or less completely by the suggestions of other and related impressions.[16]

Memory, however, was not always consistent, it depended, according to Sully, on the mind's readiness to 'look at the impression the required way', an intrinsically contingent and flawed process that mirrored the eye's blurring of afterimages with present impressions: 'Sometimes the meaning of an impression flashes on us at once, and the stage of pre-perception becomes evanescent. At other times the same impression will fail for an appreciable interval to divulge its meaning' (30–1). Sully effectively constructs the retina as a screen that the mind is required to look at in 'the required way' so that it can decode the right message from the images projected on its surface. Citing Wilhelm Wundt's neurological account of the physiology of attention that argued that 'the reaction of attention' depended upon the reinforcing affects of 'nervous excitation', Sully emphasised the centrality of nerve impulses to learned or habitual responses to perceptual stimuli (31). Given the mutual influence of Wundt, the parallels between Munsterberg and Sully are hardly surprising. Both men shared an interest in the way the mind perceives the illusion of movement, whether or not the movement actually takes place in real time, or in the mind of the observer. It is this psychological preoccupation that made film such a captivating medium for Munsterberg. It materialised the way the mind creates movement through afterimages generated by the eye, mediating the world as a series of rapidly moving pictures, independent of the movements of actual space and time. This, in turn, generated patterns of psychological response – primarily memory and attention – that Hepworth and his contemporaries, such as Paul, struggled to channel back through the cinematographic apparatus.

Cinematic Minds

Hugo Munsterberg, although little known now, was a famous figure in America at the time of the publication of 'The Photoplay: A Psychological Study' in 1916. Although he had begun his career in experimental psychology under the tutelage of Wilhelm Wundt and was mentored by William James, who also included Sully in his extensive international psychological network, Munsterberg made his reputation in broader intellectual circles as the originator of applied psychology.[17] Works, such as *On the Witness Stand: Essays on Psychology and Crime* (1909), *Vocation and Learning* (1912), *Psychology and Industrial Efficiency* (1912), *Business Psychology* and *Psychology: General and Applied* (1916) extended Munsterberg's influence into the non-academic community, another aspect of his approach to the general communication of theories of mind that linked him to the nineteenth-century tradition of popularising science that David Brewster had so ardently championed. Like Brewster, Munsterberg was also a controversial querulous figure. His negative comparisons of American with German culture in the lead up to the First World War gradually alienated the initially strong support he had received from colleagues and general audiences alike.

By 1916 Munsterberg's fame was veering towards infamy, a grim circumstance that may have prompted him to seek the comforting darkness of the movie theatre. In a short illustrated essay, 'Why We Go to the Movies', published in the popular magazine *The Cosmopolitan* in 1915, he described his first film experience with a similar enthusiasm to Hepworth:

> I may confess frankly that I was one of those snobbish late-comers. Until a year ago I had never seen a real photoplay. Although I was a passionate lover of the theatre, I should have felt it undignified for a Harvard professor to attend a moving picture show, just as I should not have gone to a vaudeville performance or to a museum of wax figures or to a phonograph concert. Last year, while I was travelling a thousand miles from Boston, I and a friend risked seeing *Neptune's Daughter* [a romantic fantasy directed by Herbert Brenon], and my conversion was rapid. I recognized at once that marvelous possibilities were open, and I began to explore with eagerness the world which was new to me.[18]

This exploration initially involved avid movie watching: 'I went with a crowd to Anita Stewart and Mary Pickford and Charles Chaplin; I saw Pathe and Vitagraph, Lubin and Essanay, Paramount and Majestic, Universal and Knickerbocker' (172). Further research followed: 'I read books on how to write scenarios; I visited the manufacturing companies, and, finally, I began to experiment myself' (172). Like Hepworth, film excited his interest in the science of the cinematic apparatus, but unlike Hepworth, Munsterberg's primary focus was on experimenting with the parallels between mind and technology, not on improving the technology itself to the point where it would be able to supplement the eye and mind's intrinsic perceptual flaws. While Munsterberg actively participated in the process of film production, his film shorts, which were produced in conjunction with Paramount Pictures and screened before feature films, took the form of applied psychological tests and were part of a series called 'Paramount Pictographs: the Magazine for the Screen' entitled 'Testing the Mind'.[19] As he wrote to a friend in 1916:

> In order to popularize the ideal of mental tests and to stimulate public interest last year I constructed scenarios for moving pictures which allowed everyone in the audience to take part in the tests. The Paramount Pictures Corporation brought them out with unusual success. As two million people have seen those tests on the screen, the idea had a chance to spread, and, it seems to me, awakened interest all around.[20]

Munsterberg traced the genealogy of the cinema back to early nineteenth-century experiments with the afterimage, or persistence of vision, in his account of 'The Outer Development of the Moving Pictures' in the first section of *The Photoplay*. Beginning in the 1830s, he moves from Plateau's phenakistoscope, to the popularity of the zootrope or bioscope, 'a revolving black cylinder with vertical slits, on the inside of which paper strips with pictures of moving objects in successive phases were placed' (47). Munsterberg argued that the

> scientific principle which controls the moving picture world of today was established with these early devices. Isolated pictures, presented to the eye in rapid succession but separated by interruptions, are perceived not as single impressions of different positions, but as a continuous movement. (48)

To demonstrate the viability of this lineage Munsterberg draws on the child's knowing suspension of the logic of perception when it creates the illusion of movement with a simple thaumatrope – in which different images on either side of a circular disc blend into one with the turn of a hand – to explain the doubleness of the observer's simultaneous awareness of the flatness of the screen as an 'object of perception' and perception of the illusion of depth and movement (72). Both the thaumatrope and the cinema generate forms of positive afterimages, he argues, the difference being one of degrees of psychological and technological complexity:

> In the case of the picture on the screen this conflict is much stronger. *We certainly see the depth, and yet we cannot accept it.* There is too much which inhibits belief and interferes with the interpretation of the people and landscape before us as truly plastic. They are surely not simple pictures. The persons can move toward us and away from us, and the river flows into a distant valley. And yet the distance of our real space, such as the theater shows, and the persons themselves are not flesh and blood. It is a unique inner experience, which is characteristic of the perception of the photoplays. *We have reality with all its true dimensions; and yet it keeps the fleeting, passing surface suggestions without true depth and fullness, as different from a mere picture as from a mere stage performance.*[21]

Intrinsically ephemeral, the perception of moving images involves what Mary Ann Doane describes as 'a temporal lag, a superimposition of images, an inextricability of past and present'.[22] The psychology of the afterimage is inseparable from the reticular movements of memory, a non-linear temporality, which Doane argues, against Deleuze's theory of the 'movement-image', cannot be defined 'as a succession of instants' (77).

Moving forward from the thaumatrope, to the daguerreotype to the perfection of the photographic plate to the stop-motion photography of Eadweard Muybridge and Etienne-Jules Marey, and then on to Thomas Edison, the Lumière brothers and Robert Paul, Munsterberg narrates a conventional history of technological and scientific progress that paradoxically captures the generative interplay between residual and emergent media. Munsterberg's acute sense of the vitality of past forms is also fundamentally linked to the alternative temporality of the mind that shapes 'The Inner Development of the Moving Pictures.' He aligns the development of cinema from the documentary form of the actuality, to the extended narrative form of fiction films, such as Hepworth's adaptation of Alice, as an internal development, in which the medium mirrors the psychological interplay between memory and attention:

> The advance was first of all internal; it was an aesthetic idea. Yet even this does not tell the whole story of the inner growth of the moving pictures, as it only points to the progress of the photoplay. It leaves out of account the fact that the moving pictures appeal not merely to the imagination, but that they bring their message also to the intellect. They aim towards instruction and information. Just as, between the two covers of a magazine, artistic stories stand side by side with instructive essays, scientific articles, or discussions of the events of the day, the photoplay is accompanied by a kinematoscopic rendering of reality in all its aspects. (54)

Munsterberg's rhetoric here reveals his imbrication in nineteenth-century conceptions of the moving image. Recalling the familiar nineteenth-century terminology of instructive entertainment that had provided the rationale for generations of optical recreations, he evaluates cinema's dual appeal to the imagination and intellect. He also reinforces the parallels between engaging with the early multi-perspectival moving picture format and the multi-medial miscellaneous appeal of reading magazines such as the *Strand Magazine*, where, as the previous chapter discussed, readers could move freely between illustrated fiction by notable contemporary writers, as well as essays on scientific and historic events, such as a textual remediation of Robert Paul's seminal film of the Prince's Derby in 1896.

The ultimate realisation of the cinematic medium, however, according to Munsterberg, lay in the transition from the novelty of filming coronations, parades, derbys, and the natural wonders of the world, to the artistic rendering of fictional plots. This transition prompts him to ask, 'What was the real principle of the inner development on this artistic side?' (57). One of the answers to this question, he suggests, is that fictional constructs reinforce the pivotal supplementary role imagination and memory play in the way the mind experiences moving images. To clarify this claim, he reminds his readers of the constitutive role illusion plays in everyday perception, when 'we believe that we see something which only our imagination supplies' (75). To further reinforce this point he invokes the analogy of the involuntary creative substitution that is intrinsic to the process of reading: 'If an unfamiliar printed word is exposed to our eye for the twentieth part of a second, we readily substitute a familiar word with similar letters' (76-7). He then asks, 'Are we not also familiar with the experience of supplying, by our fancy, the associative image of a movement when only the starting point, and the end point are given if a skillful suggestion influences our mind?' (76). This argument, in turn, nicely sets up the parallels between the inner experience of reading and perception and the inner experience of 'the film world' as Munsterberg calls it:

> *the motion which he sees appears to be a true motion, and yet it is created by his own mind.* The afterimages of the successive pictures are not sufficient to produce a substitute for the continuous outer stimulation; the essential condition is rather the inner mental activity which unites the separate phases in the idea of connected action.[23]

Like Hepworth, Munsterberg's theory of the moving image is grounded in an acute sense of the fragility of human eye, as well as the importance of countering the eye's limitations with mechanisms that trigger the 'inner mental activity' of association that ultimately blurs the line between present and past and creates the illusion of connection and continuity (78). The film on the screen is mirrored and then expanded by the film in the viewer's mind, suggesting new ways of conceiving of the use and value of the cinematic apparatus.

The fictional photoplay only amplifies these effects, taking the mere perception of movement into new psychological and aesthetic territory:

> The mere perception of the men and women and of the background, with all their depth and their motion furnishes only the material ... We must accompany those sights with a wealth of ideas. They must have a meaning for us, they must be enriched by our own imagination, they must awaken the remnants of earlier experiences, they must stir up our feelings and emotions,

they must play on our suggestability, they must start ideas and thoughts, . . . they must draw our attention constantly to the important and essential element of the action. (79)

But channelling this associative process, Munsterberg insists, requires the careful management of distractions. These include the distraction of musical accompaniment and the 'words on screen' that substitute 'for the speech of the actors' (82). While the 'so-called "leaders" between the pictures . . . prescribe the line in which the attention must move and force the interest of the spectator toward the new goal', they must remain secondary to the pictures themselves (82). Film surpasses the most absorbing novel, musical piece or theatrical performance, Munsterberg contends, by providing the ultimate mechanism for capturing and holding the attention of the easily distractible human eye, the close-up:

A clerk buys a newspaper on the street, glances at it and is shocked. Suddenly we see that piece of news with our own eyes. The close-up magnifies the headlines of the paper so that they fill the whole screen. . . . Whenever our attention becomes focused on a special feature, the surrounding adjusts itself, eliminates everything in which we are not interested, and by the close-up heightens the vividness of that on which our mind is concentrated. It is as if that outer world were woven into our mind and were shaped not through its own laws but by the acts of our attention. (88)

It is precisely the appeal of this closing in on the forensic details of a scene that late nineteenth-century writers, such as George Sims, found so captivating about the new medium's potential 'to capture and display humanity', as Stephen Bottomore has recently argued.[24] The movement of a hand, a flicker of emotion playing across a face, or a significant word or headline could be the key to unlock the plot, a reciprocity between screen and mind that Munsterberg argues exemplifies the way cinema uniquely objectivises both the mechanisms of attention and memory.

In addition, narrative film reflects the multi-temporal nature of memory, according to Munsterberg, the way the mind moves across and between 'parallel currents with their endless interconnections' (95). The cinematograph, for example, allows multiple details of a scene to be fleetingly and simultaneously viewed:

We see the banker, who had told his young wife that he has a directors' meeting, at a late hour in a cabaret feasting with a stenographer from his office. She had promised her poor old parents to be home early. We see the gorgeous roof garden and the tango dances, but our dramatic interest is divided among the frivolous pair, the jealous young woman in the suburban cottage, and the anxious old people in the attic. Our mind wavers among the three scenes. The photoplay shows one after another. Yet it can hardly be said that we think of them as successive. It is as if we were really at all three places at once. (95)

This non-linear dissolution of time frames, Munsterberg argues, exemplifies that, as with the perception of depth and movement, the experience of cinematic time is ultimately all in the mind: '*Events which are far distant from one another so that we could not be physically present at all of them at the same time are fusing in our field of vision, just as they are brought together in our consciousness.*'[25] This alignment of cinematic and psychological temporality also provides the key to understanding cinema's status as art. Munsterberg argues that like the novel, painting, theatre, or music, cinema possesses its own unique capacity to transform the real into an aesthetic experience. Indeed, Munsterberg suggests that film comes closest in this regard to 'the art of musical tones':

> They have overcome the outer world and the social world entirely, they unfold our inner life, our mental play, with its feelings and emotions, its memories and fancies, in a material which seems exempt from the laws of the world of substance and material. (127)

The challenge is to train people to look beyond the machine as they do when they read, as Munsterberg insists, a 'printed book of lyric poems is also machine-made' (159). To achieve the same recognition as a true art alongside the lyric or 'a true novel', however, Munsterberg argued that film ultimately had to move away from the novel, a claim that simultaneously revealed the powerful conceptual hold the immersive psychology of literary experience continued to have over early film makers and theorists, such as Hepworth and Munsterberg (142).

Residual Flickers of Alice

Making *Alice in Wonderland* (1903) was 'an ambitious effort' according to Hepworth's account in *Came the Dawn*:

> This was the greatest fun and we did the whole story in 800 feet – the longest ever at that time. Every situation was dealt with with all the accuracy at our command and with reverent fidelity, so far as we could manage it, to Tenniel's drawings. I had been married about a year and my wife, broken-in to film work, played the part of the White Rabbit. Alice was played by Mabel Clark, the little girl from the cutting room, growing exasperatingly larger and smaller as she does in the book. The beautiful garden was the garden of Mount Felix, at Walton; the Duchess, the kitchen, the mad tea-party, the Cheshire Cat, the royal procession – all were there. The painting of the whole

pack of cards human size was quite an undertaking and the madly comic trial scene at the end made a suitable and hilarious finale. (63)

Reinforcing the alignment with Carroll's plot, Hepworth's inter-titles were equally reverential in their adherence to the original, with one minor detour that is in itself symptomatic of the challenges of executing a film narrative in a period when 'a specific cinematographic language did not exist', as Andre Gaudreault has argued, echoing the seminal theory of Christian Metz.[26] Hepworth included a scene where Alice plays with the Hepworth family dog in the above-described 'beautiful garden', an oddly disruptive addition which was accompanied by an inter-title that read, 'Alice, now very small, has gained access to the Garden where she meets a Dog and tries to make him play with her.' Kamilla Elliot notes that this moment in Hepworth's film is one of the earliest examples of the generative tension between word and image that shaped early cinema. 'Despite claims of film as a universal language', Elliot argues, 'early inter-titles like these indicate that for audiences, film was a foreign language needing translation into their own'.[27] The words duplicate the images on the screen, but they also provide vital information that the silent images cannot. The inter-title names Alice, encourages the audience to identify with her point of view and establishes her transition to the 'beautiful garden' of Wonderland. The viewer's eye is thus directed to read narrative content into the cinematic frame, and also to fill the space between frames with an associative network of words and ideas.

Aside from this brief departure from its literary source, the success of Hepworth's *Alice in Wonderland* depended on audience recognition of the details of Carroll's plot and Tenniel's illustrations. The ability of audiences to move between media is assumed, a realistic expectation given the miscellaneous habits of reading and viewing that were required of turn-of-the-century readers on a daily basis. As Munsterberg notes, early film audiences were trained to navigate their way through increasingly dense and complex information networks by the hybrid format of popular magazines. In this media environment watching a film, like reading a fictional work and then dipping into an informative essay, was a networked socially organised experience that was also inherently plural and contingent on 'a particular site, phase and mode of exhibition', to invoke Miriam Hansen.[28] Andrew Shail has also recently reinforced this symbiosis of late nineteenth-century film and print culture in his analysis of the proliferation of allusions to the cinematograph in short fiction published in turn-of-the-century popular magazines. Shail argues that short fiction which relied on the cinematograph as a central fictional conceit, including George Sims' detective stories, were significant 'components of the larger effort to absorb and make sense of the new technology, at a point when no consensus on the purpose and propensities of the cinematograph existed'.[29]

With a running time of roughly twelve minutes, *Alice in Wonderland* was the longest film in existence at that time. Yet despite its technological novelty, the structure of the film was indebted to existing commercial magic-lantern slide sets of literary texts, illustrating episodes and relying on the supplementary reading of lecturers and audiences. Consumers and exhibitors could purchase Hepworth's film in parts and selectively project individual sequences. Indeed, this was the favoured form of presentation and consumption at this time, given that short films fitted more easily into the variety format in which they were most commonly featured as part of fairground attractions and music-hall programmes. The Mad Hatter's tea party sequence, for example, proved a popular choice with contemporary exhibitors. Hepworth also continued a long tradition of privileging Tenniel's illustrations, which I discussed in Chapter 5. Indeed, he was so concerned that the film be true to Tenniel's illustrations that he spent an inordinate amount of time making costumes and building sets to do the original images justice.

Although the recently restored copy of *Alice in Wonderland* is damaged, which reinforces its truncated structure, the surviving frames reveal Hepworth's impressive editorial and technical mastery of visual effects, including the convincing portrayal of Alice's magical physical transformations.[30] The film begins inside Alice's dream. The first inter-title reads 'Alice dreams that she sees the White Rabbit and follows him down the Rabbit-hole, into the Hall of Many doors.' The following sequence depicts Alice pulling aside a velvet curtain to reveal a small door that she tries unsuccessfully to unlock. She then drinks from a bottle that says 'drink me', shrinks and then eats to grow large enough to grasp the key from the table before shrinking again with the aid of a magic fan.

Another inter-title cues the transition into the garden beyond where Alice somewhat mysteriously encounters the previously mentioned dog, before the next inter-title sets up a further sequence depicting Alice entering the White Rabbit's house, resuming her normal size and finding herself trapped. The following sequences move quickly from her escape from the White Rabbit to her encounter with pig and pepper with no textual framing – a series of narrative transitions that would have made little sense to an audience unfamiliar with Carroll's text. This sequence ends with the inter-title, 'The Duchess's Cheshire Cat appears to Alice and directs her to the house of the Mad Hatter – The Mad Tea-Party.' Hepworth's Cheshire Cat then emerges from a mist and Alice alternates between waving a handkerchief and reaching out to pat him, a far remove from Carroll's oracular feline. The action then abruptly cuts to the Mad Hatter's tea party literally visualising the preceding textual cue. Again, this scene would have been inexplicable without prior knowledge of Carroll's plot.

The penultimate sequence of frames is set up with another inter-title: 'The Royal Procession – The Queen invites Alice to join – Alice unintentionally offends the Queen who calls the Executioner to behead her. But Alice boxes his ears and in the confusion which results she awakes.' The cards march up the garden path while Alice stands by applauding and patting them on the head. The Queen pauses and Alice joins the procession, but all quickly dissolves into chaos, including an axe-wielding child whom Alice pushes away. The subsequent melee resolves into a chase with Alice fleeing down the path followed by the pack of cards with the Queen of Hearts bringing up the rear. This final scene ultimately dissolves into an image of Alice awakening from her dream.

As this description of the film suggests, each scene consists of what Tom Gunning has described as 'a sort of micro-narrative, showing a single location and a complete action'.[31] The continuity between these micro-narratives, Gunning argues, consequently relied on 'the audience's foreknowledge of the story' to maintain 'a sort of sluggish continuity, rather than emphasizing disruptions between shots' (91). This 'tableau style' interplay between discontinuity and continuity, Gunning suggests, locates films like *Alice in Wonderland* at a transitional point between discontinuous and continuous films, such as Hepworth's slightly later popular chase film, *Rescued by Rover* (1905) in which continuous action over a series of cuts 'establishes a coherent synthetic geography' (91). Hepworth's stress on the importance of the continuity between frames in *Animated Photography* reveals the impetus behind this gradual technical refinement of continuous form. Addressing himself to his fellow exhibitors he urges them to

> Remember, an audience is a thing of ideas. Keep it always and continuously entertained and interested; give it no time to notice and remember the many faults in your pictures; do not distract its attention by pauses and evident uncertainties. (83)

Holding the attention of the viewer is vital to the effective experience of the moving image. As a consequence, Hepworth continues, 'a living photograph show', while necessarily episodic, must ease the transition between frames so that the audience 'does not suffer from the weariness which is the inevitable result of watching a herd of heterogeneous pictures – no matter how excellent – jumbled together without rhyme or

reason' (84). Although continuity did not always mean linear chronological progression, as he remarks in the context of one of his earlier
visual tricks:

> With some machines it is possible to work the mechanism backwards if
> desired; and certain films, shown *a la* 'Alice through the Looking Glass,' the
> effect is extremely funny. It is a variation of the usual order of things which,
> if confined to once in an evening, is sure to raise a laugh. (87)

As these playful comments suggest, the robust commercialism and
technological modernity of Hepworth's work was far removed from the
aesthetic constraints of genteel literary culture. And yet, as his observations in both *Animated Photography* and *Came the Dawn* also reveal,
Hepworth was in many ways captivated by the same fascination with
how to produce vivid images in his audience's mind that compelled
Coleridge and Wordsworth, to return to my introductory arguments at
the beginning of this study. While Hepworth obviously did not share
Coleridge and Wordsworth's horror of the commercialism of popular
visual entertainment, he did share their interest in training the eye of the
reader/viewer to see familiar scenes anew, from a slightly altered perspective, and thus to make images move in the mind with a dynamism
that far exceeded the two dimensional limits of either screen or page.

Notes

1. Hepworth, *Came the Dawn. Memories of a Film Pioneer*, p. 16.
2. Hepworth, *Came the Dawn*, p. 22.
3. Hepworth, *Animated Photography. The ABC of the Cinematograph*, p. 19.
4. Hepworth, *Came the Dawn*, p. 31.
5. Joseph A. F. Plateau, cited in Doane, *The Emergence of Cinematic Time*, p. 71.
6. Hepworth, *Came the Dawn*, p. 31.
7. Sitney, 'Image and Title in Avante-Garde Cinema', *October* 11. Essays in Honor of Jay Leyda (Winter 1979), p. 103.
8. Munsterberg, 'The Photoplay: A Psychological Study', in *Hugo Munsterberg on Film. The Photoplay: A Psychological Study and Other Writings* p. 77.
9. Hepworth, *Came the Dawn*, p. 32.
10. Hepworth, *Came the Dawn*, p. 29.
11. Kluge's concept of film as an alternative public sphere is discussed at length in the introduction to this study.
12. Acland, 'Introduction', *Residual Media*, p. xvii.
13. Williams, *Marxism and Literature*, p. 125.
14. Doane, *The Emergence of Cinematic Time*, p. 72.
15. Brewster, *Letters on Natural Magic*, p. 27. Italics are Brewster's.
16. Sully, *Illusions – A Psychological Study* (1887), p. 30.

17. The works that established Munsterberg's reputation as an experimental psychologist were *The Activity of Will* (1889), *Contributions to Experimental Psychology* (1889), and *Aims and Methods of Psychology* (1891).
18. Munsterberg, 'Why We Go to the Movies', in *Hugo Munsterberg on Film. The Photoplay: A Psychological Study and Other Writings*, p. 172.
19. Allan Langdale provides a detailed account of the context of these films in 'S(t)imulation of Mind: The Film Theory of Hugo Munsterberg', in *Hugo Munsterberg on Film*, p. 33.
20. Hugo Munsterberg in an unpublished letter to Mr Samuel McClintock, dated 28 September 1916, in the Munsterberg Papers of the Boston Public Library's Special Collections [MS Acc.2357], reprinted in Langdale, 'S(t)imulation of Mind', p. 33.
21. Munsterberg, *The Photoplay* , pp. 70–1. The italics are Munsterberg's.
22. Doane, *The Emergence of Cinematic Time*, p. 77.
23. Munsterberg, 'The Photoplay', p. 78. Italics are Munsterberg's.
24. Bottomore, 'George R. Sims and the Film as Evidence,' in *Reading the Cinematograph. The Cinema in British Short Fiction 1896–1912*, p. 35.
25. Munsterberg, 'The Photoplay', p. 96.
26. Gaudreault, 'Film, Narrative, Narration: The Cinema of the Lumière Brothers', in *Early Cinema. Space, Frame, Narrative*, p. 71.
27. Elliot, *Rethinking the Novel/Film Debate*, p. 92.
28. Hansen, *Babel and Babylon*, p. 14.
29. Shail, 'Reading the Cinematograph. Introduction', in *Reading the Cinematograph*, p. 2.
30. Cecil Hepworth and Percy Stow (directors), *Alice in Wonderland* (1903). The British Film Institute recently restored the film which now runs at just eight minutes of the original twelve. The film was a family affair with Hepworth's wife appearing as the Red Queen, the family cat as the Cheshire cat and Hepworth himself as the Frog Footman.
31. Gunning, 'Non-Continuity, Continuity, Discontinuity. A Theory of Genres in Early Films', in *Early Cinema. Space, Frame, Narrative*, p. 91.

Bibliography

Abercrombie, John. 'Correspondence', *Edinburgh Journal of Science*, New Series no. 4, (1830), 218–19.

—. *Inquiries Concerning the Intellectual Powers and the Investigation of Truth*. Edinburgh: Waugh and Innes, 1830.

Acland, Charles R. 'Introduction,' in Charles R. Acland (ed.). *Residual Media*. London: University of Minnesota Press, 2007, pp. xiii–xxvii.

Alhambra Theatre, 'Theatre of Varieties' Programme, Monday 20 April 1896. Museum of London Collection of Music Hall Programmes.

'*Alice's Adventures in Wonderland*. By Lewis Carroll', *Athenaeum* (16 December 1865), 844.

'*Alice's Adventures in Wonderland*', *The Scotsman* (22 December 1866), 5.

Altick, Richard. *The Shows of London*. Cambridge, MA: Belknap Press, 1978.

Anderson, Patricia. *The Printed Image and the Transformation of Popular Culture 1790–1860*. Oxford: Oxford University Press, 1991.

Armstrong, Isobel. *Victorian Glassworlds*. Oxford: Oxford University Press, 2008.

Bain, Alexander. *Senses and the Intellect*. 1855. Repr. London: Longmans, Green and Co., 1894.

Barnes, John and Richard Maltby. *The Beginnings of Cinema in England, 1894–1901*. Exeter: Exeter University Press, 1997.

Barthes, Roland. *The Rustle of Language*, trans. Richard Howard. New York: Hill and Wang, 1986.

Batchen, Geoff. *Burning With Desire: The Conception of Photography*. Cambridge, MA: MIT Press, 1999.

Baudelaire, Charles. *The Painter of Modern Life*, trans. and ed. Jonathan Mayne. London: Phaidon, 1995.

Benjamin, Walter. *Illuminations*, ed. Hannah Arendt, trans. Harry Zohn. New York: Schocken, 1968.

Bennett, Scott. 'John Murray's Family Library and the Cheapening of Books in Early Nineteenth-Century Britain', *Studies in Bibliography* 29 (1976), 141–67.

Bennett, Tony. 'Texts, Readers, Reading Formations', *The Bulletin of the Midwest Modern Language Association* 16:1 (Spring 1983), 3–17.

Blanchot, Maurice. 'Everyday Speech', *Yale French Studies* 73 (1987), 12–20.

Bolter, Jay David and Richard Grusin. *Remediation: Understanding New Media*. Cambridge, MA: MIT Press, 2000.

Bottomore, Stephen. 'George R. Sims and the Film as Evidence', in Andrew Shail (ed.), *Reading the Cinematograph. The Cinema in British Short Fiction 1896–1912*. Exeter: University of Exeter Press, 2010, pp. 22–36.

Brewster, David. *Treatise on the Kaleidoscope*. London and Edinburgh: n. p., 1819.

—. *Letters on Natural Magic, addressed to Sir Walter Scott*. London: John Murray, 1833.

—. *The Stereoscope: its History, Theory and Construction, with its Application to the Fine and Useful Arts, and to Education etc*. London: n. p., 1856.

—. *The Kaleidoscope. Its History, Theory and Construction with its Application to the Fine and Useful Arts*. London: John Murray, 1858.

Brokedon, William, et al. *Finden's Illustrations of the Life and Works of Lord Byron*. London: John Murray, 1832–4.

Brooker, Jeremy. 'Paganini's Ghost: Musical Resources of the Royal Polytechnic Institution', in Richard Crangle, Mervyn Heard and Ine van Dooren (eds), *Realms of Light: Uses and Perceptions of the Magic Lantern from the Seventeenth to the Twenty-First Century*. London: Magic Lantern Society, 2005.

Brougham, Henry. *Practical Observations upon the Education of the People, Addressed to the Working Class and Their Employers*. London: Longmans, 1825.

—. *Works of Henry Lord Brougham*, 11 vols. Edinburgh: Adam and Charles Black, 1872–3.

Brown, Thomas. *Lectures on the Philosophy of the Human Mind*, 4 vols. Edinburgh: Tait, 1820.

Buzard, James. *The Beaten Track: European Tourism, Literature, and the Ways to 'Culture' 1800–1918*. Oxford: Clarendon Press, 1998.

Byron, Lord. '*Childe Harold's Pilgrimage, Canto III*', *Portfolio*, Political and Literary 1:4 (23 November 1816), 73–7.

—. *The Poetical Works of Lord Byron: Poetry*, 7 vols, ed. Ermest Hartley Coleridge. London: John Murray, 1898–1904.

Caine, Barbara. *Victorian Feminists*. Oxford: Oxford University Press, 1992.

Calè, Luisa. *Fuseli's Milton Gallery: 'Turning Readers into Spectators'*. Oxford: Clarendon Press, 2006.

Carpenter, William. *Principles of Human Physiology with Their Chief Applications to Psychology, Pathology, Therapeutics, Hygiene, and Forensic Medicine*. London: Churchill, 1853.

—. *Principles of Psychology*. London: Henry S. King, 1874.

—. *Principles of Mental Physiology* [1874], 2nd edn. London: Henry S. King, 1875.

Carroll, Lewis. 'Alice on Stage', *The Theatre* 9:52 (April 1887), 179–84.

—. *The Diaries of Lewis Carroll*, 2 vols, ed. Roger Lancelyn Green. London: Cassell & Company, 1953.

—. *Alice's Adventures in Wonderland and Through the Looking-Glass and what Alice found there*, ed. Roger Lancelyn Green. Oxford: Oxford University Press, 1971.

—. Preface to *Sylvie and Bruno* (1889), in *The Complete Illustrated Works of Lewis Carroll*. London: Chancellor Press, 1982, pp. 239–45.

—. *Lewis Carroll and the House of Macmillan*, ed. Morton N. Cohen and Anita Gandolfo. Cambridge: Cambridge University Press, 1987.

Carroll, Noel. 'Film/Mind Analogies: The Case of Hugo Munsterberg', *Journal of Aesthetics and Art Criticism* 46:4 (Summer 1988), 489–99.

Castle, Terry. *The Female Thermometer: Eighteenth-Century Culture and the Invention of the Uncanny*. Oxford: Oxford University Press, 1995.

Chandler, James K. and Kevin Gilmartin (eds). *Romantic Metropolis: The Urban Scene of British Culture, 1780–1840*. Cambridge: Cambridge University Press, 2005.

Chew, Samuel. *Byron in England: His Fame and After-Fame* [1924]. New York: Russell & Russell, 1965.

Christensen, Jerome. *Lord Byron's Strength: Romantic Writing and Commercial Society*. Baltimore: Johns Hopkins University Press, 1993.

Clarence, Sylvester. 'Mr Charles Kean's Sardanapalus', *Theatrical Journal* (20 July 1853), 223–4.

Cobbe, Frances Power. 'Unconscious Cerebration. A Psychological Study', *Macmillan's Magazine* 23:133 (November 1870), 24–37.

—. 'Dreams, as Illustrations of Unconscious Cerebration', *Macmillan's Magazine* 23:138 (April 1871), 512–23.

—. *Darwinism in Morals and Other Essays*. London: William and Norgate, 1872.

Cohen, Morton N. *Lewis Carroll: A Biography*. New York: Vintage, 1995.

Cohn, Albert Mayer. *A Bibliographical Catalogue of the Printed Works Illustrated by George Cruikshank*. London: Longmans, 1914.

Cole, John William. *The Life and Theatrical Times of Charles Kean*. London: R. Bentley, 1859.

Coleridge, Samuel Taylor. *Biographia Literaria; or, Biographical Sketches of My Life and Opinions* [1817], in *Coleridge's Poetry and Prose*, ed. Nicholas Halmi, Paul Magnuson and Raimonda Modiano. New York: Norton, 2004.

—. *Collected letters of Samuel Taylor Coleridge*, 6 vols, ed. E. L. Griggs. Oxford: Oxford University Press, 1956–71.

—. *The Friend*, 2 vols, ed. Barbara Rooke. London: Routledge & Kegan Paul, 1969, vol. 1, pp. 16–17.

—. 'On Poesy or Art', in *Biographia Literaria, with his Aesthetical Essays*, 2 vols, ed. John Shawcross. 1907. Repr. Oxford: Oxford University Press, 1979, vol. 2: pp. 259–60.

—. *Lectures on Literature 1808–19*, 2 vols, ed. R. A. Foakes. London: Routledge, 1987.

—. 'The Garden of Boccaccio', in *Poems*, ed. John Beer. London: J. M. Dent, 1993, pp. 473–6.

Collins, Philip. 'Dickens on Ghosts: An Uncollected Article', *Dickensian* 59 (1963), pp. 5–14, 8–9.

—. *Dickens: The Critical Heritage*. London: Routledge, 1971.

—. *Charles Dickens: The Public Readings*. Oxford: Oxford University Press, 1975.

Crary, Jonathan. *Techniques of the Observer: On Vision and Modernity in the Nineteenth Century*. Cambridge, MA: MIT Press, 1990.

Cripps, Elizabeth. '*Alice* and the Reviewers', *Children's Literature* 11 (1983), 33–48.

Cruikshank, George. *Twelve Sketches Illustrative of Sir Walter Scott's Demonology and Witchcraft*. London: James Robins and Co., 1830.

Dallas, E. S. *The Gay Science*, 2 vols. London: Chapman Hall, 1866.

Dames, Nicholas. *The Physiology of the Novel: Reading, Neural Science, and the Form of Victorian Fiction*. Oxford: Oxford University Press, 2007.

D'Arcy Wood, Gillen. *The Shock of the Real: Romanticism and Visual Culture, 1760–1860*. Basingstoke: Palgrave, 2001.

Dart, Gregory. '"Flash Style": Pierce Egan and Literary London 1820–28', *History Workshop Journal* 51 (2001), 181–205.

Davidoff, Leonore and Catherine Hall. *Family Fortunes: Men and Women of the English Middle Class 1780–1850*. London: Routledge, 1987.

Davis, Michael. *George Eliot and Nineteenth-Century Psychology: Exploring the Unmapped Country*. Aldershot: Ashgate, 2006.

De Certeau, Michel. *The Practice of Everyday Life*, trans. Steven Rendall. Berkeley: University of California Press, 1984.

Decherney, Peter. 'Film Study and Its Object', *Film History* 12:4 (2000), 443–60.

Deleuze, Gilles. *The Logic of Sense*, trans. Mark Lester. New York: Columbia University Press, 1990.

—. *Cinema 1: The Movement-Image*, trans. Hugh Tomlinson and Barbara Habberjam. London: Athlone, 1992.

Deleuze, Gilles and Felix Guattari. *A Thousand Plateaus: Capitalism and Schizophrenia*, trans. Brian Massumi. Minneapolis: University of Minnesota Press, 1987.

Della Porta, Giambattista. *Natural Magick* (Naples, 1558). First English edn. London: Thomas Young and Samuel Speek, 1658. Repr., ed. Derek J. Price. New York: Basic Books, 1957.

Dendy, Walter Cooper. *The Philosophy of Mystery*. London: Longmans, 1841.

Description of A View of Mont Blanc, The Valley of Chamounix and the surrounding mountains (London, 1837). John and Robert Burford, The Panorama of Leicester Square Tracts 1826–49, British Library Collection.

De Quincey, Thomas. 'On the Poetry of Pope', in *De Quincey's Collected Writings*, 14 vols, ed. David Masson. Edinburgh: Adam and Charles Black, 1890, vol. 11, pp. 52–8.

Dickens, Charles. *The Haunted Man and the Ghost's Bargain, A Fancy for Christmas-Time*. London: Bradbury and Evans, 1848.

—. 'The Amusements of the People', *Household Words* 1 (30 March 1850).

—. *Christmas Books: A Reprint of the First Editions, with the illustrations, and an introduction, biographical and bibliographical, by Charles Dickens the Younger*. London: Macmillan, 1892.

—. *The Letters of Charles Dickens*, ed. Kathleen Tillotson et al., 11 vols. Oxford: Clarendon, 1965–99.

—. *Bleak House* [1853]. London: Penguin, 1969.

—. *Selected Journalism, 1850–1870*, ed. David Pascoe. London: Penguin, 1997.

—. *Pictures from Italy* [1846], intro. Kate Flint. London: Penguin, 1998.

Dimmock, Wai-Chee. 'Feminism, New-Historicism and the Reader', in Andrew Bennett (ed.). *Readers and Reading*. London: Longman, 1995, pp. 112–31.

Dircks, Henry. *The Ghost! As Produced in the Spectre Drama, popularly illustrating the marvellous optical illusions obtained by the apparatus called the Dircksian Phantasmagoria*. London: E. and F. N. Spon, 1863.

Doane, Mary Ann. *The Emergence of Cinematic Time: Modernity, Contingency, the Archive*. Cambridge, MA: Harvard University Press, 2002.

Dolby, George. *Charles Dickens as I Knew Him: The Story of the Reading*

Tours in Great Britain and America (1866–1870). London: Fisher & Unwin, 1855.

Drury Lane bills, Theatre Museum London.

Duncan, Ian. *Modern Romance and Transformations of the Novel: The Gothic, Scott, Dickens*. Cambridge: Cambridge University Press, 1992.

During, Simon. *Modern Enchantments: The Cultural Power of Secular Magic*. Cambridge, MA: Harvard University Press, 2002.

Edgeworth, Maria and Richard Lovell. *Practical Education* [1798]. New York: Harper Brothers, 1855.

Egan, Pierce. *Life in London*. London: Sherwood, Neely & Jones, 1821.

—. *The True History of Tom and Jerry; or The Day and Night Scenes, of Life in London*. London: Charles Hindley, 1821.

—. *Tom and Jerry. Life in London or the Day and Night Scenes of Jerry Hawthorn, Esq. and his elegant friend Corinthian Tom in their Rambles and Sprees through the Metropolis*. London: John Camden Hotten, 1869.

Eisenstein, Sergei. 'Dickens, Griffith, and the Film Today', *Film Form: Essays in Film Theory* [1949], repr. San Diego: A Harvest Book, 1977.

Elfenbein, Andrew. *Byron and the Victorians*. Cambridge: Cambridge University Press, 1995.

Eliot, George. *Middlemarch* [1874]. Harmondsworth: Penguin, 1969.

Elliot, Kamilla. *Rethinking the Novel/Film Debate*. Cambridge: Cambridge University Press, 2003.

Ellis, Alec. *Books in Victorian Elementary Schools*. London: The Library Association, 1971.

Ellis, Stuart Marsh. *Henry Kingsley, 1830–1876*. London: Grant Richards, 1931.

Epstein Nord, Deborah. *Walking the Victorian Streets: Women, Representation and the City*. Ithaca, NY: Cornell University Press, 1995.

Evans, K. Jane. *Tabart of Fonthill: From England to Van Diemen's Land*. Published privately for the Tabart Family, 1991.

'Family Library, Vol. XVI, – *Letters on Demonology and Witchcraft, addressed to J. G. Lockhart, Esq.* By Sir Walter Scott, Bart. London, 1830. Murray (Unpublished)', *Athenaeum* 151 (September 1830), 577–82.

Fenwick, Eliza. *Visits to the Juvenile Library Or, Knowledge Proved to be the Source of Happiness* [1805], ed. Claire Tomalin. New York: Garland, 1977.

Ferriar, John, MD. *An Essay Towards the Study of Apparitions*. London: Cadell & Davies, 1813.

Field, Kate. *Pen Photographs of Charles Dickens's Readings. Taken from Life* [1868]. Repr. Boston: James Osgood, 1871.

Fielding, Raymond. 'Hale's Tours: Ultrarealism in the Pre-1910 Motion Picture', in John F. Fell (ed.), *Film Before Griffith*. Berkeley: University of California Press, 1983, pp. 116–27.

Fineman, Joel. 'The History of the Anecdote', in H. Aram Veeser (ed.), *The New Historicism*. New York: Routledge, 1989, pp. 49–77.

Flint, Kate. Introduction to Charles Dickens, *Pictures from Italy* [1846]. London: Penguin, 1998, p. vii.

Foster, John. *The Life of Charles Dickens*. London: Chapman and Hall, 1872.

Gallagher, Catherine and Stephen Greenblatt. *Practicing New Historicism*. Chicago and London: The University of Chicago Press, 2000.

Gardiner, Marguerite, Countess of Blessington. *The Magic Lantern; or, Sketches of Scenes in the Metropolis*. London: Longman, Hurst, Rees, Orme and Brown, 1823.

Garofalo, Daniela. 'Political Seductions: The Show of War in Byron's Sardanapalus', *Criticism* 44:1 (Winter 2002), 43–63.

Gaudreault, Andre. 'Film, Narrative, Narration: The Cinema of the Lumière Brothers,' in Thomas Elsaesser (ed.), *Early Cinema. Space, Frame, Narrative*. London: BFI Publishing, 1990, pp. 68–75.

Geer, Jennifer. '"All sorts of pitfalls and surprises": Competing Views of Idealized Girlhood in Lewis Carroll's *Alice* Books', *Children's Literature* 31 (2003), 1–24.

Gernsheim, Helmut and Alison. *L. J. M. Daguerre: The History of the Diorama and the Daguerreotype*. London: Secker & Warburg, 1956.

Gilbert, Ann Taylor. 'Remonstrance', in Josiah Conder (ed.), *The Associate Minstrels*. London: G. Ellerton for T. Conder, 1810, p. 23.

Gitelman, Lisa. *Scripts, Grooves and Writing Machines: Representing Technology in the Edison Era*. Stanford: Stanford University Press, 1999.

Goble, Mark. *Beautiful Circuits: Modernism and the Mediated Life*. New York: Columbia University Press, 2010.

Goethe, Johann Wolfgang. *Italian Journey* [1786], trans. W. H. Auden and Elizabeth Mayer. New York: Pantheon, 1962.

Gordon, Margaret. *The Home Life of Sir David Brewster*. Edinburgh: Edmonston and Douglas, 1869.

Graff, Gerald. *Professing Literature: An Institutional History*. Chicago: University of Chicago Press, 1987.

Griffiths, Alison. *Shivers Down Your Spine: Cinema, Museums and the Immersive View*. New York: Columbia University Press, 2008.

Groth, Helen. 'Domestic Phantasmagoria: The Victorian Domestic and Experimental Visuality', *South Atlantic Quarterly* 108:1 (Winter 2009), pp. 147–69.

Groth, Helen and Natalya Lusty. *Dreams and Modernity: A Cultural History*. London: Routledge, 2013.

Guida, Fred. *A Christmas Carol and Its Adaptations*. Jefferson, NJ: McFarlane, 2000.

'Guide to the Panorama of Niagara Falls', in *A Collection of Descriptions of Views Exhibited at the Panorama, Leicester Square, and Painted by H. A. Barker, Robert Burford, John Burford and H. C. Selous, London, 1798–1856*. London: British Library, n. d.

Guillory, John. *Cultural Capital: The Problem of Literary Canon Formation*. Chicago: The University of Chicago Press, 1993.

Gunning, Tom. 'The Non-Continuous Style of Early Film 1900–1906', in Roger Holman (ed.), *Cinema 1900/1906: An Analytical Study*. Brussels: Federation International des Archives du Film, 1982, pp. 219–30.

—. 'Non-Continuity, Continuity, Discontinuity. A Theory of Genres in Early Films', in Thomas Elsaesser (ed.), *Early Cinema. Space, Frame, Narrative*. London: BFI Publishing, 1990, pp. 86–94.

—. 'Now You See It, Now You Don't: The Temporality of the Cinema of Attractions', *Velvet Light Trap* 32 (1993), 3–12.

—. 'An Aesthetic of Astonishment: Early Film and the (In)Credulous Spectator', in Linda Williams (ed.), *Viewing Positions: Ways of Seeing Film*. New Brunswick, NJ: Rutgers University Press, 1995, pp. 114–33

—. 'Before Documentary', in Daan Hertogs and Nico de Klerk (eds), *Uncharted Territory: Essays on Early Nonfiction Film*. Amsterdam: Stichting Nederlands Filmmuseum, 1997, pp. 9–24.

—. 'Hand and Eye: Excavating a New Technology of the Image in the Victorian Era', *Victorian Studies* 54:3 (Spring 2012), 495–515.

Gurney, Edmund, Frederic W. H. Myers, and Frank Podmore. *Phantasms of the Living*, 2 vols. London: Trubner, 1886.

Haining, Peter. *Movable Books: An Illustrated History*. London: New English Library, 1979.

Halliday, Andrew. 'Mr Whelks Combining Instruction with Amusement', *All the Year Round* 15:376 (7 July 1866), pp. 610, 611.

Hancher, Michael. 'Alice's Audiences', in James Holt McGavran Jr (ed.), *Romanticism and Children's Literature in Nineteenth-Century England*. Athens: University of Georgia Press, 1991, pp. 190–207.

Hankins, Thomas L. and Robert J. Silverman. *Instruments and the Imagination*. Princeton: Princeton University Press, 1995.

Hansen, Miriam. 'Universal Language and Democratic Culture: Myths of Origin in Early American Cinema', in Dieter Meindl and Friedrich W. Horlacher with Martin Christalder (eds), *Myth and Enlightenment in American Literature*. Erlangen: University of Erlangen-Nürnberg, 1985, pp. 321–51.

—. *Babel and Babylon: Spectatorship in American Silent Film*. Cambridge, MA: Harvard University Press, 1991.

Harris, John. *The Comic Adventures of Old Mother Hubbard, and Her Dog: in which is shewn the Wonderful Powers that Good Old Lady possessed in the Education of her Favourite Animal*. London: John Harris, 1819.

Hawkins, Ann R. 'Marketing Gender and Nationalism: Blessington's *Gems of Beauty/l'Ecrin* and the mid-century book trade', *Women's Writing* 12:2 (2005), 225–40.

Hazlitt, William. *Lectures on the English Poets*. London: Taylor and Hessey, 1818.

—.*Complete Works*, 21 vols, ed. P. P. Howe. London: J. M. Dent and Sons, 1930–4.

Headrick, Daniel R. *When Information Came of Age: Technologies of Knowledge in the Age of Reason and Revolution, 1700–1850*. Oxford: Oxford University Press, 2000.

Heidegger, Martin. 'The Age of the World Picture', in *The Question Concerning Technology and Other Essays*, trans. William Lovitt. New York: Harper & Row, 1977, pp. 115–54.

Helmholtz, Hermann von. *Treatise on Physiological Optics* [1867] 3 vols, ed. James P. C. Southhall. New York: Dover, 1962.

Hendricks, Gordon. *Beginnings of the Biograph*. New York: Beginnings of American Film, 1964.

Henson, Louise. 'Investigations and fictions: Charles Dickens and ghosts', in Nicola Brown, Carolyn Burdett and Pamela Thurschwell (eds), *The Victorian Supernatural*. Cambridge: Cambridge University Press, 2002.

Hepworth, Cecil M. *Came the Dawn: Memories of a Film Pioneer*. London: Phoenix House, 1951.

—. *Animated Photography. The ABC of the Cinematograph*. 1897; repr. New York: Arno Press & the New York Times, 1970.

Herschel, John F. W. *A Preliminary Discourse on the Study of Natural Philosophy* [1851] Chicago: University of Chicago Press, 1987.

Hibbert, Samuel. *Sketches of the Philosophy of Apparitions*. Edinburgh: Oliver & Boyd, 1824.

Holland, Henry. *Chapters on Mental Physiology*. London: Longman, Brown, Green and Longmans, 1852.

Hooper, William. *Rational Recreations, in which the principles of numbers and natural philosophy are clearly and copiously elucidated, by a series of easy, entertaining, interesting experiments. Among which are all those commonly performed with the cards*, 4 vols. London: L. Davis, 1774.

Howell, Margaret J. *Byron Tonight: A Poet's Plays on the Nineteenth-Century Stage*. Surrey: Springwood Books, 1982.

Hume, David. *A Treatise on Human Nature* [1740], ed. L. A. Selby-Bigge. Oxford: Clarendon Press, 1976.

Hyde, Ralph. *Panoramania!: The Art and Entertainment of the 'All-Embracing' View*. London: Trefoil in association with Barbican Art Gallery, 1988.

James, Henry. *A Small Boy and Others*. New York: Scribners & Co., 1913.

James, William. *A Pluralistic Universe* [1909], intro. Henry Samuel Levinson. Lincoln: Nebraska University Press, 1996.

James, William. *The Principles of Psychology* [1890], 2 vols. London: Dover Books, 1969.

Jay, Martin. *Downcast Eyes: The Denigration of Vision in Twentieth-Century French Thought*. Berkeley: University of California Press, 1993.

—. 'Photo-Unrealism: the Contribution of the Camera to the Crisis of Ocularcentrism', in Stephen Melville and Bill Readings (eds). *Vision and Textuality*. Durham, NC: Duke University Press, 1995, pp. 345–61.

Jeffrey, Francis. 'Review of Lord Byron's *Giaour*', *Edinburgh Review* 21 (July 1813), 299–309.

—. 'Lord Byron's Tragedies', *Edinburgh Review* 36 (1822), 416–17.

John, Juliet. *Dickens and Mass Culture*. Oxford: Oxford University Press, 2010.

Kant, Immanuel. *Critique of Pure Reason* [1781], trans. Norman Kemp Smith. London: St Martin's Press, 1965.

Kaplan, Fred. *Dickens: A Biography*. New York: William Morrow, 1988.

Kean, Charles. *Sardanapalus. Adapted for representation by Charles Kean*. London: Thomas Hailes Lacy, 1853.

Keating, Peter (ed.), *Into Unknown England, 1866–1913: selections from the social explorers*. London: Fontana, 1976.

Keats, John. *The Letters of John Keats*, ed. Maurice Buxton Forman. Oxford: Oxford University Press, 1935.

Keen, Paul. *Literature, Commerce, and the Spectacle of Modernity, 1750–1800*. Cambridge: Cambridge University Press, 2012.

Kent, Charles. *Charles Dickens as a Reader*. London: Chapman & Hall, 1872.

King, Andrew. 'A Paradigm of Reading the Victorian Penny Weekly: Education of the Gaze and *The London Journal*', in Laurel Brake, Bill Bell and David Finkelstein (eds), *Nineteenth-Century Media and the Construction of Identities*. Basingstoke: Palgrave, 2000, pp. 77–92.

King, Norman. 'The Sound of Silents', *Screen* 25:3 (May–June 1984), 15–28.

Kingsley, Charles. *The Water-Babies: A Fairy Tale for a Land Baby*. London: Macmillan, 1863.

Kittler, Friedrich A. *Discourse Networks 1800/1900*, trans. Michael Metteer with Chris Cullens. Stanford: Stanford University Press, 1990.

—. *Gramophone, Film, Typewriter*, trans. Geoffrey Winthrop-Young and Michael Wutz. Stanford: Stanford University Press, 1999.

Klancher, Jon. *The Making of English Reading Audiences 1780–1832*. Wisconsin: University of Wisconsin Press, 1987.

Kluge, Alexander, Thomas Y. Levin and Miriam B. Hansen. 'On Film and the Public Sphere', *New German Critique* 24/25, Special Double Issue on New German Cinema (Autumn 1981–Winter 1982), 206–20.

Knox, Vicesimus. *Winter Evenings, or, Lucubrations on Life and Letters*, 2 vols. London: Charles Dilly, 1790.

Kofman, Sarah. *Camera Obscura of Ideology*, trans. Will Straw. London: Athlone Press, 1998.

Koven, Seth. *Slumming: Sexual and Social Politics in Victorian London*. Princeton: Princeton University Press, 2004.

Lamb, Charles. *The Works of Charles Lamb*, 2 vols. New York: Harper and Brothers, 1838.

—. 'The Barrenness of the Imaginative Faculty in the Productions of Modern Art', in *Complete Works and Letters*, 5 vols, New York: Modern Library, 1935, vol. 3, pp. 186–203.

Laxton, William. 'Steam Navigation', *Journal, Scientific and Railway Gazette*, 10 (April 1847), 116–19.

Le Sage, Alain-René. *The Adventures of Gil Blas de Santillane* [1715–35], trans. Tobias Smollett (1749), 3rd edn, 4 vols. London: T. Osborne, J. Rivington, R. Baldwin, T. Longman et al., 1766.

Lefebvre, Henri. *Everyday Life in the Modern World*. London: Continuum, 2002.

'Letters on Demonology and Witchcraft. By Sir Walter Scott, Bart – London, 1830', *Fraser's Magazine* (December 1830), 507–19.

Lewes, George Henry. 'Voluntary and Involuntary Actions', *Blackwood's* 86 (1859), 99–113.

—. *The Physiology of Common Life*, 2 vols. Edinburgh: Blackwood and Sons, 1860.

—. 'Heart and Brain', *Fortnightly Review* 1 (1865), 66–74.

—. 'Charles Kean and Sardanapalus'. Reprinted in *Dramatic Essays*, 3 vols, ed. William Archer and Robert W. Lowe. London: Walter Scott, 1896, vol. 3, pp. 250–2.

—. 'Dickens in Relation to Criticism', *Fortnightly Review* 11 (February 1872), 141–54.

—. *Problems of Life and Mind*, 5 vols. London: Trübner and Co, 1874–9.

—. *On Actors and the Art of Acting*. Leipzig: Bernhard Tauchnitz, 1875.

—. *The Physical Basis of Mind*. London: Trübner, 1877.

—. *The Principles of Success in Literature* [1865], ed. F. N. Scott. Boston: Allyn and Bacon, 1892.

Lewis Carroll's Library: A Facsimile Edition of the catalogue of the auction sale following C. L. Dodgson's death in 1898, with facsimiles of three subsequent booksellers' catalogues offering books from Dodgson's library, ed. Jeffrey Stern. Virginia: University of Virginia Press, 1981.

Lightman, Bernard. 'Lecturing in the Spatial Economy of Science', in Aileen Fyfe and Bernard Lightman (eds), *Science in the Marketplace: Nineteenth-Century Sites and Experiences*. Chicago: The University of Chicago Press, 2007.

'Literature of the Day: – The New Magazine', *The Metropolitan Journal of Literature. Science, and the Fine Arts* (May to August 1831), 19.

Locke, John. *The Educational Writings of John Locke: A Critical Edition with Introduction and Notes*, ed. James L. Axtell. Cambridge: Cambridge University Press, 1968.

Lockhart, John Gibson. *Memoirs of Sir Walter Scott*, 5 vols. London: Macmillan, 1900.

London as it is To-Day: Where to Go, and What to See. London: H. G. Clarke, 1850.

Luhmann, Niklas. *Social Systems*, trans. John Bednarz, Jr with Dirk Baecker. Stanford: Stanford University Press, 1995.

—. *Art as a Social System*, trans. Eva M. Knodt. Stanford: Stanford University Press, 2000.

Macready, William Charles. *The Diaries of William Charles Macready 1833–1851*, 2 vols. London: G. P. Putnam & Sons, 1912.

Manning, Peter. 'Childe Harold in the Marketplace: From Romaunt to Handbook', *Modern Language Quarterly* 52 (1991), 170–90.

Mannoni, Laurent. *The Great Art of Light and Shadow: Archaeology of the Cinema*. Exeter: University of Exeter Press, 2000.

Marcus, Laura. 'Literature and Cinema', in Laura Marcus and Peter Nicholls (eds). *The Cambridge History of Twentieth Century Literature*. Cambridge: Cambridge University Press, 2005, pp. 335–8.

Marsh, Joss. 'Dickensian "Dissolving Views": The Magic Lantern, Visual Story-Telling, and the Victorian Technological Imagination', *Comparative Critical Studies* 6:3 (2009), 333–46.

Martin, Sarah Catherine. *The Comic Adventures of Old Mother Hubbard, and Her Dog: Illustrated with Fifteen Elegant Engravings on Copper-plate*. London: John Harris, 1805.

Marx, Karl and Friedrich Engels. *The German Ideology*, 2 vols, trans. C. J. Arthur. London: Lawrence Wishart, 1965.

Marx, Karl. *Grundrisse*, trans. Martin Nicolaus. New York: Random House, 1973.

Matthews, Brander. 'The Kinetoscope of Time', *Scribner's Magazine* 18:6 (1895), 733–44.

Mavor, Carol. *Pleasures Taken: Performances of Sexuality and Loss in Victorian Photographs*. Durham, NC: Duke University Press, 1995.

Mole, Tom. *Byron's Romantic Celebrity: Industrial Culture and the Hermeneutic of Intimacy*. Basingstoke: Palgrave, 2007.

Morely, Henry. 'New Discoveries in Ghosts', *Household Words* (1852).

Morely, Henry and W. H. Wills. 'The Ghost of the Cock Lane Ghost', *Household Words* 6 (1853).

Morely, John and W. H. Wills. 'The Stereoscope', *Household Words* (10 September 1853), p. 42.

Morrell, J. B. 'Brewster and the early British Association for the Advancement of Science', in Morrison-Low, A. D. and J. R. R. Christie (eds). *'Martyr of Science': Sir David Brewster 1781–1868*. Edinburgh: The Royal Scottish Museum, 1984, pp. 25–9.

Morrison-Low, A. D. and J. R. R. Christie (eds), *'Martyr of Science': Sir David Brewster 1781–1868*. Edinburgh: The Royal Scottish Museum, 1984.

McKernan, Luke and Stephen Herbert (eds). *Who's Who of Victorian Cinema: a worldwide survey*. London: BFI, 1996.

Munsterberg, Hugo. 'The Photoplay: A Psychological Study', in *Hugo Munsterberg on Film. The Photoplay: A Psychological Study and Other Writings*, ed. Allan Langdale. London: Routledge, 2002.

Murray, John. Preface, in *A Handbook for Travellers on the Continent*, 3rd edn. London: John Murray, 1842, n. p.

Musser, Charles. 'Rethinking Early Cinema: Cinemas of Attraction and Narrativity', *Yale Journal of Criticism* 7:2 (1994), 203–33.

Myers, Frederic W. H. 'The subliminal consciousness: Chap 2, The mechanism of suggestion', *Proceedings of the Society for Psychical Research* 1 (1892), 355–75.

Nead, Lynda. *The Haunted Gallery: Painting, Photography, Film c.1900*. New Haven: Yale University Press, 2007.

Neel, Alexandra. '"A *Something-Nothing* Out of Its Very Contrary": The Photography of Coleridge', *Victorian Studies* (Winter 2007), 208–17.

Newman, William and Hain Friswell. *The Laughable Looking Glass for Little Folks*. London: Dean and Son, 1857.

Newnes, George. Editorial, *Strand Magazine* 1 (1891), 1–2.

North, Christopher (John Wilson). 'The Magic Lantern, or Sketches of Scenes in the Metropolis', *Blackwood's Edinburgh Magazine* 11:65 (June 1822), 715–22.

North, Michael. *Camera Works: Photography and the Twentieth-Century Word*. Oxford: Oxford University Press, 2005.

Nunokawa, Jeff. *The Afterlife of Property: Domestic Security and the Victorian Novel*. Princeton: Princeton University Press, 1994.

Oettermann, Stephan. *The Panorama: History of a Mass Medium*. New York: Zone Books, 1997.

Opie, Iona and Peter. *A Nursery Companion*. Oxford: Oxford University Press, 1980.

'Optical Magic of Our Age', *Chambers's Edinburgh Journal* 278 (April 1849), 259–63.

Otis, Laura. *Networking: Communicating with Bodies and Machines in the Nineteenth Century*. Michigan: University of Michigan Press, 2001.

Otto, Peter. *Multiplying Worlds: Romanticism, Modernity, and the Emergence of Virtual Reality*. New York: Oxford University Press, 2011.

'Panorama of the Battle of Waterloo', *London Saturday Journal* 3:68 (16 April 1842), 187–9.

'Panoramas and Dioramas', *Leisure Hour* (January 1886), 45–8.

Paris, John Aryton. *Philosophy in Sport Made Science in Earnest, Being an Attempt to Illustrate the First Principles of Natural Philosophy by the Aid of Popular Toys and Sports*, 3 vols. London: Longman & Rees, 1827.

Pepper, John Henry. *The Boy's Playbook of Science*. London: Routledge, Warne and Routledge, 1860.

—. *The True History of the Ghost; and all About Metempsychosis*. London: Cassell & Co., 1890.

Pittard, Chrisopher. '"Cheap, Healthful Literature": *The Strand Magazine*, Fictions of Crime, and Purified Reading Communities', *Victorian Periodicals Review* 40:1 (Spring 2007), 1–23.

Plumb, J. H. 'The New World of Children in Eighteenth-Century England', *Past and Present* 67 (May 1975), 64–95.

Plunkett, John. 'Moving Books/Moving Images: Optical Recreations and Children's publishing 1800–1900', *19: Interdisciplinary Studies in the Long Nineteenth Century* 5 (2007), www.19.bbk.ac.uk, 1–27.

Polytechnic Programmes Collections, University of Westminster.

Pound, Reginald. *The Strand Magazine 1891–1950*. London: Heinemann, 1966.

Price, Leah. 'From the History of a Book to a "History of the Book"', *Representations* (Fall 2009), 120–38.

Proust, Marcel. *Remembrance of Things Past*, trans. C. K. Scott Moncrieff and Terence Kilmartin. New York: Chatto and Windus, 1982.

Rancière, Jacques. *The Future of the Image*, trans. Gregory Elliot. London: Verso, 2007.

Reichertz, Ronald. *The Making of the Alice Books: Lewis Carroll's Uses of Earlier Children's Literature*. Montreal and Kingston: McGill-Queen's University Press, 1997.

Reiman, Donald H. (ed.), *The Romantics Reviewed*, 5 vols. New York: Garland Press, 1972.

Rev. of *Sardanapalus*, *Athenaeum* (18 June 1853), 745.

Rev., *The Sunderland Herald* (25 May 1866), 2.

Rev., *The Times* (17 August 1876), 175.

Rev., *The Times* (26 December 1865), 5.

Richards, I. A. 'A Theory of Communication', in *Principles of Literary Criticism*. 1926. Repr. London: Harcourt and Brace, 1961.

Richardson, Alan. *Literature, Education, and Romanticism: Reading as Social Practice, 1780–1832*. Cambridge: Cambridge University Press, 1994.

Roach, Joseph R. 'G. H. Lewes and Performance Theory: Towards a "Science of Acting"', *Theatre Journal* 32:3 (October 1980), 312–28.

Roberts, William. 'Rev. of *Sardanapalus*', *British Review* 19 (March 1822), 72–3.

Rorty, Richard. *Philosophy and the Mirror of Nature*. Princeton: Princeton University Press, 1979.

Rose, Gillian. *Mourning Becomes the Law: Philosophy and Representation*. Cambridge: Cambridge University Press, 1996.

Rovee, Christopher. *Imagining the Gallery: The Social Body of British Romanticism*. Stanford: Stanford University Press, 2006.

Rubery, Matthew. *The Novelty of Newspapers: Victorian Fiction after the Invention of News*. Oxford: Oxford University Press, 2009.

Ruskin, John. *Praeterita: The Autobiography of John Ruskin* [1889]. Oxford: Oxford University Press, 1983.

Ryan, Vanessa L. *Thinking with Thinking in the Victorian Novel*. Baltimore: Johns Hopkins University Press, 2012.

Rylance, Rick. *Victorian Psychology and British Culture 1850–1880*. Oxford: Oxford University Press, 2000.

Scarry, Elaine. *Dreaming by the Book*. Princeton: Princeton University Press, 1999.

Schmid, Susanne. 'The Countess of Blessington: Reading as Intimacy, Reading as Sociability', *Wordsworth Circle* (Summer 2008), 88–93.

Scott, Walter. 'The Field of Waterloo', in *The Vision of Don Roderick, the Field of Waterloo, and Other Poems*. London: A. Constable & Co., 1821, pp. 191–225.

—.*Letters on Demonology and Witchcraft. Addressed to J. G. Lockhart*. London: John Murray, 1830.

—. *The Journal of Sir Walter Scott*. Westport, CT: Greenwood Press, 1978.

Secord, James A. *Victorian Sensation: The Extraordinary Publication, Reception, and Secret Authorship of 'Vestiges of the Natural History of Creation'*. Chicago: University of Chicago Press, 2000.

—. 'Portraits of Science: Quick and Magical Shaper of Science', *Science* 297:5587 (6 September 2002), 1648–9.

—. 'How Scientific conversation Became Shop Talk', in Aileen Fyfe and Bernard Lightman (eds). *Science in the Marketplace*. Chicago: The University of Chicago Press, 2007, pp. 23–59.

Sennett, Richard. *Flesh and Stone: The Body and the City in Western Civilization*. New York: W. W. Norton & Co., 1994.

Shail, Andrew 'Reading the Cinematograph. Introduction', in Andrew Shail (ed.), *Reading the Cinematograph. The Cinema and Short British Fiction 1896–1912*, Exeter: Exeter University Press, 2010, pp. 1–17.

Shelley, Percy Bysshe. *The Letters of Percy Bysshe Shelley*, 2 vols, ed. Frederick L. Jones. Oxford: Clarendon, 1964.

Sherer, Susan. 'Secrecy and Autonomy in Lewis Carroll', *Philosophy and Literature* 20:1 (1996), 1–19.

Sherson, Erroll. *London's Lost Theatres of the Nineteenth Century*. London: B. Blom, 1969.

Shuttleworth, Sally. '"The malady of thought." Embodied memory in Victorian psychology and the novel', in Matthew Campbell, Jacqueline M. Labbe and Sally Shuttleworth (eds), *Memory and Memorials 1789–1914*. London: Routledge, 2000.

Simmel, Georg. 'The Metropolis and Mental Life', in *The Sociology of Georg Simmel*, trans. and ed. Kurt H. Wolff. New York: Free Press, 1964, pp. 409–24.

Sims, George Robert. *The Social Kaleidoscope*. London: J. P. Fuller, 1881.

—. *How the Poor Live*. London: Chatto & Windus, 1883.

— (ed.). *Living London: Its Work and its Play, its Humour and its Pathos, its Sights and its Scenes*, 3 vols. London: Cassell and Co., 1901–3.

—. *Biographs of London: Life-pictures of London's Moving Scenes*. London: Chatto & Windus, 1902.

—. *My Life: Sixty Years' Recollections of Bohemian London*. London: Chatto & Windus, 1917.

'Sir David Brewster and The Kaleidoscope' (advertisement), *Illustrated London News* (31 March 1866), 306.

Sitney, P. Adams. 'Image and Title in Avant-Garde Cinema', *October* 11, Essays in Honor of Jay Leyda (Winter 1979), 97–112.

Skelton, Percival. 'The Home and Grave of Byron', *Once a Week* 2:49 (2 June 1860), 539–42.

Slater, Michael (ed.). *Dickens' Journalism: Sketches by Boz and other early papers 1833–1839*. London: Phoenix, 1996.

Smajić, Srdjan. 'The Trouble with Ghost-Seeing: Vision, Ideology, and Genre in the Victorian Ghost Story', *ELH* 70 (2003), 1107–35.

Small, Helen. 'A pulse of 124: Charles Dickens and a pathology of the mid-Victorian reading public', in James Raven, Helen Small and Naomi Tadmor (eds), *The Practice and Representation of Reading in England*. Cambridge: Cambridge University Press, 1996.

Smiles, Samuel. *A Publisher and His Friends: Memoir and Correspondence of the Late John Murray*, 2 vols. London: Murray, 1891.

—. *Self-Help. With Illustrations of Conduct and Perseverance*, ed. Asa Briggs. London: John Murray, 1969.

Smith, Adam. *The Theory of Moral Sentiments*, ed. D. D. Raphael and A. L. Macfie. Indianapolis: Liberty fund, 1984.

Smith, Albert (ed.), *'Gavarni in London: Sketches of Life and Character,' with illustrative essays by Popular Writers*. London: David Bogue, 1849.

Smith, Grahame. *Dickens and the Dream of Cinema*. Manchester: Manchester University Press, 2003.

Smith, Greg. *Thomas Girtin: The Art of Watercolour*. Millbank: Tate Publishing, 2002.

Southey, Robert. 'State and Prospects of the Country', in George Lewis Levine (ed.), *The Emergence of Victorian Consciousness, the Spirit of the Age*. New York: Free Press, 1967, pp. 24–48.

Spencer, Herbert. *Principles of Psychology*. London: Longman, Brown, Green and Longmans, 1855.

St Clair, William. 'The Impact of Byron's Writings: an Evaluative Approach', in *Byron: Augustan and Romantic*, ed. Andrew Rutherford. New York: St Martin's Press, 1990, pp. 52–62.

Stewart, Dugald. *Elements of the Philosophy of the Human Mind*, 3 vols. London: A. Strahan and T. Cadell, W. Creech, 1792–1827.

Stewart, Garrett. *Between Film and Screen: Modernism's Photosynthesis*. Chicago: University of Chicago Press, 1999.

—. 'Curtain Up on Victorian Popular Cinema; Or, The Critical Theater of the Animatograph', http://www.branchcollective.org/, 1–11.

Sully, James. *Illusions – A Psychological Study*. London: Kegan Paul, Trench & Co., 1887.

—. 'The Dream as a Revelation', *Fortnightly Review* 53:315 (March 1893), 354–65.

Sutherland, John. *The Life of Walter Scott: A Critical Biography*. Oxford: Blackwell, 1995.

Taylor, Isaac. *Home Education* [1838]. London: Bell and Daldy, 1867.

Taylor, Jane. *Memoirs, correspondence, and poetical remains of Jane Taylor*. London: Holdsworth and Ball, 1831.

Taylor, Jane and Ann Taylor. *Signor Topsy-Turvy's Wonderful Magic Lantern: or, The World Turned Upside Down*. London: Tabart & Co., at the Juvenile and School Library, 1810.

Taylor, Jenny Bourne. 'Forms and fallacies of memory in nineteenth-century psychology: Henry Holland, William Carpenter and Frances Power Cobbe', *Endeavour* 23:2 (1999), 60–4.

Telescope, Tom (John Newbury). *The Newtonian system of philosophy adapted to the capacities of young ladies and gentlemen and familiarized and made entertaining by objects with which they are intimately acquainted: being the substance of six lectures read to a select company of friends*. London: Ogilvy and Speare, 1794.

Thackeray, William Makepeace. 'De Juventute – Roundabout Papers No. VIII', *Cornhill Magazine* 2:10 (October 1860), 501–12.

—. *Roundabout Papers, Little Travels, and Roadside Sketches*, in *The Works of William Makepeace Thackeray*, Kensington Edition, vol. xxvii. New York: Scribners, 1904.

'Theatres', *The Times* (17 June 1876), 587.

Theatre Notices, *Observer* (13 April 1834).

'The Caleidoscope and the Tetrascope', *The Literary Journal* (17 May 1818), 122.

'The Prince's Derby. Shown by Lightning Photography', *Strand Magazine* 12 (July 1896), 134–40.

Thomas, Ronald R. *Dreams of Authority: Freud and the Fictions of the Unconscious*. Ithaca: Cornell University Press, 1990.

Thompson, E. P. *Making of the English Working Class*. London: Vintage, 1966.

Thoren, Victor E. *The Lord of Uraniborg: A Biography of Tycho Brahe*. Cambridge: Cambridge University Press, 1990.

Thorington, J. Monroe. *Mont Blanc Sideshow. The Life and Times of Albert Smith*. Philadelphia: The John C. Winston Company, 1934.

Throsby, Corin. 'Byron, commonplacing and early fan culture', in *Romanticism and Celebrity Culture, 1750–1850*, ed. Tom Mole. Cambridge: Cambridge University Press, 2009, pp. 226–7.

'Through the Looking Glass', *The Spectator* (30 December 1871), 1607–9.

Trotter, David. *Cinema and Modernism*. Oxford: Blackwell, 2007.

Vogler, Richard. *Graphic Works of George Cruikshank*. London: Dover, 1979.

Voskuil, Lynn M. *Acting Naturally: Victorian Theatricality and Authenticity*. Virginia: University of Virginia Press, 2004.

Vrettos, Athena. 'Defining Habits: Dickens and the Psychology of Repetition', *Victorian Studies* (Spring 1999/2000).

Walkerdine, Valerie. 'Developmental Psychology and the Child-Centered Pedagogy: The Insertion of Piaget into Early Education', in Julian Henriques et al. *Changing the Subject: Psychology, Social Regulation and Subjectivity*. London: Methuen, 1984, pp. 155–75.

Whale, John. 'Sacred Objects and the Sublime Ruins of Art', in John Whale and Stephen Copley (eds), *Beyond Romanticism*. London: Routledge, 1992, pp. 227–35.

Wilkie, Edmund H. 'Professor Pepper – A Memoir', *The Optical Magic Lantern Journal and Photographic Enlarger* II (June 1900).

Williams, Raymond. *Marxism and Literature*. New York: Oxford University Press, 1977.

Wolfson, Susan J. '"A Problem Few Dare Imitate": Sardanapalus and "Effeminate Character"', *ELH* 58:4 (Winter 1991), 867–902.

Wordsworth, William. Preface, 1800 version, in *Wordsworth and Coleridge: Lyrical Ballads*, ed. Nicholas Roe. London: Routledge, p. 294.

—. *William Wordsworth: The Poems*, 2 vols, ed. John O. Hayden. 1977. Repr. Harmondsworth: Penguin, 1982.

Ziter, Edward. 'Kean, Byron, and Fantasies of Miscegenation', *Theatre Journal* 54:4 (2002), 607–26.

Index